William Hunt

History of Italy

With maps

William Hunt

History of Italy
With maps

ISBN/EAN: 9783337239695

Printed in Europe, USA, Canada, Australia, Japan

Cover: Foto ©ninafisch / pixelio.de

More available books at **www.hansebooks.com**

Historical Course for Schools.

HISTORY
OF
ITALY.

BY

WILLIAM HUNT, M.A.,

VICAR OF CONGRESBURY.

SECOND EDITION. WITH MAPS.

London:
MACMILLAN AND CO.
1883.

LONDON:
R. CLAY, SONS, AND TAYLOR,
BREAD STREET HILL.

CONTENTS.

CHAPTER I.
	PAGE
THE EMPEROR AND THE BARBARIANS	1

CHAPTER II.
THE EMPEROR AND THE POPE	16

CHAPTER III.
THE EMPEROR AND THE CITIES	36

CHAPTER IV.
THE GREATNESS OF THE GUELFS	53

CHAPTER V.
THE GHIBELIN LORDS	70

	PAGE
THE GREAT STATES	91

CHAPTER VII.

ITALY INVADED	116

CHAPTER VIII.

ITALY CONQUERED	145

CHAPTER IX.

ITALY ENSLAVED	169

CHAPTER X.

ITALY DIVIDED	196

CHAPTER XI.

ITALY FREE AND UNITED	224
INDEX	261

CHRONOLOGICAL TABLE.

	A.D.
End of the separate Western Empire	476
The Invasion of the Lombards	568
Italy revolts from Leo the Iconoclast	728
Charles the Great crowned Emperor	800
The Saracens invade Sicily	827
Bari taken by the Emperors Lewis and Basil	871
End of the Carolingian Empire	887
Otto the Great crowned Emperor	962
Decree of Conrad II.—Heribert Archbishop of Milan	1037
Civitella—Leo IX., and the Normans	1053
War of Investitures—Henry IV., at Canossa	1077
The Concordat of Worms	1122
Coronation of Frederic I.—Arnold of Brescia	1154
Battle of Legnano	1176
Peace of Constanz	1183
End of the Norman Kingdom of Sicily	1194
Battle of Corte Nuova—Success of Frederic II.	1237
Defeat of the Florentine Guelfs at Monteaperto	1260
Battle of Tagliacozzo	1268
The Sicilian Vespers	1282

CHRONOLOGICAL TABLE.

	A.D.
Defeat of the Pisans off Meloria	1284
Beginning of the Babylonish Captivity	1305
Henry VII., in Italy	1310
Coronation of Lewis of Bavaria	
Death of Castruccio Castrucani and of Galeazzo Visconti	1328
John of Bohemia leaves Italy	1333
The Duke of Athens driven from Florence	
Accession of Joanna I., of Naples	1343
Niccolo di Rienzi, Tribune of Rome	1347
The Plague	1348
The Return of the Pope to Rome	1376
The Insurrection of the Ciompi	
The Great Schism begins	1378
The War of Chioggia begins	
Death of Duke Gian-Galeazzo Visconti	1402
Pisa becomes subject to Florence	1406
The Kingdom of Sicily joined to Aragon	
The Council of Pisa	1409
The Council of Constanz	1415
The Peace of Ferrara	
Sigismund crowned Emperor	1433
Banishment of Cosimo de' Medici	
Death of Duke Filippo Maria Visconti	1447
Francesco Sforza enslaves Milan	1450
The Peace of Lodi	1454
The Conspiracy of the Pazzi	1478
Charles VIII. enters Italy	
Flight of Piero de' Medici	1494
Fra Girolamo Savonarola put to death	1498
Lewis XII. conquers the Duchy of Milan	1500
Cesare Borgia made Duke of Romagna	1501

CHRONOLOGICAL TABLE.

	A.D.
Ferdinand of Spain and Sicily conquers Naples	1504
Pisa reconquered by Florence	1509
War of the League of Cambray	
Julius II., forms the Holy League	1511
The battle of Ravenna	1512
The Medici return to Florence	
Marignano—the French Masters of Lombardy	1515
Pavia—Charles Master of Lombardy	1525
The Sack of Rome	1527
The Medici driven out of Florence	
Charles V. crowned Emperor	1530
The Fall of Florence	
The Society of Jesus formed	1540
The Fall of Siena	1555
The Peace of Câteau-Cambresis	1559
The Victory of Lepanto	1571
Complete Restoration of Duke Emmanuel Filibert	1574
The Treaty of Lyons	1601
Insurrection in Naples under 'Mas Aniello	1647
Insurrection in Messina	1674
Francesco Morosini conquers Peloponnêsos	1684
Bombardment of Genoa by Lewis XIV.	
End of the Habsburg Kings of Spain	1700
Peace of Utrecht—Austrian power in Italy	1713
Victor Amadeus II. King of Sicily	
Victor Amadeus II. King of Sardinia	1718
End of the Medici	1737
Treaty of Vienna—Spanish Bourbons in the Two Sicilies	1738
The War of the Austrian Succession	1740
The Revolt of Genoa	1746
The Peace of Aix-la-Chapelle	1748

CHRONOLOGICAL TABLE.

	A.D.
Abolition of the Society of Jesus	1773
Invasion of Italy by Buonaparte	1796
Treaty of Campo Formio	1797
Buonaparte King of Italy	1805
The Congress of Vienna	1815
Insurrection in Naples	1820
Insurrection in the Kingdom of Sardinia	1821
Insurrection in Central Italy	1831
The Raid of G. Mazzini	1833
The Bandiera Attempt	1844
Election of Pope Pius IX.	1846
The First War of Independence	1848
The Battle of Novara—the Accession of King Victor Emmanuel II.	1849
The Fall of Rome and Venice	1849
The Siccardi Law	1850
Sardinia takes part in the Crimean War	1855
The Freedom of Lombardy	1859
The Freedom of Central Italy	1860
Garibaldi delivers Sicily and Naples	1860
Victor Emmanuel King of Italy	1861
Defeat of Garibaldi at Aspromonte	1862
The September Convention	1864
The Freedom of Venetia	1866
The Mentana affair	1867
Rome the Capital of Italy	1870

LIST OF MAPS.

1. Italy *cir.* 668, showing the Lombard kingdom and duchies after the visit of Constans.
2. Italy in 1402, showing the Visconti dominions at the death of Gian-Galeazzo.
3. Italy in 1557, showing the extinction of the Republics and the predominance of Spain.
4. Italy in 1713, showing the arrangements of the Peace of Utrecht and the predominance of Austria.
5. Italy in 1815, as arranged by the Allied Sovereigns.
6. Dominions of the House of Savoy :—
    1. *Cir.* 1250, showing advance both in Italian and Burgundian lands.
    2. 1557-1574, their reconstruction as a power mainly Italian.
    3. 1601, showing the confirmation of their Italian character by the Treaty of Lyons.
    4. 1860, they become the kingdom of Italy.

ITALY.

CHAPTER I

THE EMPEROR AND THE BARBARIANS.

Geography of Italy (1)—Italy in the absence of the Emperor (2)—governed by his representatives (2, 3)—re-united to the Empire (4)—the Lombards (5)—conquer Italy (6)—and found a kingdom (7)—Rome deserted by the Emperor (8)—defended by the Pope (8)—the Franks called in (9)—Charles the Great crowned Emperor; revival of the Empire of the West; its division into kingdoms (10)—the Saracens (11)—revival of the Greek power in South Italy; decay and end of the Carolingian Empire (12).

1. **Physical Geography.**—Italy is a long narrow peninsula with a vast sea-board, and we find accordingly that its southern parts, and the island of Sicily, have been much influenced by the commerce and wars of the Mediterranean. It would seem to be quite shut out from any interference by land by the great northern boundary of mountains; but unhappily this has often been overpassed, and no country has suffered more from foreign invasion. The Alps, which completely close in Italy on the north, slope rapidly down to the large and fertile plain of Lombardy. They are joined on their south-east by the Apennines, which run right through the peninsula. The Apennines pass along the coast and shelter the *Riviere* (shores) of the Gulf of Genoa from the north wind;

they then take a wider sweep, and towards the south divide into two ranges, one passing down each of the two smaller southern peninsulas. Their forms are round and wavy, unlike the sharp needle-like rocks of the Alps, and they are mostly covered with vegetation. They are of considerable height, so that the land to the south-west of them has a second bulwark against the northern nations. There are two great volcanic districts in Sicily and South Italy connected by the Lipari Islands; that in Italy may be traced nearly as far north as Parma and Modena. The chief rivers on the east of the Apennines are the Po, with its numerous tributaries, which rises at the meeting of the Alps with the Apennines, and the Adige, which rises in the Tyrol. These two drain the great northern plain. The Po flows swiftly, and has made great deposits of earth. This is also the case with the smaller rivers to the north and south of it, so that the coast-line has become much changed, and Ravenna, once an important seaport, is now inland. The most remarkable effect of these deposits is the Lido, or long strip of land which encloses the Lagoons or salt-water lakes of Venice. On the west of the Apennines there are no rivers of any size save the Arno; for the Tiber is now a very small stream. The climate of Italy is warm and delicious, and the sky is clear and deep blue. The people are thus able to discuss matters out of doors, and this power in the days of freedom helped to give every man an interest and part in the government of his city or state. The soil is fruitful, especially in the well-watered northern district; and in the volcanic district of the south and in Sicily grow the vine, the date, and the aloe. Parts of Italy, especially round Rome and the Tuscan *Maremma* (sea-coast), are unhealthy, but this is to a great extent the result of war, bad government, and neglect. The Italians belong to the same branch of the Aryan family as the Greeks, and were welded into one people by the power of Rome. Sicily and South Italy were colonized by Greeks, and the Greek language was spoken in those parts as late as the middle of the thirteenth century: though it was then giving way to the speech of the rest of Italy. This was of course a sort of Latin, though very different from the speech of Cicero. This difference was not recognized for a long time, because the Italians wrote in good Latin, while they talked corrupt Latin or *Romance*. The Italians of the North are a brave and noble people, with great talents for poetry and the arts, with warm affections, quick perception, and lively imagination; but they lack, to some extent, depth of mind and fixity of purpose. These defects, as well as that of indolence, and a want of sufficient regard for truth, especially belong to the Italians of the South. Many evil things in the Italian character are the results of foreign slavery, and will doubtless to a great extent disappear now that the people are again free.

2. **Zeno sole Emperor**, 476.—The history of the Italian nation begins with the invasion of the *Lombards*. As long as the Emperor remained in Italy, or was able to protect her, no independent national life could arise. The barbarian invaders of Italy tore her away from the Empire, and in doing so they made her people into a separate nation. When an Emperor of the Romans was again acknowledged in Italy, he had less real power there than in any other part of his dominions. The tie was not broken at once; Italy first became used to the Emperor's absence, before she saw his rule shaken off. In 476, *Romulus Augustulus*, the Emperor reigning over Old Rome, was deposed, and the Senate voted that there should be only one Emperor; so *Zeno*, the Emperor reigning in New Rome or Constantinople, was made lord of the whole Empire without any rival in the West. When this happened, the chief power in Italy was in the hands of *Odoacer*, an Herulian, leader of the mercenary bands which had taken

the place of a native army. He was King over his own people, and regent for the Emperor over the other inhabitants of Italy. He was in name the servant of the Emperor, but he was really independent of him. The government of Odoacer gave way before the invasion of the *East-Goths* under *Theodoric*.

3. **Theodoric, Lieutenant of the Emperor,** 493-526.—Like Odoacer, Theodoric conquered and ruled by a commission from the Emperor, but the splendour and prosperity of his reign weakened the tie which bound Italy to the Emperor. Unlike Odoacer, he aimed at setting up a dynasty. He recognized his own people as the conquerors, and at the same time he impartially administered their own laws to the conquered Italians. Religious jealousy marred the happiness of his reign and the success of his plans. The Gothic rule was short-lived: the northern race was unsuited to a life of inactivity, and the scandals of the Court after the death of Theodoric greatly weakened the power of the East-Goths.

4. **Italy re-united to the Empire,** 539-563.—Justinian seized the opportunity of regaining the oldest and noblest province of the Empire, which had become detached in all things save in name. The chief strength of the Ostrogoths lay in North Italy, for they were not sufficiently numerous to colonize the whole land. The descendants of the Greek colonists in Sicily and South Italy gladly welcomed Belisarius the general of the Emperor. The Greek city Naples was forced by the barbarians to resist: at its fall Apulia and Calabria were restored to the Empire. After a long struggle the Imperial armies, first under Belisarius, and afterwards under Narses, destroyed the name and nation of the East-Goths. Italy was thus again made in reality a subject of the Emperor, who was represented by an *Exarch* or ruler, dwelling not at Rome but at Ravenna. The Gothic war

brought the unhappy Italians to the greatest poverty and distress, and they had only a short respite before they were made a prey to the fiercest of the northern nations.

5. **The Lombards.**—The destruction of the Goths left the North of Italy undefended, and the Exarch had no forces at command strong enough to keep back fresh invaders. The *Lombards*, a wild Teutonic people, had come down from the eastern banks of the Elbe to the Danube. For a time they served under Narses, and gained for the Emperor the country between the Danube and the Adriatic. Justinian instigated them to fight against the *Gepidæ*, who had seized the country south of the Danube, and were threatening the now undefended passes into Italy. The Lombards crossed into *Pannonia*, under their King *Audoin*, and began a war which lasted for thirty years. The savage bravery of the King's son *Alboin* made him the chief among the Lombards. While yet young, he slew the son of the King of the Gepidæ in the great battle of *Asfeld*, and received from the hands of the sorrowing father the arms of the slain. When Alboin became King, he found useful allies in the *Avars*, who had fled westwards, driven forward by the constant advance of kindred Turkish hordes. He slew Cunimund, the King of the Gepidæ, took his daughter Rosamund to wife, and utterly destroyed the Gepidæ. The way into Italy now lay open, and the Lombards did not hesitate to advance. They met with unexpected encouragement. Narses, the eunuch, had conquered Totila, and Teias, the last King of the Ostrogoths, and had delivered North Italy from a fierce raid of the Franks and Alamanni. Nevertheless, his avarice caused his disgrace at the Imperial Court, and he was deprived of the Exarchate. Stung by an ungenerous taunt of the Empress, he incited the Lombards to invade Italy.

6. **The Lombards invade Italy,** 568.—Alboin crossed the Julian Alps, and entered Friuli unopposed. The people were

wasted with misery, and the new Exarch Longinus could not inspire the same confidence as Narses had done. Verona, the city of Theodoric, submitted to the barbarians. Milan had but a few years before been burnt by a savage host of Franks and Alamanni, and could make no resistance. Alboin was soon master of all the north of Italy—of that rich land of Lombardy, which has so long kept the name of its conquerors. Two extremes only escaped him. In the east, the islands of *Venice* remained to the Emperor, and the Island of *Grado* gave a home to the flying Patriarch of Aquileia. In the west, the Ligurian cities were sheltered by the wall of the Apennines, and the Archbishop of Milan found a refuge in *Genoa*. *Pavia* alone closed her gates against Alboin, and was besieged for three years. Meanwhile, detached bands overran Tuscany, and desolated the country as far as the gates of Rome. At last Pavia was forced by famine to yield, and the Lombard King made the city which dared to withstand him the place of his abode and the capital of his kingdom. He did not live long to enjoy his conquests. Rosamund his wife, the daughter of Cunimund, had him slain, and thus avenged her father. The Lombard people met at Pavia, and chose Cleph, the bravest of themselves, to be King. He also was soon assassinated, and for ten years thirty chiefs each seized some city for himself. Some among them made raids on the lands of the Franks and Alamanni, and the Emperor Tiberius tried to regain the lost province by bribing Chilperic the Frank to avenge these attacks. This danger called forth *Autharis*, the son of Cleph. He was chosen King by the voice of the people, and saved them by his courage and ability. The last and greatest attack was led by Childebert, and instigated by the Emperor Maurice. It was foiled by the superior generalship of Autharis, who avoided coming to any engagement, and allowed the heat of summer to defeat the invaders. The victorious King marched through the land, to Spoletum, to Beneventum, to Rhegium, and there he touched with his lance a column which stood washed by the waves of the strait, and cried that so far should stretch the bounds of the Lombards.

7. **The Lombard Kingdom**, 568-774.—The Imperial power in Italy had now almost ceased. The Exarch ruled over the land east of the Apennines, from the Po to Ancona. Rome, with the country between Terracina and Civita Vecchia and the Duchy of Naples, also owned his authority. Of these, Naples soon became really independent. The islands of Sardinia, Corsica, and Sicily also still held to the Emperor; but his name was nowhere so much honoured as in the little group of islands which formed in after-time the Republic of Venice. The invasion of Attila, and the destruction of Padua and the neighbouring country, had driven the unhappy people to take shelter in the small islands of the Lagoon. The invasion of Alboin and the fall of Aquileia increased the importance of the settlement by causing a fresh number to take refuge there. Besides the Lombard kingdom in the north of Italy, the Duchy of Spoletum kept watch over Rome and Ravenna, and the Duchy of Beneventum held in check the Greek maritime cities of the South. The Lombards were Arians, and they therefore hated all Catholic persons and places: they spared neither church nor fortress, monastery nor farm. The Gothic war had crushed the spirit of the people, and the conquest of Italy had weakened the power of the Bishop of Rome, who would naturally have been a centre round whom to rally. He became a servant of the Emperor, and was put under the orders of the Exarch; but he did not gain any protection for himself or his city from the power he was forced to acknowledge. The Lombards threatened Rome. The Emperor could only incite the Franks to make a raid upon them, and the Exarch irritated, but could

not hurt, his powerful neighbours who kept pressing down on
the remnants of the Imperial territory. In the midst of these
dangers, *Gregory* was elected Bishop of Rome (590-604), and
saved the city. The weakness and absence of the Emperor
left Gregory the sole defender of Rome and of Italy, and the
greatness of the Papal power arose from the noble way in which
he discharged this trust. If an Emperor had been in Rome,
the position of Gregory within the city would have been lower,
and he would certainly have had no political power in Italy.
By the wisdom of his internal government he relieved the
people of the pestilence and famine which oppressed them.
He made peace with the powerful Duke of Spoletum, who
threatened Rome from the south, and defended her against
Agilulf, the successor of Autharis, who attacked her from
the north. The Exarch all this while did nothing, and the
Emperor Maurice rather hindered than helped. The wisdom
and vigour of Gregory the Great made the Pope the centre
of independent action in Italy in things temporal as well as
spiritual. The most lasting benefit which he conferred upon
his land was the conversion of the Lombards. He effected
this through Theodelinda, Queen of Agilulf, and widow of
Autharis. This abated the fierceness with which they had
hitherto treated the Italians; and for a time they granted
them a peace. But the Lombards could not long be without
war. In 662, Italy again received a visit from her Emperor.
Constans the Second, conscious of the hatred of the people
of Constantinople, hoped to set up the Empire again in
Rome. He landed at *Tarentum*, and attacked the territories
of Romoald, Duke of Beneventum. He destroyed the flourishing city of Luceria, but retreated with disgrace on the
advance of Grimoald, the Lombard King, who came to help
his son, the Duke. Constans turned to Rome. While he was
there, the greatness of the Pope seemed to disappear, and he
became like the Patriarch of Constantinople, who never

gained very much power, because the Emperor was always present in the city. The Emperor did nothing in his Imperial city, save that he stole its ornaments, and, above all, the brass roof of the Pantheon, which had been changed into the Basilica of St. Mary. After a stay of twelve days he went to Sicily, and, after he had done much evil, was there slain.

8. **Final Separation of Italy from the East.**—The Italians were thus left defenceless, and saw far the greater part of their land in the hands of strangers. Yet, in spite of all, they still held themselves to be the subjects of the Emperor. The Bishop of Rome had acquired a new position as the defender of the city, and was sometimes more powerful than the Exarch, yet he never, till the beginning of the eighth century, left his allegiance to the Cæsar who reigned in Constantinople. The tie which had been weakened by the decree of 476, and by the rule of the Goths, which had been broken as regards the larger part of Italy by the invasion of the Lombards, and which, though loosened by the vigour of Gregory and the indifference of the Emperor, yet still bound Rome and Roman Italy to the East, was now to be finally severed. *Leo the Isaurian* (717) declared against the worship of images practised by the Catholic Church. The violent attacks made by him and his son upon the popular worship caused many troubles in the East; but there the clergy were too much in the Emperor's power to be able to resist his dictation successfully. But if, even there, this religious change occasioned tumult and bloodshed, in Italy, far from the Emperor's presence, the opposition was fiercer and more determined. It ended in her separation from the Eastern Emperor: it led to a great increase in the power of the Pope; to the interference of the Franks in the affairs of Italy; and finally to the restoration of the Empire of the West. Pope *Gregory the Second* vainly remonstrated with the Emperor. He was in a great strait; for *Liutprand*, one

of the greatest of the Lombard Kings, began to cut the Roman territory short, and took Ravenna. The Pope made alliance with the Venetians, gathered an army, and retook the city. He was everywhere supported against the Emperor, and one Exarch was slain by the people of Ravenna. Still he hesitated to cast away any possible chance of help against the Lombards. His successor, *Gregory the Third*, was the last Bishop of Rome who received the sanction of the Emperor of the East for his consecration. He resisted the Imperial decrees concerning image-worship. Leo sent a great fleet to uphold his Exarch; it was scattered by a tempest; the Exarch fled from Ravenna, and Italy was virtually lost.

9. **The Franks called in.**—Liutprand again threatened Rome, and as the Emperor had used the help of the Franks in the earlier Lombard invasions, so now Gregory looked to the same orthodox people in his need. He sent to *Charles Martel*, the Duke of the Franks, and bade him hasten to help him. Charles died before he could obey the call, but *Pippin* his son received a most urgent summons from Pope Stephen in person. Pippin had deposed Childeric, the last of the Merwings, and had been declared King by Pope Zachary. He twice crossed the Alps, and compelled King Aistulf to yield up his conquests, which included the cities of the Exarchate and the Pentapolis. The Emperor made a claim to this territory, but Pippin gave it all to the Pope. From this donation arose the temporal sovereignty of the Bishops of Rome which lasted until 1870. In return Pippin received the title of Patrician of the Romans from the Roman people and their Bishop. This gave him some vague authority in the city, though the Emperor was still nominally acknowledged. It was in name alone that the Emperor still reigned over Italy. The real power of the Frankish patrician was small, because he was the other side of the

Alps. The Pope, by the donation of Pippin, really ruled over the remains of the Roman province.

After the death of Pippin, Desiderius, the Lombard King, ravaged Romagna, and threatened Rome. Pope Hadrian applied to King Charles, called "*the Great*," the son of Pippin, the hereditary protector of the city. In 774 Charles entered Italy, besieged King Desiderius in Pavia, took him prisoner, and put an end to the Lombard dominion over North Italy, which he added to his own territories. He kept Easter at Rome, and renewed to Hadrian the gift of his father. In the future transactions of Hadrian with Charles a desire for temporal sovereignty can be discerned; and about this time a famous forgery appeared, which purported to be a donation of Constantine to Pope Silvester and his successors, conveying, not the sovereignty of Rome only, but of all the western provinces of the Empire.

10. **The Coronation of Charles the Great,** 800.—Charles paid two more visits to Italy during the lifetime of Hadrian, and helped him to keep possession of the Exarchate. When *Leo the Third* was chosen Pope, he sent to the Patrician the keys of the Confession of St. Peter, the holiest sanctuary in Rome, and the banner of the city. Before long Leo wanted the help of Charles, for a conspiracy was made against him. He was attacked in the streets of Rome, and well-nigh slain. He escaped to Spoletum, and thence to Paderborn, where Charles was warring against the Saxons. The next year the King of the Franks entered Rome, to inquire into the charges made against the spiritual Head of Christendom. The temporal Head, the successor of Augustus, was unfitted for such a work. The West had been estranged by the heresy of the *Iconoclasts* (image-breakers). The Empire was now in the hands of Eirênê, who had deposed and blinded her son Constantine. It seemed unbearable that the lordship of Western Europe should belong to this woman, and that the Roman Empire should be

disposed of without the voice of the Roman people. Charles, on the other hand, was the undoubted Lord of the West, the champion of the Catholic faith against heathen and heretic, the Defender of the Holy See, the Patrician of the Romans, and the Guardian of the city. His voice declared the innocence of the Pope and the punishment of his enemies. He was now to receive the reward of all the good things which he and his father had done for the Papacy. On Christmas day, 800, as he knelt in the Church of St. Peter, the Pope placed a crown of gold upon his head, and the mighty multitude of Romans and Franks hailed him as the successor of Augustus. The Empire of the West, which, in 476, Zeno had made one with the Empire of the East, again rose into separate existence. Italy was again joined to the Empire, of which Rome was the head. The Italian kingdom of Charles stretched from the Alps as far as Terracina. The Duchy of Beneventum paid him tribute, but in all else remained independent. The cities of Gaeta and Naples, and the islands of Sicily and Sardinia, with the extreme ends of Calabria and Apulia, which received the high-sounding title of the Theme of Lombardy, still acknowledged the Eastern Cæsar. Venice was busy with her own affairs, and stood aloof from Italian politics. At this time, and for long after, she knew no Emperor save him who reigned in Constantinople. As long as Charles lived, Italy enjoyed a brief season of stillness. When he died, his vast Empire began to fall to pieces. All the government depended upon him personally; his different states were ruled over by officers of his own choice; he overlooked everything, and everything was referred to him. By his death the tie which bound all together was broken, and each state began to follow out its separate destiny. After the death of Charles the Great his son, *Lewis the Pious*, succeeded to the Empire. He tried in vain to satisfy the ambition of his sons Lothar, Lewis, and Charles, by constant divisions of his dominons. On his death his sons, who had perpetually fought and plotted against him, warred the more fiercely with one another. The *Peace of Verdun*, which was made between the brothers in 843, gave *Lothar* the Imperial title, and a long and narrow kingdom, which stretched from the North Sea to the southern bounds of his grandfather's Italian kingdom. Lothar gave his son *Lewis* a share in the Imperial dignity, and the special charge of the kingdom of Lombardy.

11. **The Saracen Conquests.**—In 827, the *Saracens*, who had become almost masters in the Mediterranean by the submission of Africa, Spain, and Crete, began the conquest of Sicily. It was nearly fifty years before Syracuse was taken and the whole island subdued; but meanwhile they made several attacks upon Italy. They quickly overran Calabria, and their way was made more easy by the bitter feuds between the principalities of Beneventum, Salernum, Naples, and Capua. In one of these wars, Radelchis of Beneventum called the Saracens of Sicily to his aid, and this ruinous example was too often followed by other princes and counts. These encouragements enabled the Saracens to make good their footing in South Italy, and even to pillage under the walls of Rome. The city was perhaps saved by the approach of the Emperor, *Lewis the Second*. Leo the Fourth, who was Pope 847—855, took care to protect the part of Rome which lay beyond the Tiber. He fortified it, and hence it is called after him the Leonine city. A league formed between the maritime cities of Naples, Amalfi, and Sorrento, forced the Moslems to retreat from Gaeta. They however took Bari, which commands the Adriatic, and established a garrison on the Garigliano. The cruelty, lust, and avarice of the conquerors brought great evils upon the cities of South Italy, which were enriched by commerce, and offered them a tempting bait. The Italians called the Emperor Lewis to help them, and he undertook the siege of Bari.

But it was needful to meet the Saracens by sea if the siege was to be effectual. The only power which could match them in the Mediterranean was that of the Emperor of the East. The fleet of Basil the Macedonian was helping the cities of Illyria against the same enemies, and the common danger made the two Emperors set aside their jealousies. The ships of Basil blockaded Bari, while the army of Lewis besieged it, and, in 871, the city was compelled to surrender by the united forces of the Eastern and Western Cæsars. Though Lewis gained this important victory, his influence was small in the land which he had delivered; and, though he addressed his Eastern ally as an equal, yet the Duke of Beneventum was able to seize and imprison him. After his death the Saracens again made rapid progress, and were helped by the Dukes of Naples, who, while they called themselves subjects of the Eastern Emperor, in reality acted as independent sovereigns. When Lewis died, Pope *John the Eighth* crowned his uncle King *Charles*, called the *Bald*, Emperor of the Romans. The Pope sent many letters to Charles beseeching him to come to his help; but the new Emperor had not the spirit of Lewis, and would not come. Rome itself was in danger of being taken, and the Pope was obliged to pay tribute to the Saracens, who were encouraged by the alliance of the Duke-Bishop of Naples.

12. **Revival of Greek power in South Italy**, 890.—The decay of the Carolingian line, and the ceaseless troubles of South Italy, enabled the Greeks to reap the fruits of the taking of Bari. They retook a great number of Saracen castles, and the province or theme of Lombardy stretched as far north as Salernum, while the Greek cities of Naples and Amalfi, and the Lombard rulers of Beneventum and Capua, also owned the Eastern Cæsar, though the allegiance of the Lombards was wavering and changeful. The seat of government was fixed in the newly-acquired city of Bari, and an

Imperial officer was appointed, who was first called *Patrician*, and afterwards by the more barbarous title of *Catapan*. The reconquered province was secured to the Greeks by the disputes of the different claimants for the throne of Italy, and remained part of the Eastern Empire for a century and a half (890—1043). North Italy received eight kings of the line of Charles the Great, and its history is much the same as that of the rest of his Empire. Charles did not so much create new institutions as remodel those which already existed. He left untouched the system of local government by great territorial Dukes and their inferior officers, though he restrained their power. He constantly sent his own officers on special missions to the local rulers, and by this means kept everything under his own power. He did not impose any one system of laws upon his subjects. The Lombard could claim to be tried by the laws of Rotharis and his successors, the most perfect of all the barbarian codes, and the Roman by his own more elaborate system. Thus there were many elements of disunion in his policy, but his wisdom and greatness kept all together. After his death the local powers grew stronger, and the central influence weaker, under each succeeding Emperor-King. The Counts, who were at first officers appointed by the crown, became the most powerful of the territorial nobles; and the Bishops, whom Charles had always kept in check, assumed in many cases, like the Counts, an almost independent sovereignty over their cities and lands. At the close of the ninth century, the chief powers in North Italy were the Duke of Friuli, the Count of Tuscany, and the Archbishop of Milan. They paid a merely nominal obedience to the Carolingian king. For seventy years the kingdom of Italy was joined to the Imperial dignity, either in the person of the Emperor himself or of his son or grandson. On the death of *Charles the Bald,* Emperor, and King of the

Western Franks and of Italy, Carloman, son of Lewis, King of the Eastern Franks, seized the crown of Italy during the vacancy of the Empire. This was against the will of Pope John the Eighth. The Pope was forced to flee, and took refuge with Boso, who became King in *Cisjurane Burgundy* and *Provence*. The Pope adopted Boso as his son, and on the death of Carloman wished to raise him to the Empire, and so shut out the German Carolingians. But the nobles and Bishops of North Italy were many of them of German families, descendants of the great officers and nobles of Charles the Great, and would have nothing to do with the Pope's candidate. Charles the Fat, son of Lewis the German, made the Pope crown him Emperor, and the German party had the better of the struggle. The new Emperor had no power either to still the factions of his Italian kingdom or to curb the aggressions of the Saracens. At his death in 887, the Empire of Charles fell to pieces, and the legitimate line of the Carolingian Kings of Italy ended.

CHAPTER II.

THE EMPEROR AND THE POPE.

Italian Kings and Emperors (1)—*the barbarian invasions* (2)—*degradation of the Papacy* (3)—*troubles of Italy* (3)—*Otto the Great in Italy* (4)—*the Saxon Emperors* (5)—*Otto the Third and Crescentius* (6)—*the Lombard Cities* (7)—*the Franconian Emperors* (8)—*the Normans in South Italy* (9)—*the commerce of the Italian cities* (10)—*the position of the Church towards the lay power; the War of Investitures* (11)—*the allies of the Pope* (12)—*Henry V. and the Pope* (13)—*the Concordat of Worms* (14).

1. **Italian Kings and Emperors.**—When the Empire of Charles the Fat was broken up, the kingdom of the West Franks separated itself from that of the East Franks. Italy was no longer bound to accept a descendant of Charles the

Great as her King, since the Empire had departed from his line, and as yet it was by no means necessary that the Imperial dignity should be united to the East Frankish crown. A strong anti-German feeling had grown up in Italy. Men began to feel that the King of Italy at least, and, if possible, the Emperor of the Romans, should be an Italian. The East Franks, or Germans, chose *Arnulf* King. Italy was divided by two competitors,—*Berengar of Friuli*, and *Guido of Spoleto*. Berengar was generally supported by the Lombards, and Guido by some of the great nobles, and especially by *Adalbert*, Count of Tuscany, a descendant of Boniface, who had received the county or marquessate from Charles the Great. Guido was victorious, and was crowned Emperor, and Berengar called the German Arnulf to help him. Arnulf came, and terrified North Italy into submission. Pope Formosus favoured the German party, and the conqueror looked forward to obtaining the Imperial crown, but for a time he was driven back by the heat. Guido died, and his son Lambert obtained the crown of Italy and the Empire. While Arnulf was away, Lambert met with no opposition. But the Germans came back, and Arnulf entered Rome, and was crowned Emperor almost without a blow. The violence and disorder of the German army made Arnulf much hated, and this strengthened the opposite party. Arnulf and Lambert soon died. It was said that both of them were murdered. Adalbert, the great Count of Tuscany, had set Berengar upon the throne, but he soon called *Lewis* of Provence, son of Boso, to overthrow him. After a while Adalbert turned against him also and overthrew him, because Lewis allowed the Tuscan kingmaker to see that he was jealous of his power. All these revolutions, which in twenty years gave the crown of Italy to five different claimants, brought nothing but evil to the unhappy land. Those who contended for it were unable or unwilling to defend it. They were no true

Italians—Arnulf was a German, and the rest were Italians only in name. In all else they were Germans. Because the Popes called in the Germans, Pippin and Charles, to defend Italy, the land now had to bear the ambition and violence of these Counts.

2. **The Northmen, Saracens, and Magyars.**—Italy, in the tenth century, like the rest of Europe, suffered severely from barbarian invasions. The *Northmen*, under their great leader Hasting, were wasting the kingdom of Provence, when they heard of the riches of Rome. They sailed across the gulf, and, it is said, mistook the Magra for the Tiber. They landed near Luna, which the Italians held to be the oldest city in the land. Hasting pretended to be converted, and was baptized by the bishop. Soon after the citizens were told that Hasting had died in his camp. He was borne into the city by his followers, to be buried in holy ground. Thus the Normans gained an entrance into Luna. Then Hasting, who was only pretending to be dead, sprang from the bier, and he and his men killed the priests and many people. They burned the city, and sailed away with much spoil. This story may not be true, but it is certain that the Northmen took Luna by craft and destroyed it. Two other foes abode longer, and worked greater evils. The *Saracens* of the South, from their fortress on the Garigliano, commanded the road to Rome, and were a curse to all the country round them. The warlike Pope, John the Tenth, formed a league of some powerful nobles, and, in 916, supported by the ships of Constantine the Seventh, the Eastern Emperor, he took the field in person, and inflicted a bloody defeat upon the intruders. The greatest scourge of all were the *Magyars* or *Hungarians*, a Turanian horde, who swept over Central Europe in the early part of the century. They brought with them the severest evils which a heathen and barbarous nation can inflict upon countries which have risen to Chris-

tianity and civilization. They poured down upon Italy; and the land which was as the garden of Eden before them, behind them was a desolate wilderness. King Berengar brought them to bay by the river Brenta. They asked leave to retreat, and rid the land of their presence. The King haughtily refused. His army was routed, and the savages overran the land without further opposition. In after-times the King allied himself with these barbarians against his private enemies.

3. **Degradation of the Papacy.**—Though Berengar was crowned Emperor, he did nothing against the enemies of Italy or of the Pope. He employed himself entirely in seeking to counteract the intrigues of the nobles, which were chiefly set on foot by Ermengarde, daughter of Adalbert of Tuscany, and widow of Adalbert of Ivrea. Rudolf of Burgundy was set up against him, and for the moment succeeded in seizing the crown. Berengar was assassinated. After his death a new claimant appeared. This was *Hugh* of Provence, the son of Bertha, widow of Adalbert, and half-brother of Guido, the reigning Marquess of Tuscany, and of Ermengarde, widow of the Marquess of Ivrea. He thus united the interests of both these great houses. He landed at Pisa in 926, and was received as King by Pope John. Rome was in the power of an infamous woman called Marozia. This is the darkest period in the history of the Papacy. Two celebrated women, Theodora and Marozia, were supreme. Marozia was the mother, the mistress, and, perhaps, the murderer of a Pope. She now married King Hugh. The Romans would not allow the foreigner to come within their walls, and he was forced to keep his court in the Castle of St. Angelo. He was driven away by *Alberic*, a son of Marozia, who restored to the city some republican institutions. Alberic ruled over Rome till he died. He was succeeded by his son, who ruled the city as Consul under the name of *Octavian*, and as Pope under

that of *John the Twelfth*. Although Hugh was driven out from Rome, he ruled over the rest of Italy. His life was hateful for its shameful immorality, and he used his kingly power simply as a means of robbery. Conspiracies were formed against him. The most formidable was one to give the throne to Berengar, Marquess of Ivrea, the greatest noble of North Italy. He had married Willa, a daughter of Boso, the brother of King Hugh. Willa stirred up her husband against her uncle, who, not without reason, was hated by her family. The King found out the conspiracy, and would have blinded Berengar, but he was warned by Lothar, the King's son, and so fled and escaped. The King brought upon himself the hatred of the great nobles, ecclesiastical and civil, because he gave so much to his foreign followers, and so they left him for Berengar, who again came into Italy. Hugh went back to Provence, and left his son *Lothar* to bear the title of King. In a short time Lothar died, and his death is put down to Berengar, whom he had once saved from his father's anger. After his death Berengar and his son Adalbert took the title of King.

4. **Otto the Great in Italy**, 951.—Berengar sought Adelheid, the young and beautiful widow of Lothar, in marriage for his son. On her refusal he shut her up in prison, and used her very cruelly. News of her sad fate were carried across the Alps, and *Otto the Great*, the German King, came down and delivered her with a strong hand, and afterwards married her. Berengar was powerless before him, and became his man at Pavia. Otto returned home in triumph, and the North of Italy was left to the evil government of King Berengar, until the German came again and claimed the kingdom and the Empire. Otto was the representative of the Dukes of Saxony. His father *Henry* had been elected King of the Germans, and had given the *Magyars* or *Hungarians* the first great check on the field

of *Merseberg*. The work of ridding Europe of this dreadful scourge was carried on by Otto after he came back from Italy. The invasion was ended by the battle of *Lechfeld*. The Hungarians were made to settle down, and are henceforth to be reckoned among the nations of Europe. In 957 the discontent which Berengar's oppression caused in Italy was heard by the great German King. His son Ludolf entered Italy, but died shortly after, and Berengar's oppression was increased by jealousy. At last Otto came into Italy with a large army, and, in 962, was crowned King and Emperor. Berengar and his wife ended their days in Germany, and the shadowy line of Italian Kings and Emperors came to an end.

5. **The Saxon Emperors, 962–1002.**—Both the crown of the Italian kingdom or of Lombardy, and the crown of the Empire, which brought with it rights over Rome and the Lombard Duchies, were now again worn by a German King. From this time the belief began to grow that he who was chosen King by the Germans had a right to be crowned King of Italy at Milan, and Emperor at Rome. The coronation of Otto was a revival of the Empire, for the Italian Emperors had been no more than Kings of part of Italy with a highsounding, but, in their case, a meaningless title. From this time forward the armies of the German Kings made the title of Augustus again venerable. If the Imperial dignity had remained in the hands of Italian Princes, it would certainly have lacked the vast and splendid theories which clustered round it, but possibly an Italian King, aided by so great a name, might have formed a free and united Italy. As it was, the Empire gained in strength by being joined to the German Kingship. As regards Italy, however, the effect of this union was that her lawful Sovereign was a man of another nation, and dwelt across the Alps. As soon as Otto had left Rome, the wicked Pope, *John the Twelfth*, began to conspire

with Berengar, and even with the Magyars. He inherited the influence of his father Alberic; and the Romans, who hated to be governed, rose against the German soldiers. The Pope was deposed by Otto for his treachery and other crimes, and the Roman people were put down again and again, until at last the Emperor took away all their independent institutions, and committed the care of the city to *Leo the Eighth*, a Pope of his own choosing. Thus Otto made himself complete master of the city and of the Pope. In South Italy the Emperor tried to secure the allegiance of the Lombard Princes, which wavered between the two Empires. He carried on a war against the Eastern Emperor. In this he had no great success, and on the death of *Nikêphoros Phôkas* he made peace with his successor *John Tzimiskês*, and married his son Otto to *Theophanô*, daughter of the Emperor *Rômanos*. This marriage made Otto the Second anxious to join South Italy to his Empire. He made an attempt upon it with the help of Pandulf Ironhead, who united under his rule the principalities of Capua, Benevento and Salerno. He was defeated by the Saracens and Greeks, and the battle of *Crotona* saved the Theme of Lombardy for the Eastern Emperor, *Basil the Second*. After this victory the power of the Eastern Emperor in the South greatly increased. The Lombard duchy of Benevento finally fell to pieces at the death of Pandulf Ironhead, and the Eastern Emperors gained considerable power over the small parts into which it was broken up.

6. **Otto the Third and Crescentius.**—The absence of Otto the Second and the minority of his son gave the Romans fresh hope, and they again set up an independent municipal government under a *Consul* named *Crescentius*. This popular leader was a citizen of wealth and of noble family. He was descended from Theodora and Pope John the Tenth, from the great and wicked house who had ruled so long in Rome.

John the Fifteenth, who was a Roman, after a short attempt at resistance, acknowledged the Consul's powers. But, in 996, *Otto the Third* came down into Italy, and was crowned Emperor by *Gregory the Fifth*, a German Pope of his own appointment, and, for a time, the consular government seemed at an end. When Otto left Italy, Crescentius regained his power, set up a Greek Antipope, and turned to the Eastern Empire for help. The Emperor soon came back. He deposed and cruelly tortured the Consul's Antipope, and besieged Crescentius in the Castle of St. Angelo. He persuaded Crescentius to come to terms and to surrender, and then faithlessly had him put to death. Thus he put an end to the *self-government* of the Romans, as his grandfather had done. Otto the Third held that he inherited some rights over the Eastern Empire from his mother, as he had over the Western Empire from his father. His lofty ambition was to reign over the world, and, to this end, he sought a Greek wife, still further to strengthen his claims over the East. Thus both the Emperor and his Roman rebels looked to Constantinople for the furtherance of their designs. At the head of Otto's world-wide Empire was to be Rome, the mistress of the world, and the mother of churches of the world. He therefore earnestly carried on the regeneration of the Papacy which his grandfather had begun, and drew Italy into close connexion with himself and his Teutonic kingdom. His magnificent plans were soon ended, for he was poisoned, when he was only twenty-five, by *Stephania*, the widow of Crescentius, who had met with shameful treatment from the Germans. At his death the city and the Church again turned to the popular government of the house of Crescentius, and, after a while, fell to a lower state of degradation under the Popes and Counts of the great house of Tusculum.

7. **The Lombard Cities.**—The large cities of North Italy seem to have kept, under one form or another, a good part

of the municipal liberty which they had in earlier times. From the beginning of the Empire their internal government had been in the hands of the higher class. This *Order* (*Ordo Decurionum*) was responsible to the Imperial treasury for the taxes; it thus represented the city, and was a sort of governing corporation, and, though it was much weakened by taxation and general distress, it must still have been the foremost power in Pavia and other large cities. The smaller cities, for the most part, must have fallen under the power either of some great secular lord or bishop, and even Milan had often enough to do to keep her Archbishop in check. The lord's officer commanded the militia of the city, and was judge in the more important cases, while other matters were managed by officers chosen by the citizens. The troubles which came upon Italy at the break up of the Carolingian dominion, the disputes for the throne and the invasion of the Hungarians, made the cities rise in power and importance, as places which either could be made capable of defence, or had been already fortified in older times. In the eleventh century the government was generally carried on by two or more Consuls, chosen by the people. Their duties were to dispense justice, to call out and head the militia, and to preside over the councils of the city. Each of these infant republics had generally two councils. The smaller one carried out the laws and policy of the city, and in after-time was called the *Consiglio di Credenza*. The other consisted of more members, and was called the *Great Council* or *Senate*. In this larger Council new measures were debated. The highest power in the city was in the whole body of the citizens themselves. On great occasions the common bell of the city was tolled, and all the citizens gathered together in "*Parliament*" in the square of the city-palace. These municipalities gained importance at the death of Otto the Third, for then there was another dispute for the crown. The nobles of Lombardy chose *Ardoin*, Marquess of Ivrea, to be King, and Pavia, the old capital of the kingdom, espoused his cause. The cause of the German King, *Henry of Bavaria*, was upheld by the city of Milan, and he was crowned there. A strong anti-Milanese party, headed by Pavia, clung to Ardoin, until he retired to a monastery. The war between the two cities marks the beginning of their independent life and action. Henry never had much power in Italy, and the severity with which he punished Pavia confirmed the hatred of his enemies. On his death the national party offered the kingdom to Robert, King of the French, and then to William, Count of Poitou; but they both refused it.

8. The Franconian Emperors.—In 1024, the Germans chose *Conrad of Franconia* to be king, and *Heribert*, Archbishop of Milan, invited him into Italy, and crowned him with the iron crown of the kingdom. Several of the Italian cities had Bishops for their Counts. These cities quickly became independent, because there was often a disputed election, and then the candidate for the bishoprick would make many promises in order to gain a strong party. This was the case with Milan. Heribert the Archbishop (1018) greatly increased the power of his city. He made a successful war with Lodi. He ruled despotically over his nobles, and the most important part of his career was his war with them. In this war the Archbishop invented a sacred ensign, as a rallying-point for his army. It was a tall mast, with two white pennants hanging from the top, and with an image of the Crucified half-way down. It was fixed in a car, and was thence called the *carroccio*. This standard, like the ark of Israel, was looked upon with deep veneration, and its loss implied the most crushing defeat. In after-time it was richly ornamented with devices, and most of the other cities adopted a similar ensign. The war between Heribert and the lesser nobles was a type of a widely-spread struggle. As the power of the Carolingian Kings declined, the successors of the great officers whom Charles had appointed became lords of the soil, and the other nobles sank in proportion, because they became their vassals, whereas in olden time they had only owed allegiance to the Emperor. In order to check the power of the greater ecclesiastical and civil lords, Conrad the Second issued a decree, in 1037, in his great council (*placitum*), that all fiefs should descend from father to son, and that no one should lose his fief but by the course of law and the judgment of his equals. The cause of the war between Heribert and his nobles was his refusal to extend this privilege to them. The absence of the Emperor enabled civil discord to go on unchecked. Milan was for some time disturbed by a war between the nobles and the people headed by a noble called *Lanzo*. In this war *Henry the Third*, who succeeded his father, refused to interfere.

The Papacy sank low under the Tusculan Popes. It was raised by the wise appointments of German Popes by the Emperor Henry the Third. The climate proved fatal to his first two Popes; the third, his own kinsman, *Leo the Ninth*, began a work of reformation, which, in time, made the Papacy so strong that it became the rival of the Empire. The two main causes of weakness in the Church were simony and the marriage of the clergy. Simony robbed it of its sanctity as a profession and enabled the temporal power to interfere with its preferments. The marriage of the clergy tended to make ecclesiastical benefices hereditary, lessened the veneration of the laity for the priesthood, and hindered the priests from devoting themselves to a struggle for power. Both these customs were vigorously attacked by Leo. No defence was offered for simony, but it was too wide-spread to be quickly rooted out, and the attack upon it gradually was merged in the War of the Investitures. The attempt to enforce clerical celibacy gave rise to a bitter struggle in Milan. The Church of St. Ambrose withstood that of St. Peter; and the married clergy, in Milan, in other Lombard cities, and in Florence, were for a long time able to resist not only Leo the Ninth, but even the mightier Gregory the Seventh.

9. **The Normans in South Italy.**—While the cities of the North were rising into some degree of independence, Southern Italy was attacked by a fresh invader. The Northmen, who were settled in Normandy, had by no means lost their love of adventure. Whether on a pilgrimage or a military expedition, they were to be found wherever there was hope of plunder or renown. A band of these wandering knights, in 1010, helped *Gaimar*, a Lombard prince of Salerno, against the Saracens. A little later they made alliance with *Melo* of Bari, who revolted from the Greek Empire. They attacked the Theme and were defeated. The Emperor *Henry the Second* favoured their settlement in Southern Italy to counteract an alliance made between the Emperor Basil and Pandulf, Prince of Capua. They established themselves in *Aversa*, which was confirmed to them by *Conrad*. Their numbers soon increased. A Norman force under three of the sons of Tancred of Hauteville, in 1037, took service with the Catapan *George Maniakês*, and helped him to conquer a large part of Sicily from the Saracens for the Emperor Rômanos the Third. Maniakês displeased his new allies. They turned against him, and, under the command of Counts, chosen by themselves, they soon conquered Apulia. This conquest by a body of military adventurers, at once avaricious, prodigal, and without restraint, pressed very heavily upon the people. A league was formed against them by Pope *Leo the Ninth*, who applied to the Emperors *Henry the Third* and *Constantine the Tenth* to help him against the common enemy. Both of them had work to do at home, and the Pope himself led an army composed of some Italians, Greeks, and Swabians

against the Normans. His foes were few in number, but they were all men of war, and, in 1053, under Counts Humfrey, Richard, and the famous *Robert Wiscard*, sons of Tancred, they totally defeated the Papal army at the battle of *Civitella*. The Pope was taken prisoner. The devout Normans reverenced their captive, and, it is said, received from him the investiture of their present and future conquests in Apulia, Calabria, and Sicily. These they consented to hold as a fief of the Holy See. These conquests were carried on by Robert Wiscard, and were confirmed to him by Pope *Nicolas the Second*. Robert, in 1059, took the title of Duke of Apulia and Calabria. The submission of the Normans, and their acknowledgment of Leo as Lord of South Italy and Sicily, was a most important step in the greatness of the Papacy. After a long war, Sicily was subdued. Robert gave the island to Roger his brother, who took the title of Count. In 1071 Bari, the residence of the Catapans, fell. The Lombard duchies were extinguished, one after another, and the Norman dominions were united, in 1127, under Roger, the Great Count of Sicily, son of Count Roger. He completed the work of conquest and took the title of King of Sicily, of Apulia and Capua.

10. **Commerce of the Italian Cities.**—The conquest by the Normans crushed the Greek maritime cities of Naples, Gaeta, and Amalfi, which had carried on the trade of the Mediterranean, and brought the riches of the East into Europe. Their place was taken by Venice, Pisa, and Genoa. *Venice* still stood aloof from the Empire of the West and from the rest of Italy. She still boasted herself the subject of the Eastern Emperor. In alliance with Alexios Komnênos, she filled the Adriatic with a powerful fleet, and successfully checked the aggressions of Robert Wiscard, who had attacked the Empire of New Rome. Early in the eleventh century the fleet of Pisa drove the Saracens out of Sardinia, and colonized the island. This conquest was

THE REPUBLICS OF THE NORTH.

disputed by *Genoa*, but as yet *Pisa* was far ahead of her rival, and in the beginning of the next century she also took the Balearic Isles. The Crusades greatly increased the wealth and importance of the Italian maritime cities. Before the decided check which these holy wars gave to the Saracens, the number of pirates made the Levant, and even the Adriatic unsafe. The Italian cities, which took a considerable part in the Crusades, reaped great benefits from them. They conveyed the merchandise of the East to Italy, and thence passing down the Rhine, it was dispersed through Europe by the cities of Germany. From the beginning of the twelfth century, Venice, Pisa, and Genoa began to dispute between themselves the mastery in the Levant, and even, at last, in the Bosporos. For a century and a half Pisa was the strongest and had the largest trade. The splendour of her *Duomo*, her *Baptistery*, and her famous *bell-tower*, recall the time when she received and traded in the riches of the East. The cities of Italy, however, were not entirely dependent upon imports, for they carried on large manufactures of silk and woollen stuffs. The spirit of independence and the love of freedom and self-government had already begun to appear in the cities of the North. Before long the cities of Tuscany, freed from the dominion of their great Counts, began to run the same course. The history of the republics of the North gathers round Milan. Their career was short and brilliant. The nobles found that they were not able to stand against such powerful neighbours, and in most cases were forced to become their citizens. When they entered their new homes, they filled them with confusion, and the burghers of humble birth had no little trouble in keeping their more noble fellow-citizens in order, and often severely punished them when they disturbed the peace of their city, or were unmindful of its welfare. After these cities had for a short time been free, the citizens listened to evil counsels, and fell under the yoke of absolute rulers, or, as they were called in Greece, *tyrants;* that is to say, men who in some way or other got the lordship over a state which had once been a commonwealth. These men used the swords of the citizens, or more often of mercenaries hired by their money, to annex other places, and thus Italy became split up into separate lordships. When the Lombard republics began to decay, and to fall under Tyrants, Florence was in an early stage of her career of greatness. This noble Tuscan city was for a long time the bulwark of Italian freedom, and was almost the last to fall under the yoke.

11. **War of the Investitures.**—The reform which Henry the Third brought about in the Papacy armed it against the Imperial throne. He worked its reform by becoming a maker of Popes, and the Popes only waited for strength to rid themselves of a master. For many years both before and after the death of Henry, the Court of Rome was managed by the Archdeacon *Hildebrand,* a man of great political talent, proud, ambitious in all matters which concerned his order, and of an unbending will. He aimed at making the priesthood a united spiritual army, devoted solely to the advancement of the political power of the Church, and of the Head of the Church upon earth. To this end he strove to raise the position of the priesthood by enforcing the celibacy of the clergy and by freeing ecclesiastical appointments from all lay power. In his eyes a married priest was guilty of concubinage ; and one who received the temporalities, the lands or revenues, of his benefice from a lay lord, was guilty of simony. The attack which he made upon the marriage of the clergy in the time of Leo the Ninth turned away a large number of them from him. The second doctrine struck at the root of all lay power, which was based upon the lordship of land. If it had been fully successful, it would have created throughout Christendom an order independent of all

secular government, and possessed of vast wealth. This wealth would have been held to have come from God alone, and it would therefore have been subject to no obligations towards man; it would have been exempt from taxation, from the burthen of national defence, and even from loyalty to the Sovereign. Still it was evident that the lay power over the Church needed some check. The Bishop or parish-priest received the temporalities of his benefice from the temporal lord by a ceremony called *Investiture*, and this often led to the giving of money for the sacred office, and to the appointment of unworthy and unfit persons. It also worked, along with the marriage of the clergy, in debasing their character. A priest was allowed by the lord on payment of a sum, like the temporal "*relief*," and on performance of homage, to succeed to his father's office, though he might have no education or fitness. And so the sacred office was treated like a secular benefice or fief (*beneficium*). When Hildebrand was made Pope, he determined to stop these evils, and, in 1075, he made a decree against Investitures. This caused strife between him and King Henry the Fourth. In the eyes of the Imperial party, the Pope was the first subject of the Emperor, invested by him with his bishop-rick and its possessions. Imperialists remembered how Otto the Great and Henry the Third had judged, deposed, and appointed Popes. The Churchmen held that the Emperor was lower than the Pope, as temporal things are lower than spiritual, and they reminded their opponents that it was the coronation by the Pope which alone could make a German King *Augustus*. The Pope excommunicated the King, and favoured a great rebellion which was made against him in Saxony. This rebellion obliged Henry to submit. For three days in the month of January, 1077, King Henry waited, bareheaded and shivering, at the gates of the Castle of Canossa, before the haughty Pope would listen to his penitent submission. At last the King was allowed to appear before him. The Pope, after making him promise all that he asked, in some sort forgave him. Before long the strife broke out again.

12. **The Allies of the Pope.**— In Italy the chief ally of the Pope was the *Countess Matilda*, daughter and heiress of Boniface, Count of Tuscany; and her great wealth and her wide territories, of which Florence was the head, were readily placed at the Pope's service. In Lombardy, especially in Milan, and at Ravenna, men held to their King, for Gregory's strictness had raised a strong party against him. The discontented party in Germany chose another King called *Rudolf of Swabia*. In return Henry made *Guibert of Ravenna*, Antipope. Then Pope and King declared each other deposed. On the defeat and death of his rival in Germany, in 1080, Henry came down into Italy, and was received with great joy in Lombardy. The Countess Matilda's troops had been defeated near Mantua. The King threatened her capital and then marched on to Rome. For three years his army besieged the Pope. Each summer it retreated before the heat, and returned again in the winter. The Eastern Emperor, Alexios, whose dominions were invaded by the Norman Wiscard, made an alliance with Henry, and supplied him largely with money. The Normans, however, who since the battle of Civitella had been the firm allies of the Papacy, could not help Gregory at first, for Robert was warring in the East. In one of the many intervals of the siege the Emperor's troops overran Tuscany, and several of the adherents of the Countess deserted the Pope's cause. Henry took the Leonine city which lies on the right bank of the river, and, at last, the Romans opened their gates to him. On Palm Sunday, 1084, the King's Pope, Guibert, was consecrated and took the title of *Clement the Third*, and, in return, he crowned King Henry as Emperor of the Romans.

Meanwhile Pope Gregory remained shut up, in reality a prisoner, but still unyielding, in the fortress of St. Angelo, the ancient tomb of Hadrian, once the stronghold of the Consul Crescentius. At last help came. The Norman, who had put the Eastern Cæsar to flight, now advanced against his ally and brother of the West. He had a large army, of which the Saracens of Sicily, the subjects of his brother Roger, were an important part. The Emperor retreated before him, and, in 1084, he entered Rome without meeting any resistance. But a tumult, which broke out among the citizens, so enraged the conquerors that they treated the city as though it had been taken by storm. They committed every excess of pillage and violence, and the Cœlian quarter was destroyed by fire. After the death of Gregory, other Popes still carried on the struggle with Henry the Fourth, and adopted the shameful policy of raising foes against him of his own household. His eldest son *Conrad* was persuaded to revolt by the Countess Matilda and Pope Urban the Second. He was received by Milan and some of the Northern cities which had hitherto remained faithful to his father, and was crowned King of Italy, first at Monza, and then in the Church of St. Ambrose. The cause of the Papacy was greatly helped forward by the Crusading movement, for the Pope turned the religious enthusiasm of Europe to his own account, and in the Council of Piacenza accused the Emperor of many vile acts. After the death of Conrad, the Emperor's second son *Henry* was set up against him. At last, worn out with the struggle, and heart-broken by his children's undutifulness, the Emperor died, in 1106.

13. **Henry V. and the Pope.**—The policy of the Pope met with its reward, for *Henry the Fifth* was a much more dangerous enemy than his father had been. He came into Italy with a large army, and, as he passed, all the cities, save Milan, submitted to him. He was even received by

Florence and the Countess Matilda. He entered Rome, and, in 1111, shut Pope *Paschal the Second* up in prison, and only let him out again on the condition of his crowning him Emperor. Henry was triumphant, but only for a time. As had been the case with his father, his real weakness lay in German discontent, which was much increased by his despotic rule. The Pope again took heart, and the death of the Countess Matilda put him almost in a regal position, for she left the Holy See all her vast possessions, reaching from Mantua to Pisa, and from Pisa almost to the gates of Rome. The Countess, when advanced in life, had married *Welf*, son of the Duke of Bavaria, in order to thwart the Emperor in Germany through that powerful house. Henry claimed the lands which Matilda held of the Empire as a lapsed fief, and it seems likely that he asserted the claim of the Bavarian house to her other possessions, not to put them into the hands of the Welfs, who were his enemies, but to get them away from the Pope. He entered Tuscany, and took peaceable possession of the territory, which he held undisturbed during his life; nevertheless, the Popes did not forego their claim, and it was revived in after years.

The Normans throughout the struggle continued the faithful allies and vassals of the Popes. Gregory the Seventh, Urban the Second, and Paschal the Second, each in turn found shelter in their dominions. From the time of the coronation of Conrad, most of the Lombard cities were inclined to the Papal side, but the presence of a German army in Tuscany prevented much active help being given.

14. **The Concordat of Worms**, 1122.—At last the question of Investitures was decided at Worms. Each party gave up something: the substantial gain was on the Pope's side. The Emperor surrendered the right of Investiture by ring and staff, and granted the right of free election to the clergy. On the other hand, the Pope granted that the temporalities

of the Church in Germany should be received from the Emperor, that it should in fact become a National Church. Thus the Emperor lost, while the King of the Germans gained. The contest, however, had really been for Papal independence, the forerunner of Papal ascendancy, and here too the Pope was the victor. The power which Charles and Otto and Henry the Third had exercised over the Papacy was gone for ever. The Pope became independent of the Emperor, while the Imperial crown was still conferred by the hands of the Pope. The independence of the Pope gave Italy an ally against her Emperor. The long struggle left her cities an increased importance and freedom from control. The War of Investitures made it possible for them in aftertime to combine together against the common enemy. For a while indeed they used their strength against one another. The long feud between Milan and Pavia divided the North into two great parties, and the smaller cities shared the quarrels and fortunes of the larger, who were at their head. Milan was the more successful during the early part of the twelfth century, and the conquest of Lodi and Como confirmed her headship in Lombardy. In Tuscany, Florence rose to independence at the death of the Countess Matilda, and was ruled by Consuls, like the Northern cities. During the first half of the twelfth century she began to extend her territory, and forced a great many noble families to become her citizens. During this time the Pisans were at the height of their prosperity, and were engaged in victorious wars by sea and land. They took the island of Majorca from the Saracen pirates, and brought a long war with Lucca to a triumphant end. In this war Florence was on the side of Pisa, and inflicted a severe defeat on Siena, which took the other side. As yet the rivalry between the two great Tuscan cities had not begun, and the friendship between them made them very terrible to their neighbours.

CHAPTER III

THE EMPEROR AND THE CITIES.

Lothar and Conrad (1)—*Arnold of Brescia* (2)—*Frederic Barbarossa* (3)—*his quarrel with the Pope* (4)—*with the Lombard cities* (5)—*the Lombard League* (6)—*end of the Norman kingdom* (7)—*dispute for the Empire* (8)—*the cities and the nobles* (9)—*the Latin conquest of Constantinople* (10)—*Frederic the Second, King of the Romans* (11)—*Emperor* (12)—*his quarrel with the Pope* (13)—*his success* (14)—*his failure, and death* (15).

1. **Lothar the Saxon and Conrad III.**—The death of Henry the Fifth without children in 1135 caused a dispute for the Empire between two great families. *Lothar*, Duke of the Saxons, was chosen by the German Electors, and was supported by the *Welfs* of *Bavaria*. They had for some time been allies of the Papacy, and had disturbed the peace of the Empire. The other party was headed by the *Hohenstaufens*. The greatness of this family had been much increased by the marriage of Frederic with a daughter of Henry the Fourth, who made his son-in-law Duke of the *Swabians*. The Hohenstaufens withstood the Papal party in Germany, and were supporters of Imperial law and order. Italy, like the rest of the Empire, was divided between these two parties, who soon were called *Guelfs*, or *Welfs*, and *Ghibelins*, from *Waiblingen*, a village which was the home of the Hohenstaufen family. The Papacy was also disputed between *Innocent* and *Anaclet*. The cause of Anaclet was taken up by Roger, King of Sicily, against Innocent and his ally Lothar. The succession of the Saxon Duke was decided north of the Alps. He came down into Italy, and was crowned by Pope Innocent, and it is said that, in return,

the Emperor did homage to the Pope, or became his man. A war with King Roger followed, which completed the ruin of the Greek maritime cities. Pope Innocent the Second, like his predecessor Leo the Ninth, fell into the hands of the Normans, and they again made their conquests secure by a nominal homage. On the death of Lothar, *Conrad* was chosen King. He was the son of Frederic the First and brother of Frederic the Second, Duke of the Swabians. Innocent strengthened himself against the new King by a close alliance with Roger of Sicily, who was a dangerous enemy both to the Eastern and Western Cæsar. To check his encroachment, the Emperors *Manuel* and *Conrad* formed a league and alliance by marriage.

2. **Arnold of Brescia.**—Although Pope Innocent was successful against his foreign enemies, he could not manage his own city. The Romans were stirred up by the preaching of a monk named *Arnold of Brescia*, and again strove to shake off the temporal rule of their great Bishop. In Brescia, and indeed through all Lombardy, his eloquent and stern denunciations of the ambition of the priesthood stirred men's minds. He was forced to flee to Zurich. After a few years he appeared in Rome, and there preached a reformation in the State. The Romans refused to be ruled by their Bishop; they formed a Senate and tried to imitate the institutions of the old Republic. They hoped to gain the protection of Conrad, and offered him the *Patriciate* or Headship of the City, the office which had been held by Charles the Great before his Imperial coronation. One Pope after another also wrote to beg him to suppress a revolt which was against both Emperor and Pope. But he was too much engaged with other matters to take either side, and so the Romans chose an Italian named *Giordano* for their Patrician, and continued to listen to and obey the teaching of Arnold.

3. **Frederic Barbarossa.**— When Conrad died, the

Electors chose his nephew *Frederic*, called *Barbarossa*, or *Red Beard*. In 1154 he came down into Italy. He held a great Diet at Roncaglia, and there received the submission of the Italian States. But a spirit of independence had grown up in North Italy. The Lombard cities had for some years been left without Imperial control, and had made wars and alliances between themselves like sovereign states. The Emperor had become a stranger; now at last he was prepared to assert his authority. Frederic in Germany was a great feudal sovereign, but he had higher rights as the imperial successor of Augustus. These were eagerly insisted upon by the civil lawyers who filled his court, and were gladly accepted by his German and Italian partisans. At the same time a powerful party in Italy indignantly resented any interference with their affairs. The question as to the Emperor's position in Italy soon arose. At the Diet at Roncaglia, Lodi and Como made complaint to Frederic of the many wrongs done them by Milan; and Pavia, the rival of Milan, also brought accusations against Tortona, one of the allies of that city. Milan had deeply offended Frederic by refusing to yield him his *regalian rights*. These rights were *forage*, *food*, and *lodging* for the Emperor's army, which every city was bound to provide when he entered her territory, and to refuse them was to deny his authority. Frederic decided against Milan and her party He delayed his march to Rome to destroy Asti and Chieri, and besieged and burnt Tortona. He spared the lives of the conquered, and they took refuge in Milan. He then went on to Rome, and was crowned Emperor by *Hadrian the Fourth*. In return he enabled the Pope to put Arnold to death, and by his very presence overthrew the independence of the Romans.

4. **Quarrel with the Pope.**—The friendly feelings between the Pope and the Emperor soon ended. The Pope, as the

spiritual Head of the universe, claimed universal obedience, while the Emperor, whose authority was founded on the necessity of civil law and order, could allow no rival. Thus, from the very nature of their position, these two great powers were forced into strife. There were also special causes of quarrel. The Pope refused to acknowledge the right of the Emperor to the territories of the Countess Matilda, and the submission of Lothar had done much to strengthen his claims. He also angered Frederic by making alliance with the Norman King *William*, and by investing him with his territories, to be held of the Holy See, just as Leo the Ninth and Innocent the Second had invested his predecessors. The Pope thus acknowledged a power in Italy independent of the Emperor, and nominally dependent on himself. He also made alliance with the Eastern Emperor. A bitter quarrel broke out, in which the Pope aimed at independence and temporal authority, while the Emperor refused to give up his rights over the Imperial City and his Italian dominions. Upon the death of Hadrian, in 1159, a disputed election took place. The Church party chose *Alexander the Third*, the Imperialists supported *Victor the Fourth*. Each Pope excommunicated his rival and his supporters. All Christendom was divided by these two parties. Alexander the Third received the greater support, though he would not have been able to stand against so powerful an enemy near home as the Emperor was, if it had not been for the war between Frederic and the Lombard cities.

5. **Quarrel with the Lombard Cities.**—In 1158, the Emperor had entered Italy with a large army, and was determined to make Milan acknowledge his authority. He was joined by Pavia, which, as the ancient capital of Lombardy, was naturally ever on the side of her King and Emperor, and by other cities, all of them jealous of Milan, and therefore belonging to the Imperial or Ghibelin party.

The fruitful suburbs of the city were ravaged, and famine soon began to be felt. The Milanese submitted, and made their peace with the Emperor. At the Diet held in the autumn of the same year the rights of the Emperor were defined. He claimed to appoint the civil magistrates, he forbade cities to wage private war, he fixed the regalian rights, and especially provoked Milan by a small curtailment of her territory. She again withstood the Emperor in 1159 (the year of the Schism), and was placed under the ban of the Empire. Frederic was persuaded by the Cremonese to begin the war by attacking Crema, the constant ally of Milan. He met with a strenuous resistance, and during the siege both parties were guilty of great cruelty. The citizens were reduced to the last stage of famine, and after a noble defence of six months they yielded to the Emperor. He allowed them to go forth unharmed, but gave their city up to his soldiers to pillage and destroy. The obstinate resistance of Crema weakened his army, and delayed the fall of Milan. Each year Frederic cut off all her supplies, and wasted the country round, until at length the citizens were forced to yield unconditionally. The Emperor, though he spared the lives of his rebellious subjects, utterly overthrew their city, and declared its name blotted out. While Frederic was thus victorious in the North, the kingdom of Sicily was torn by civil discords, revolts, and murders. There was no longer any place in Italy for Pope Alexander; he fled to France, and stayed there three years. The Antipope *Victor* died. His place was supplied by an Imperialist Cardinal, *Guido of Crema*, who took the name of *Paschal the Third*.

6. **The Lombard League.**—In 1165, while Frederic was kept in Germany, Pope Alexander came back to Rome. All the enemies of the Emperor immediately rallied round him. The cities of the *Veronese March* had already formed a league against the Emperor, and they now invited others to

join them. In 1167, the famous *Lombard League* was formed, and its members began to help the Milanese to rebuild their city. The League included Cremona and other cities which formerly had hated Milan, for old hostilities were overcome by a common desire for freedom. The Emperor came back and went southwards. The Eastern Emperor *Manuel Komnēnos* was at feud with the Venetians, and upheld *Ancona* their rival against them. In alliance with Venice, Frederic vainly besieged Ancona, and then marched to Rome. The Pope fled before him, but the Emperor's success was checked by a power which has often rid Rome of her foreign enemies. A pestilential fever almost destroyed his army, and he was forced to retreat in haste. The triumphant cities of the League, in order to check Ghibelin Pavia, built a city near it, which they called *Alessandria*, after the name of their patron, the Pope. The war was carried on by *Christian, Archbishop of Mainz*, who laid siege to Ancona; but, though the city was brought to great straits, he was not able to take it. When the Emperor came back, in 1174, he was stopped by the new city, Alessandria; and though its defences were so poor that he called it the "Town of Straw," its new citizens were able to keep him in check, till the army of the League forced him to raise the siege. Attempts were made to arrange the causes of dispute, but neither party would yield. At length, in 1176, the Imperial army advanced to *Legnano*, about fifteen miles from the gates of Milan. The Milanese had few of their allies with them, but they fought so gallantly round the *carroccio* of their city that the Imperial army was totally defeated, and the Emperor escaped with difficulty. This great battle decided the struggle between the Emperor and the Lombard cities, and for a time between the Emperor and the Pope. A truce was made at Venice, and Frederic and Alexander were reconciled. Frederic acknowledged Alexander as Pope, and was allowed to retain the territories of the Countess Matilda for his life, after which they were to revert to the Holy See. The Emperor also made a truce with the King of Sicily. By the time that the truce with the Lombard cities had ended, six years after the battle of Legnano, the wrath of both parties had cooled, and a lasting peace was made at Constanz, or *Constance*, a city of Swabia, in 1183. The Emperor ceded to the towns all rights within their walls; he allowed them to administer their own laws, and to make peace and war on their own account; the ancient regalian rights were retained, they were defined and provisions made against future disputes; he allowed the cities to keep their Consuls, but they were nominally invested by him, and each city was to admit an Imperial Judge of Appeal. Frederic and his house loyally kept these provisions. The Lombard cities thus remained part of the Empire, while at the same time they became virtually independent. The result of the struggle was the establishment of their political life; it filled them with men of noble thoughts, and made them the nurseries of art. Unhappily they did not always respect in others the freedom they cherished for themselves. They gave way to much jealousy and violence, which would have been checked by the power and justice of the Emperor against whom they had rebelled.

7. **End of the Norman Kingdom.**—The Norman kingdom of Sicily had been the steady ally of the Pope against the Emperor. Frederic now took away this refuge by marrying his son *Henry* to *Constance*, the daughter of King Roger. On the death of William the Second she would become the legitimate heir to the crown. Frederic died in a crusade which he made against the Infidels, and Henry came to Rome, and was crowned Emperor. On the death of King William, the Sicilians chose *Tancred*, an illegitimate descendant of King Roger, and for a time successfully resisted the advance of the Emperor, who claimed the kingdom in

right of his wife. Tancred and his eldest son soon died, and so the line of Norman Kings of Sicily ended in 1194. Henry forced the Sicilians to acknowledge him as King. He treated his new subjects cruelly, and tortured and murdered many of the chief men of the kingdom. No Emperor before him had so much power in Italy. He made his German soldiers Counts of different territories all through the land, and assigned Tuscany and all the dominions of the Countess Matilda to his brother Philip. He died in 1197, leaving an infant son named *Frederic*. All his Italian subjects were much rejoiced at his death, for he had greatly oppressed them, and no one had been strong enough to withstand him. At the time of his death *Innocent the Third* was Pope. He placed himself at the head of the League of the Lombard and Tuscan cities, and forced the Germans, under *Markwald*, the Regent, to retreat southwards. The Empress Constance acknowledged the Pope as feudal lord of Naples and Sicily, and on her death, which took place in 1198, left him guardian of her infant son Frederic. Sicily was filled with fierce German and Saracen soldiers under Markwald. Pope Innocent employed against them a famous captain named *Walter of Brienne*. For a long time the unhappy kingdom was without any sort of quiet rule; and Frederic passed his early years amidst violence, rapine, and disloyalty.

8. **Dispute for the Empire.**—When Henry died, part of the Electors, upheld by many of the German princes, chose his brother *Philip* to succeed him in the Empire. The Guelfic party chose *Otto*, the son of *Henry the Lion*, who had been Duke of Saxony and Bavaria, and who had lost a great part of his dominions. The Bavarian House had always been on the side of the Church against the Imperial Swabians, and therefore Innocent was anxious that Otto should be successful. The war which followed chiefly concerns German History. It ended in the defeat

of Otto and the acknowledgment of Philip of Swabia. After a little time the new king was assassinated, and then, in 1209, Otto received the Imperial crown. Meanwhile, from the end of the war with Frederic, the cities of North Italy had been establishing their independent governments. Their greatness and freedom would have had a firmer basis, if the leagues formed for defence against the common enemy had been made the foundation of a federal union. Jealousy between them prevented this, and did not allow the glorious struggle of the Lombard League to bear full fruit. Nevertheless from that time they became independent states, with full rights, not only of self-government, but even of making peace and war as they chose, while, at the same time, they remained members of the Empire.

9. **The Cities and the Nobles.**—The rise of the cities entailed the depression of the nobles. They found the cities round them strong in their Leagues, capable of united action, and with a recognized position in the Empire, while they were themselves without any common tie, and were divided by private jealousies and party hatred. Those who had strong castles and a large following remained independent; but when a noble found himself weaker than a neighbouring city, he applied to be admitted into the number of its citizens. Though their warlike habits made their adherence acceptable, their feuds and violence disturbed their new homes. They filled the cities with fortresses, in which they could defy the attacks of their enemies or the efforts of the civil power. Some magistrate was wanted who should be supreme over all the citizens, and who should not be connected with their party feuds. For this reason the old Consuls were for the most part no longer appointed, and a *Podesta* (from Latin *potestas*, power,) was chosen in their place. The cities gained the idea of this office from the Emperor Frederic, for he had tried to appoint over them an officer of the same

sort. The Podesta was a citizen of some city other than that over which he ruled; he was a man of good birth, and was chosen by the highest Council of the State. He held office for a year, and, before he left, he had to give an account of his administration to certain officers of the city which he had governed. The Podestas had a good deal of trouble to keep the nobles in check, for they were for ever engaged in some violent feud. In 1215, one of these quarrels began in Florence by a foolish jest, which led to blows between the young *Buondelmonte* and *Oddo Arrighi*. The many noble friends of the combatants tried to settle matters, and, to put an end to the quarrel, Buondelmonte promised marriage to the niece of his enemy, of the Amidei house. The wife of *Forese de' Donati*, one of his faction, did not like the plan, and one day she called Buondelmonte to her, and reproached him with being afraid of the other party; and offered to give him her own daughter instead, and showed her to him. She was so beautiful that Buondelmonte gladly promised to marry her, and, in spite of the anger of the Amidei and all the rest of the other party, he publicly betrothed her. Then, on Easter-day, his enemies set on him unawares and slew him. His friends placed his body on a bier, and on it sat his promised bride with his head upon her lap, and they were thus borne through the streets of Florence. From that day onwards for many years the two parties filled the city with their feuds. The Buondelmonti were mostly on the side of the Church; their enemies, of whom the *Uberti* were the most powerful, were on the side of the Emperor, and so they ranged themselves as Guelfs and Ghibelins.

10. **The Latin Conquest of Constantinople.**—Up to the end of the twelfth century the Republic of Venice had very little to do with general Italian affairs. The slight allegiance which the citizens acknowledged was to the Emperor of the East. When *Pippin*, son of Charles the Great, whom his

father had made King of the Lombard kingdom, tried to make them own his kingship, they answered that they chose to be the servants of the Emperor of the Romans. They owned him who reigned in New Rome, not the Frankish monarch, who had so lately been crowned in the Old City. This allegiance was turned into hostility in the reign of Manuel Komnênos. The Venetian fleet conquered Dalmatia from the Emperor. In the east, however, the republic suffered heavy losses. The Emperor favoured Ancona, her rival. Venice made alliance with his enemy, the Norman King of Sicily, and, in concert with the Emperor Frederic, besieged Ancona. The city made a successful stand with the help of the Byzantine fleet. These defeats caused a change of government in Venice, and from this time the power fell into the hands of an oligarchy. During the reign of Manuel Komnênos, which lasted from 1153 to 1180, the strength of the Eastern Empire was lessened by imprudent and unsuccessful wars. At last there came a quarrel about the succession, and *Alexios Angelos* came over to get help from the Princes of the West for his father, *Isaac*, who had been deposed. When he came to Italy, he found a great army assembling at Venice. A war had been preached against the enemies of the Cross, and the Crusaders wanted the Venetians to supply them with a fleet. The Venetians promised to do so, on condition that the Crusaders would take *Zara* for them from the King of Hungary. Alexios persuaded the crusading army to help him, and, in 1203, they and the Venetians under their Doge *Enrico Dandolo*, set the deposed Emperor and his son upon the throne. These Emperors were slain by the people, and, in 1204, the *Latins* took the city, and set up Baldwin, the Count of Flanders, as Emperor, and divided the greater part of the Empire. The taking of Constantinople added much to the wealth of the Italian cities. The arts and luxuries of the world were centred in that city, the sister and successor of the older Rome. As Venice had taken a prominent part in this expedition, which is called *the Fourth Crusade*, she received a large share of the conquered lands, and especially many islands and sea-coast places. Her supremacy in the Levant was unsuccessfully disputed by Genoa. By these two cities the treasures of Byzantine arts and manufactures were dispersed through Italy, and thence through the Western world. Three parts of the Eastern Empire still remained under Greek rule; a Greek *despot* reigned over *Epeiros;* and Greek princes with the title of Emperor reigned in *Nikaia* and *Trapezous*, or *Trebizond*. In 1261, the Emperor *Michael Palaiologos*, who reigned in Nikaia, won back Constantinople and set up the Empire again. But, though the Genoese had helped him a great deal, he was neither able nor willing to discourage the Venetian and Pisan traders. The merchants of Venice and Pisa had dwellings within the walls, while the Genoese settled in the suburb of *Galata*.

11. **Frederic II. King of the Romans.**—Although Otto IV. owed his crown to Pope Innocent, he did not long continue his friend. The Emperor was at peace with the Lombard League, and so he ventured to set up his right to the territories of the Countess Matilda, and even to the kingdom of Sicily, the fief of the Holy See. On this Pope Innocent turned against him. Otto was unpopular with a great many of the German Princes, who held to the Swabian house, and, with the Pope's approval, they offered the Imperial crown to Frederic, the young king of Sicily. The Pope thus formed an alliance with the Ghibelins; and Otto, the head of the Guelfs, went to war with the Pope. The cities of Italy were divided. Some Guelfic cities, like Milan, out of hatred to Frederic's house, held to Otto against the Pope; some Ghibelin cities, like Pavia, held to Frederic, the Pope's candidate against the Guelf Emperor. Thus Italian

politics seemed turned upside down. The Genoese brought Frederic in safety to their city, in spite of the Pisan fleet, which was watching for him. He went thence to Pavia, and the Pavesans brought him on his northern journey till he was met by the Cremonese. The Milanese did all they could to stop him, and defeated his Pavesan upholders with great loss. In 1212, Frederic, who was then not quite eighteen, was elected King of the Romans at Frankfort by the Electors of the Holy Roman Empire. The discomfiture of Otto was completed at the battle of *Bouvines* in 1214, where the French under *Philip Augustus* defeated his German forces, and his Flemish and English allies. Milan still fought on, though without success, against the Italian upholders of the Hohenstaufen. In 1216, Innocent the Third died, having done more than any other Pope to raise and strengthen the power of the See of Rome.

12. **Frederic II. Emperor.**—The death of Otto the Fourth, in 1218, left Frederic without a rival, and, in 1220, he was crowned Emperor by *Honorius the Third*. Frederic, King of Italy, Sicily, Sardinia, Germany, Burgundy, and Jerusalem, and Emperor of the world, was, unlike his predecessors, not simply a Teuton. His Sicilian parentage and education gave him special qualities and habits of mind. He learned much from Mahometan teachers, and in culture and thought he was far in advance of his time. He had the polish and wit which were natural to the South of Europe. He had noble and worthy aims, and his own kingdom of Sicily, where he was undisputed master, enjoyed during his reign a time of order and prosperity to which it had long been a stranger. He promoted the cultivation of arts and letters, and insisted on the supremacy of law. But his Southern home had given him a taste for voluptuous enjoyment, and his breadth of intellect and the influence of his early teachers gave him a liberality about religious matters

which shocked the feelings of the day. The many-sidedness of his character and the wide scope of his genius made him the "*Wonder of the World,*" as he was called by the men of his own time. The implacable hatred of the Popes involved him in endless troubles, cramped his usefulness, and embittered his life. The first few years of his reign were the happiest: he reduced to submission the turbulent nobles, who had been the curse of his southern kingdom, and protected the weak from their violence. He collected together the Saracen freebooters, placed them in the fortress of Lucera, and formed them into a regular body of troops, who remained faithful to him and his family. He founded the University of Naples, and encouraged those of Bologna and Salerno. During his reign the modern Italian language began to be formed; and Frederic himself wrote Italian poetry and encouraged the pursuit.

13. Quarrel with the Popes.—Pope Honorius soon quarrelled with the Emperor, because he did not go on a Crusade just when he was ordered to go, and *Gregory the Ninth* excommunicated him. Honorius was also angry, because Frederic allowed his son Henry to be elected and crowned King of the Romans without the Pope's leave. Frederic did go on a Crusade, and won Jerusalem by treaty and was crowned King there. Meanwhile, Gregory revived the Lombard League against him. The Pope even tried to set on foot a Crusade against the successful soldier of the Cross and the Head of Christendom. The attempt came to nought, and, by the *Treaty of San Germano* in 1230, peace was made between the Emperor and the Pope and the Lombard League. After this the Emperor and the Pope acted together in persecuting the heretics of Lombardy. The beginning of the thirteenth century saw a wide-spread revolt against the overweening power of the Priesthood. In Italy these heretics were called for the most part *Paterines;* they were persecuted very cruelly, especially at Milan. It seems strange that Frederic, who was in no way bigoted, should have joined in this persecution. But men had not then learned to respect those who differed from them, and the Emperor, as Head of Christendom, had a special duty to keep down the enemies of the Faith. Revolts moreover of this character were often directed against the temporal as well as against the spiritual power. The Papacy had been immensely strengthened by the establishment of the two new orders of St. Dominic and St. Francis, an impulse had been given to devotion, and the Friars by their preaching brought religion home to the souls of great multitudes. The Pope sent eloquent Dominican preachers to convert the heretics from their errors. Some of these men were very famous, especially one *Fra Giovanni of Vicenza*, who preached noble truths about peace, and persecuted the poor heretics in Vicenza, Verona, and Padua. A great number of people listened to his words and obeyed him. He was not content with spiritual power alone; he made himself Lord of Vicenza and Verona. After a while Vicenza revolted from him, and, with the help of Padua, defeated and overthrew him, and this led to his downfall.

14 **The Emperor's Success. Eccelino da Romano.**—Though there was peace between the Emperor and the Pope, the Milanese longed for war with Frederic. The opportunity came in 1234. *Henry*, King of the Romans, the eldest son of Frederic, rebelled against his father in Germany. He made alliance with the Marquess of Montferrat, with Milan, Brescia, and other cities. With this revolt Gregory would have nothing to do. The Emperor easily quelled it, and King Henry died in prison. The Imperial cause in North Italy was greatly strengthened by the vigour of *Eccelino da Romano*, the successful rival of the Guelfic Marquess of Este. With some help from the Emperor, Eccelino made himself lord of Padua, Vicenza, and Verona, and raised in the North-East

of Italy a rival power to the Lombard League. He greatly oppressed the cities which were under his dominion, and made the citizens serve in his army. Milan and Brescia, the allies of the rebel Henry, withstood him. In 1237, Frederic again entered Italy. He defeated the army of Milan in a decisive battle at *Corte Nuova*, and took their *carroc_io* from them, and sent it to Rome as a witness of his victory. He also took the Podesta of the city, *Tiepolo*, son of the Doge of Venice, and put him to death for his rebellion. This execution so enraged the Venetians, who had hitherto taken no part in the struggle, that they joined the Lombard League. A large number of fugitives were succoured by *Pagano della Torre*, a neighbouring noble, and his timely kindness to Milan was the beginning of the future greatness of his family. Frederic besieged Brescia with a large army, of which Italians and his faithful Saracens were a part. The battle of Corte Nuova nearly ruined the Guelfic party in Italy. The tide of success now turned. Brescia made a successful resistance. Pope Gregory gained Venice and Genoa to his side, and pronounced sentence of excommunication against the Emperor. He wished to get this sentence confirmed by the voice of Christendom, and he therefore called a General Council to meet at Rome. The Transalpine Bishops were to be brought to Rome by Genoese ships. They were met off the island of *Meloria* (1241) by the Imperial fleet from Sicily, and from Pisa, the constant enemy of Genoa. There was a fierce battle, in which the Genoese were defeated. Many prelates and others of the clergy were taken prisoners; and so the Pope's Council came to nought.

15. **The Emperor's Failure.**—After the death of Gregory, *Innocent the Fourth*, an Italian of noble family, was chosen Pope. He hated the Emperor with a fierce personal hatred, and he accused him of many crimes before the *Council of Lyons*. The Emperor was nobly defended by his eloquent

counsellor, *Thaddeus of Sessa*. He was, however, again excommunicated; the Electors might choose another Emperor; the Pope would appoint another King of Sicily. The Emperor's enemies engaged in plots against his life, he was nowhere safe, and he was thus driven to be suspicious and even unjust. In the North, Eccelino kept constantly advancing his own power and that of the Emperor's party, but his horrid cruelties made men look on him with hatred and on his master with distrust. In 1247, Parma revolted from the Emperor, and disgracefully routed his army. The Florentine Ghibelins drove out the Guelfs and delivered their city into the hands of his natural son, *Frederic of Antioch*. His gallant son *Enzio* was taken prisoner by the Bolognese, who kept him in prison all the rest of his life. The Emperor died at the close of the next year, 1250, worn out by the continued struggle in Germany and Italy, which was kept alive by the hatred of *Gregory the Ninth*, and still more by *Innocent the Fourth*. To these his enemies no severity seemed too great, and no weapon too shameful, to be used against him. In Italy his cause was much injured by the violence and cruelty of his supporters. In Sicily, even to the end, his rule was a blessing, and in the hottest of his struggle with the Pope he protected the rights of the Church. With his death the great power of the Emperors in Italy ended: the towns in the north became so strong that they were able to withstand the occasional visits of a German army, and in the south the power passed into other hands. The Empire itself never recovered the troubles which came upon it, and the Emperor had enough to do in the German kingdom to make him stay for the most part north of the Alps.

CHAPTER IV.

THE GREATNESS OF THE GUELFS.

The Interregnum (1)—*Manfred, King of Sicily* (2)—*Charles of Anjou* (3)—*change in the Papal policy* (4)—*the Sicilian Vespers* (5)—*Florence and Pisa* (6)—*Venice and Genoa* (7)—*Neri and Bianchi* (8)—*Henry VII., King and Emperor* (9)—*Italian architecture to eleventh century* (10)—*eleventh to fourteenth century* (11)—*other arts, literature, and wealth* (12).

1. The Interregnum.—Frederic the Second was succeeded in the kingdom of Sicily by his son *Conrad*. The new king had to contend in Germany with *William of Holland*, to whom Innocent the Fourth had offered the Imperial crown. His illegitimate brother *Manfred* took charge of the kingdom of Sicily for him; but the Pope raised up a revolt in Naples, and offered the crown to the wealthy *Richard of Cornwall*, brother of *Henry the Third*, King of England. Richard refused it. King Henry foolishly accepted it for his son *Edmund*, and had to pay dearly for the empty honour, for the Pope wanted a great deal of money. Conrad had to fight for his kingdom, and, in 1254, both he and his young brother *Henry* died. The hatred of the Pope and the Guelfs made them charge Conrad with the death of Henry, and Manfred with the death of Conrad, though there was no ground for these vile stories. Conrad left an infant son *Conradin*, and Manfred governed for him. During this time the Guelfs gained a good deal of power, for there was no Emperor to head the Ghibelins, the King of Sicily was a child, and the government was unsettled. They came back to Florence, from which they had been driven by the young Frederic, and under their government the city gained great power in Tuscany. In 1254, called the Year of Victories, the

Florentines took Volterra and Siena, and humbled Pisa. The tyrant Eccelino still oppressed the Veronese march, ruling almost as a sovereign, and his cruelties were imitated by his brother *Alberigo* in Treviso. Milan, which might have checked them, was torn by feuds between the nobles and people. At last a Crusade was preached against Eccelino by the Archbishop-elect of Ravenna, legate of *Alexander the Fourth*. An army was enlisted at Venice, both of those who had fled from the tyrant's cruelty, and of many citizens of the Republic, which was endangered by Eccelino's great power. The crusading army took Padua, but for a time the war was ineffectual. In 1259 Eccelino crossed the *Adda*, hoping to be joined by the Milanese nobles. He was met by an army composed not only of Guelfs, but even of Ghibelins; he was defeated, wounded, and taken. In prison he tore the bandages from off his wounds, and so died. The next year his brother Alberigo and all his family were taken and slain with great cruelty.

2. **Manfred, King of Sicily.**—The Papal power was much increased by the vacancy of the Empire. Nevertheless both Innocent the Fourth and Alexander the Fourth found a power in their own city which they were forced to obey. The Roman people, as in the time of Arnold of Brescia, hoped for the restoration of their former greatness. They made *Brancaleone* of Bologna their *Senator*, and gave him almost unlimited power. He restrained the disorders of the nobles; he forced the Bishop of Rome to dwell in his own city, and made alliance with Manfred, the Regent of Sicily. The Senator, despite the Pope and the nobles, kept his office, save for two years, until his death, which happened in the full tide of his power and popularity. Manfred, after he had won the southern Kingdom for his nephew, reigned for a while in his name. In 1258, on a rumour of the death of Conradin, he was chosen King, and this raised the hopes of the Italian

Ghibelins. All Tuscany, except Pisa and Siena, had become Guelfic; and the exiled Ghibelins of Florence, with *Farinata degli Uberti* at their head, begged the new King to help them. The King readily granted their request, and sent a body of German cavalry to Siena, the head-quarters of their League. Meanwhile the Guelfs, not only of Tuscany, but of Genoa, of Modena, and even of Lombardy, flocked to the army of Florence. In 1260, the two armies of the Guelfs and Ghibelins met at *Monteaperto* on the Arbia. For a long time the battle was undecided, but just as Jacopo de' Pazzi and the Guelfic horsemen, which were in the centre of the Florentine line, were about to charge, *Bocca degli Abati* betrayed them, and rode off to the Ghibelins with a body of horse. Then the day was lost. A great number of Florentines were slain, and the *carroccio* was taken. The city fell into the hands of the Ghibelin confederates, and they took counsel to destroy it. But Farinata loved his city better than his party, and made such an eloquent appeal for her that Florence was saved. The loss of the Guelfs at Monteaperto was heavy, and for a time their power in Tuscany was at an end. Manfred now held a strong position, not only in his own kingdom, but also as the head of the triumphant Ghibelins throughout Italy.

3. **Charles of Anjou.**—The plans of Pope Alexander the Fourth had come to nought. He gained nothing from King Henry save money, and not as much of that as he wanted. He lived to see his party cast down, and the man whom he had made his enemy everywhere victorious. He died in 1261. He was succeeded by a Frenchman, who took the title of *Urban the Fourth*. The new Pope sought a more vigorous ally than the English King. The Empire was disputed between Richard, Earl of Cornwall, brother of our Henry the Third, and Alfonso the Tenth, King of Castile. The Pope wished to keep the Empire vacant as long as he

could, and therefore he would not take the side of either candidate, or give either the great advantage which the crown of Sicily would bring. As he was a Frenchman, he naturally first asked *Lewis the Ninth*, the French King, to take the crown. The good King would not claim that which was not rightfully his. His brother *Charles, Count of Anjou*, did not feel any such scruples, and when Pope Urban offered the crown to him, he accepted it readily. The Count of Anjou was valiant and ambitious; he had great riches, for he had married Beatrix daughter of the Count of Provence, and held that large county in her right. Her three sisters were all queens, and, it is said, that she had a mind that she also should be the wife of a king, and that she therefore stirred up her husband to undertake the conquest of Sicily. Charles was received in Rome by *Clement the Fourth*, the successor of Pope Urban, and was declared Senator of the city. The Pope made him promise that, if at any time his heirs failed, then the kingdom of Sicily was again to be in the gift of the Pope; that it should never be held by the Emperor; and that he should pay tribute and homage to the Pope as his over-lord. In this way the Pope hoped to prevent anyone shutting him in, as Henry the Sixth and Frederic the Second had done, on the North and South. Pope Clement raised an army for his new ally. He declared the war, which was about to begin, to be a Holy War or Crusade, and therefore he levied the taxes on the Churchmen which were always paid for an expedition against the Infidels. By the influence of the Pope and by the money he raised, an army of French Crusaders was gathered together, and was brought down into Italy to the Count of Anjou. King Manfred was betrayed by a number of those whom he trusted. Nevertheless he set himself to resist the French manfully. In the early part of 1266, the King met the army of the Count at *Grandella* near Benevento. The fight was long and fierce.

The Saracens, whom Manfred's father had placed in garrison in *Lucera*, followed him in great numbers, and did much hurt to the enemy with their arrows, until they were put to flight by the French men-at-arms. The French in turn were checked by the German horsemen, who charged with shouts of "*Swabia!*" but the Apulian subjects of the King did not stand firm. Manfred was slain, and his army fled. The King was buried by the bridge of Benevento. The Archbishop of *Cosenza* had his body taken up and left exposed upon the banks of the *Marino*. This battle and the death of King Manfred made the Count of Anjou master of the kingdom. He entered Naples in triumph. The Ghibelins throughout Italy were confounded. The Guelfs were now again in full power. They came back to Florence, from which they had been forced to flee by the battle of Monteaperto, and Charles was chosen "Signor" of the city for two years. Pisa, jealous of the power of her rival, and hating the Guelfs, joined with the Ghibelin nobles to set up the young Conradin as King of Sicily. Their army was defeated by Charles at *Tagliacozzo*, 1268, and the unfortunate youth was beheaded at Naples by the order of his cruel enemy. This last blow crushed the hopes of the Italian Ghibelins.

4. **Change in the Papal Policy.**—The Guelfic cities triumphed in the victories of their ally, but Charles was not content with being their ally, he wished to be their master. It was fortunate for Italian liberty that for two years he was absent on a crusade against the Infidels. Soon after his return, *Tebaldo Visconti* of Piacenza was chosen Pope, and took the title of *Gregory the Tenth*. He deserves to be remembered for his fair conduct, and his desire for peace. Charles would soon have been master of Italy, and might even have gained the Imperial crown, if it had not been for Pope Gregory. The Pope restored the balance of power in Italy by bringing back the Ghibelin exiles. At the same

time he made them for a while live peaceably with the Guelfs. He also checked the French man by restoring the Empire. *Rudolf of Habsburg*, founder of the second house of Austria, was elected in 1273. He promised not to interfere with Charles in his Kingdom, or in Tuscany. Pope Gregory might have done more if he had not been so set upon a crusade to recover the Holy Land. He desired peace that he might prepare the way for this Holy War, which was to be headed by the new Emperor. *Nicolas the Third*, who succeeded Pope Gregory in 1277, followed a more distinctly Ghibelin policy. Partly by persuasion, and partly by force, he deprived Charles of the Vicariate of Tuscany, and of the Senatorship of Rome, and raised the Ghibelin power everywhere in Italy. Nicolas was able to pursue this independent policy, because he obtained from Rudolf a renunciation of all claims upon Rome, and upon the vast territories of the Countess Matilda. The Emperor thus recognized the Pope as a sovereign in Italy. Nicolas was also helped in his plans by Milan. Ever since the battle of Corte Nuova the family of *Pagano della Torre* had had great influence in the city. In order to counteract them, the Archbishop elect, *Otho Visconti*, gathered round him a strong party of Ghibelin nobles. By their help he got the upper hand, and Milan became a powerful ally of the Ghibelins in Lombardy. On the death of Pope Nicolas, Charles took good care that the Cardinals should elect a Frenchman. The new pope, *Martin the Fourth*, was quite obedient to his wishes. Charles soon got back nearly all the power he had lost, and would no doubt have gained much more, if it had not been that a conspiracy, which had been formed some time before, suddenly broke out, and nearly sent him back to France again.

5. **The Sicilian Vespers.**—*Peter*, King of Aragon, had married *Constance*, the daughter of Manfred, and laid claim to the kingdom of Sicily in her right. He sent for help to

Michael Palaiologos, the restorer of the Eastern Empire. The Emperor agreed to his proposals, for Charles of Anjou threatened his Empire. These negotiations were, it is said, carried on through *Giovanni di Procida*, a Sicilian exile, who, as the story goes, had suffered cruel wrongs from the French. Charles knew something of the plans of the allies, and both parties were preparing for war, when affairs were brought to a crisis by a chance occurrence. On March 30, 1282, a brutal insult was offered by a French soldier to a bride in the presence of her friends and neighbours outside the walls of *Palermo*. The smothered hatred of the people broke out into open violence. The cry "Death to the French" was raised, and all who belonged to that nation in Palermo were slain without mercy. This massacre, which is called *The Sicilian Vespers*, spread through the whole island. The yoke of the oppressor was broken and the land was delivered. Charles laid siege to *Messina*. He was forced to retire by Peter of Aragon, who landed and was received as King. Pope Martin in vain excommunicated the rebels and their allies. In 1284, Charles received a great blow, for his son was defeated and taken prisoner by *Roger of Leria*, the Admiral of the Catalan fleet. Charles of Anjou died in 1286, and two years later his son, also called Charles, ransomed himself from prison. After a desultory war of twenty years in Sicily and Apulia, and after the death of Peter, his younger son *Frederic* was chosen by the Sicilians to be their King. The Angevin house continued to reign in Naples, which from this time was the capital of the kingdom on the mainland. The Angevins of Naples upheld the Guelfic party. The Aragonese of Sicily, who had been set up against the will of the Pope, were Ghibelins.

6. **Florence and Pisa.**—The coming of Charles of Anjou secured the triumph of the Guelfs in Florence. They marked their accession to power, in 1266, by a change in the

constitution. The citizens were divided into companies of different trades called "Arts," which had governors of their own, like our Teutonic guilds. Each Art had its own council, its chief magistrate, and its leader or *Gonfaloniere*. These Arts were now made the foundation of the constitution, and the government was vested in them. Their whole number was twelve, but only the seven greater Arts had as yet any power in the State. Several nobles joined these Arts to gain some part in the government of the city. The criminal jurisdiction was in the hands of the *Podesta*, and the *Captain of the People*, who acted together. The expedition of Charles of Anjou was hailed with delight by the Florentines, who were for the most part Guelfs in politics. They foolishly gave him the *Signoria*, or lordship of the city. This office did not give the holder of it for the time any right to meddle in the home policy of the State; it rather made him a sort of patron, or protector of the city in its affairs with foreign powers. But in many cases this protectorship was exercised by the lord for his own benefit, and often endangered popular liberty. The Florentines happily were too jealous of their freedom to allow Charles to encroach upon it in any way. The predominance of the Guelfs, which was firmly established by Charles, worked more lasting results. In 1266, they formed a kind of society called the *Parte Guelfa*, with its own magistracy and common funds, to watch and defeat Ghibelin movements. The constitution of 1266 was developed in 1282. The chief executive government of the city had, after the Consuls had ceased, been committed to a body of Fourteen *Buon' uomini* (good men); it was now vested in six *Priors*, who held office for two months. This body was called the *Signoria*, and its members were chosen, one from each of the greater Arts, save that of the lawyers. They lived in the public Palace and at the charge of the State. After 1266, Florence was prosperous in war, and fought successfully against Pisa, and the remainder of the Ghibelin party in Tuscany. The power of Pisa was broken by a signal defeat which she received from Genoa off the island of *Meloria* in 1284. The scene of the defeat of Pisa had, forty-three years before, been the scene of her victory over the Genoese fleet, which was bringing bishops to sit in Pope Gregory the Ninth's projected Council. The Pisan Admiral, *Ugolino della Gheradesca*, and his two sons were afterwards starved to death by his enemies in the city. Pisa never recovered this disaster, and Florence became all the more powerful in Tuscany. These wars of Florence gave too much power to the nobles, who were ever striving to be above the laws. Some severe measures were brought in against them by *Giano della Bella*, who headed the democratic party. He caused the appointment of a *Gonfaloniere of Justice*, an officer whose duty was to head the City Militia, and to carry out the sentences of the magistrates. He had a law made that the nobles should not be chosen Priors; and that common fame declared by two witnesses should be held sufficient to condemn a noble. Thus they were treated unfairly, because they were so strong and turbulent that special means had to be taken to keep them quiet. The Constitution was again altered in 1324-8, and a system was introduced by which all respectable Guelf citizens were first balloted for, and then chosen by lot to fill the different offices of the city. Most Guelfic republics were governed more or less like Florence.

7. **Venice and Genoa.**—Venice was brought into general Italian politics for the first time by the execution of Tiepolo. The state was at first a loose federation of island villages, inhabited by those who had fled from the mainland before the barbarians, in the middle of the fifth century. They were presided over by a *Doge* or Duke, who was chosen for life. A war with Manuel, the Eastern Emperor, 1173, vested the administration in an oligarchy. The Great

Council made the laws, the Senate helped the Doge to carry them out, and there was a Council for criminal jurisdiction. The Doge and his six councillors were somewhat in the same position as the Florentine Priors, save that the Doge held office for life. The Great Council was self-elective, and was always filled by members of the houses of the greater nobles, and thus not only the people but the lesser nobility were shut out from all share in the government. In 1297, the Council was closed against every one who was not a member of one of the great noble families. This gave rise to much popular discontent, and, in 1310, a secret *Council of Ten* was associated with the Doge and his six councillors to find out and punish all crimes. This Council had unlimited power, and effectually kept the people under the nobles. Soon after this, the right of sitting in the Great Council was declared hereditary. Whoever could prove his descent from the member of the Council, as it then was, had a right to sit in it, and all others were shut out. Genoa had at last become the successful rival of Venice in the Levant. Her jealousy of Pisa made her for the most part Guelfic, but still the two parties were often at feud. For a time the nobles were supreme in the city. In 1339, their power was counteracted by a Doge being chosen. The old noble families lost their political power, but they still continued to lead the fleets and armies of their fellow-citizens. A few great plebeian families gained an undue power, and disturbed the city by their ambition and strife. In the cities of Lombardy the supreme power had fallen into the hands of single men. Milan was really ruled over by the powerful Ghibelin, Matteo Visconti; Verona by the family of Scala; and Ferrara, Modena, and Reggio, by that of Este.

8. **Neri and Bianchi.**—Tuscany was divided at the end of the thirteenth century by a feud which began in Pistoia. One party was called the *Neri* or Blacks; they were violent

Guelfs, and were headed by Corso Donati: the other party, the *Bianchi* or Whites, were moderate Guelfs, and in time the violence of their enemies made them Ghibelins. *Pope Boniface the Eighth* was a violent Guelf. In order to check the Bianchi, he invited into Italy *Charles of Valois*, brother of *Philip the Fourth* of France. In 1301, the Florentines let him into their city. He was joined by Corso Donati and the Neri faction, and the triumphant Guelfs took cruel vengeance upon their enemies. Charles and his French cavalry seized all the plunder they could get, and then went away into Sicily to support the Guelfic cause against the Ghibelin King *Frederic* of Aragon. As Charles, when he was sent into Tuscany to bring peace, only left war, so, when he went into Sicily to make war, he only made peace. After a while he died, having done much evil and no good. The violence of Pope Boniface, and of his ally Charles of Valois, did harm to the Guelfic cause in Italy, and turned many moderate Guelfs into Ghibelins. Amongst the many Bianchi of Florence, who were sent into exile when the Neri triumphed, was the poet *Dante*. In the end Pope Boniface worked his own ruin by his pride and arrogance, for he quarrelled with King Philip of France. The King was joined by the noble Roman family of Colonna, which had been almost crushed by the Pope. Boniface was taken by his enemies and died in prison.

9. **Henry VII., Emperor.**—No Emperor had come into Italy since the death of Frederic the Second. Neither Rudolf nor his two successors had been crowned Emperor. On the death of *Albert* of Austria, the King of the Romans, in 1308, the electors chose *Henry, Count of Luxemburg*. In 1310, Henry entered Italy with a small German army. Unlike most of these Imperial expeditions, this was approved of by the Pope. The French King, Philip the Fourth, was really master of Pope *Clement the Fifth*, who did not live in

Italy, but sometimes within the French kingdom, or in the English territory of Bordeaux, or in Avignon, a city of the Empire. Clement did not like bearing the French yoke, and was fearful lest some one of greater talents than Charles of Valois should make an attempt on Italy, and render it impossible for the Pope to get free from the power of the French. He therefore favoured the expedition of King Henry, and hoped that it would revive the Ghibelin party and counteract the influence of the Guelfs, who were on the side of France. Dante tells us the feelings which were roused by the coming of the King. He seemed to come as God's vicegerent, to change the fortunes of men and bring the exiled home; by the majesty of his presence, to bring the peace for which the banished poet longed, and to administer to all men justice, judgment, and equity. Henry was worthy of these high hopes; for he was wise, just, and gracious, courageous in fight and honourable in council; but the task was too hard for him. At first all seemed to go well with him. The Ghibelins were ready to receive him as their natural lord; the Guelfs were inclined towards him by the Pope. In Milan the chief power was in the hands of *Guido della Torre*, the descendant of *Pagano della Torre*, who had done good service to the city after the battle of Corte Nuova. He was a strong Guelf, and was at the head of a large number of troops, for he was very rich. His great enemy was the Ghibelin *Matteo Visconti*, who continually struggled with Guido for the mastery. The King was willingly received by the Milanese, and Guido was no thebindhand in bidding him welcome. While he was at Milan, on Christmas Day, 1310, he was crowned with the iron crown of the Italian kingdom, which was made of steel in the shape of laurel leaves, and studded with gems. He made both parties enter into an outward reconciliation, and the chiefs of both vied with one another in making him large presents.

The King's need of money soon tired out the Milanese, and an insurrection was made in which both Matteo and Guido joined. Matteo betrayed his rival. Guido and all the Guelfs were driven out of Milan, and the city henceforth remained in the power of the Ghibelin Visconti. The King's demands for money made him unpopular, and each city, as he left it, rose against him. Pisa, and the other Tuscan enemies of Florence, received him with joy. But the great Guelfic city shut her gates against him, and made alliance with *Robert*, the Angevin King of Naples, the grandson of Charles of Anjou, and afterwards gave him the signoria. Rome received a garrison from Naples, and the Imperial coronation had to be performed in the Church of *St. John Lateran.* Henry was forced into war. He put Florence and the King of Naples under the ban of the Empire, and made alliance with Frederic the Aragonese King of Sicily. He marched with a powerful army towards Siena, but he fell sick, and on August 24th, 1313, he died somewhat suddenly. His death was probably caused by the heat and bad air of the summer, though, at the time, it was put down to poison. He was buried in his faithful Pisa. The expedition of Henry marks the last revival of true Imperial feeling in Italy. No other Emperor after him was looked upon as the vicegerent of God and the successor of Augustus. Those who came to Italy came as the avowed allies of some home faction or foreign power; he alone seemed to have come to bring peace and order.

10. **Italian Architecture before Eleventh Century.**—The style of building which is native in Italy is marked by the *round arch*, supported either by massive piers or by columns. It is called *Romanesque*, because from the earliest times the round arch was the special mark of a Roman building. The admiration which the Romans felt for everything Greek in art made them overlay their piers and arches

with Greek columns and entablatures. This fashion, which marred their buildings, after a long time gave way to the arch resting simply on the capitals of the columns. This improvement was first made in the Palace of Diocletian at Spálato, but generally, until the eleventh century, the round arch rests on massive piers, which are commonly square, and surrounded by attached shafts. The pier is more closely connected with the earliest specimens of Roman art; the column with the Roman style under Greek influence. In Romanesque work the Greek element became no longer a senseless addition, it was made a means of perfecting the original idea. The oldest churches in Italy are those called *basilicas*, a Greek word, meaning halls built for judicial or mercantile purposes. When the Empire became Christian, these were taken for the new worship. They consisted of a long and lofty nave, divided by arcades from two narrow aisles, and ending in an apse. In Rome, where, as was natural, men sought to preserve rather than to invent, these basilican churches are almost universal. In Ravenna Theodoric followed the Roman model in his buildings, as he did also in his government, and accordingly his works are marked by the long columnar arcades of the basilica. In other parts of Italy this shape has been often changed. The Lombard Romanesque buildings, with some rare exceptions, are marked up to the eleventh century by long low naves, with flat, though highly decorated, west fronts, and by the church being often in the form of a cross. The round arches rest on massive piers, the capitals of which are ornamented with fanciful and grotesque carving. The churches of *St. Michael* at Pavia and of *St. Ambrose* at Milan are noteworthy examples of this style.

11. **Architecture from Eleventh Century.**—In the eleventh and twelfth centuries there was a return to a shape which was akin to the old basilica; and, as centuries before

at Rome and Ravenna, the arches of the churches at Pisa and Lucca rest upon rows of columns. This then was a return to an earlier style of building, and in one respect especially was an improvement upon it. In the old churches of Ravenna there is a member between the column and the arch, which looks like a sort of fragment of the old Greek entablature, and which is quite out of character with the arch above. In the eleventh century this was left out, and the arch was again made to rest immediately upon the column. The strange carvings of the capital gave way to decoration of another sort, and the fronts were adorned with rich arcades of different stones or marbles. Profuse decoration increased very much during the twelfth and thirteenth centuries, and may be observed in the *Baptisteries* of Pisa and Parma, though they are finished in a later style. The most remarkable feature in Lombard architecture is the glorious bell-tower or *campanile*. These towers, which are detached from the main building, are mostly square, tall and thin, without any buttresses, and with the ornament increasing at the top. The most famous of these is the Leaning Tower of Pisa, which belongs to the latter part of the twelfth century. Contrary to the general rule, the Pisan tower is round, as are also most of the bell-towers at Ravenna. The Romanesque style, of which Italy is the home, spread from Rome to the other lands of Western Europe which received the Faith from her. In England, the older form of Romanesque building was changed by the Normans, and those who imitated them, so that most of our round-arched buildings are called *Norman* in architecture. But there are even in England earlier buildings, and especially some towers, which give us an idea of what the style is like in its real home. The special connexion of certain parts of Italy with the Emperors who reigned in Constantinople, is marked by the *Byzantine* character of some of their buildings. The

F 2

church of *St. Vital* and others at Ravenna, the city of the Exarch; the church of *St. Mark* at Venice, the handmaid of the Eastern Cæsar; the smaller church at Torcello in the Venetian archipelago, and the Duomo of Ancona, the last city of the Eastern Empire, are all in some degree Byzantine. For a like reason *Saracen* influence can be easily traced in Palermo and other parts of Sicily; and the *Arabian* use of the *pointed arch* had probably much to do with the early date of some pointed arches in Italy. In the thirteenth century the Italians began to leave their native Romanesque for what is called the *Gothic* style of building, which is distinguished by the pointed arch. This way of building was brought into Italy from the north of the Alps. It is a stranger in the land, and so has never reached the same perfection there as it has in its own countries. In many buildings pointed and round arches are mixed up together; and in others Gothic ornament overloads and disfigures Lombard work. The most splendid specimen of Gothic architecture in Italy, the Cathedral at Milan, belongs to a far later date; it was begun in 1387. This style is often found in the great secular buildings of Italy. The best examples of it are the Merchant-house of Bologna and the Public Palace of Siena.

12. **The other Arts and Literature.**—Sculpture began to rise again in Italy about the time when men turned to the Gothic style of building. The first great Italian sculptor of Christian times was *Niccola Pisano* who lived in the middle of the thirteenth century. He was also a famous architect. The pulpit in the Baptistery of Pisa is his work. He was succeeded by his pupils: by his son Giovanni who designed the Spina Chapel and the Campo Sante at Pisa, and by Andrea Pisano who worked (about 1300) in bronze and marble for the Baptistery and Cathedral Church of Florence. The end of the thirteenth century saw the rise of a purely Italian school of painting. The earlier Italian pictures have the

hard lines and unnatural figures which speak the influence of the East. At length, first *Cimabue* and then *Giotto* sought beauty in nature. Giotto indeed attained a freshness and vitality which are not found in the works of the sterner Cimabue. It was a long time before the Italians found out that they had ceased to speak Latin, for long after it had ceased to be spoken it was always used in writing. Italian was first used as a written language at the end of the twelfth century. It received great encouragement at the Sicilian Court of Frederick the Second. He and his sons and some of his courtiers wrote poems in Italian, which for a while was called the *Sicilian tongue*. Up to the time of Dante, the poets of Northern Italy used the Provençal dialect. That which really fixed the Italian language was the magnificent poem of *Dante, Alighieri*, called the *Divine Comedy*. This was written, partly at least, during his exile at the court of Can' Grande della Scala, lord of Verona. It is a religious epic, and describes the author as visiting Hell, Purgatory, and Heaven, and beholding and talking with those who had been most known for good or evil, and especially those who belonged to his own land and had played a part in the history of Florence, his native city. The great poem of Dante stands alone in the literary history, not only of his own city and country but of the world. The study of the literature and the law of Rome in early days strongly implanted in men's minds reverence for the Emperor, a feeling often to be disappointed and at last crushed by a near acquaintance with the bearer of this mighty title. This feeling comes out very strongly in the poems and prose writings of Dante, and most of all in the treatise *De Monarchia*. Italy had also made a rapid advance in material wealth. Milan had introduced the manufacture of cloth from Germany, and a brisk trade for raw material was carried on with Spain, England, and other countries. Clothmaking was largely followed by the Florentines, who were also skilful in making brilliant dyes. The manufacture of silk was carried on chiefly by Lucca and Genoa. But the Italians were most celebrated for their trade in money. Tuscans and Lombards collected and distributed the wealth of the West by bills of exchange and loans. They managed the finances and the mints of princes, and the Florentine *florin*, a beautiful gold coin, stamped with a lily, the device of the city, became a general standard of value.

CHAPTER V.

THE GHIBELIN LORDS.

The Ghibelin lords (1)—*Lewis of Bavaria, Emperor* (2)—*John of Bohemia* (3)—*the Duke of Athens* (4)—*the war in Naples; the Free Companies* (5)—*the Great Plague* (6)—*Rome without a Pope* (7)—*the Visconti, Lords of Lombardy, threaten Florence* (8)—*rise of the Medici* (9)—*the insurrection of the Ciompi* (10)—*the Great Schism* (11)—*the war of Chioggia* (12)—*Gian-Galeazzo Visconti* (13)—*mercenary troops* (14)—*literature of the fourteenth century* (15).

1. **The Ghibelin Lords.**—The expedition of Henry the Seventh made Robert of Naples the acknowledged head of the Guelfic party. He established the power of the great Ghibelin lords, and especially of Matteo Visconti in Milan, and from this time the cities of the North for the most part fell under the power of some lord. From the beginning of the fourteenth century onwards, different men, either by craft, or valour, or through the quarrels of others, became lords over the cities of Lombardy, and continually struggled for the mastery there, and then, if they gained it, they strove to be masters in Tuscany also. The Ghibelins were for a while victorious in Tuscany, for, in 1315, Pisa inflicted a severe defeat upon the Florentines with other Tuscan Guelfs, and their

Neapolitan allies, at *Montecatini*, a little to the north-west of Florence. Soon after this, Pisa went to war with the King of Aragon, and lost Sardinia, and was nearly ruined. In Lombardy the Ghibelins were triumphant. After the death of Eccelino da Romano, the family of the *Scala* rose to power in Verona, and *Can' Grande della Scala* was not only lord of that city, but had conquered Vicenza, Padua, and Treviso. In the west, *Matteo Visconti* made himself master of Pavia, Tortona, Alessandria, and other cities. In the east, *Federigo de Montefeltro* was lord of Urbino. In Tuscany, *Castruccio Castracani* had been chosen by the citizens to rule Lucca, and, in alliance with Pisa, he threatened the safety of Florence. Robert of Naples, the head of the Guelfs, hoped for the crown of Italy, for there was a disputed election in Germany after the death of Henry the Seventh. King Robert was encouraged by Pope *John the Twenty-Second*, who was a Frenchman, and reigned at Avignon, and who owed his election to the King. The Ghibelins of Genoa, headed by the great families of Doria and Spinola, had been driven from the city by the Guelfs. The side of the exiles was taken by the Ghibelins of Lombardy, by the Pisans, and by Frederic, King of Sicily, who besieged the city. It was defended by King Robert and the Florentines, during a long war which wasted the coast district. In this war the Guelfs, though they suffered much, were on the whole successful, for they made inroads on the territory of Lucca, and so prevented Castruccio from strengthening the besieging army. The Pope sent *Philip of Valois* (afterwards King of France) to help the Guelfs. Philip was not able to do anything against Matteo Visconti, and went back over the Alps without risking a battle. The Pope also tried his spiritual weapons against the Ghibelin leaders, and especially against the great Matteo, whom he accused of heresy and witchcraft, and accordingly excommunicated.

Meanwhile *Raymond of Cardona*, the general who had been hired to lead the Guelfs, was defeated by the Visconti, and Castruccio ravaged the valley of the Arno. In these straits the Pope again sought help beyond the Alps.

2. **Lewis of Bavaria.**—On the death of Henry the Seventh, part of the electors chose *Lewis of Bavaria*, and part *Frederic of Austria*, to be Emperor. A dispute also arose about two of the votes. Pope John took the side of the Austrian, and invited his brother *Henry* to come and help the Guelfs in Italy. This new ally did not do the Guelfic cause much good, for Frederic was overthrown, in 1322, at the battle of *Mühldorf*, and Lewis of Bavaria was acknowledged as King of the Romans. About the same time Matteo Visconti died. His place was taken by his son *Galeazzo*, who carried on the war in Lombardy against the Papal party with considerable success. King Lewis made alliance with Galeazzo and with the rest of the Ghibelins, for King Robert of Naples was, it seemed, aiming at the crown of Italy. This Ghibelin alliance made the Pope very angry, and he excommunicated Lewis. Meanwhile the Florentines were in great danger. Castruccio was constantly intriguing to get hold of Pisa. In 1325, he made himself Lord of Pistoia, defeated the Florentines, and, in alliance with Galeazzo, plundered and destroyed the neighbouring towns and villages. The Florentines sent to King Robert. He promised to help them on condition that his son *Charles, Duke of Calabria*, should receive the lordship of the city for ten years. When the Austrian party was finally crushed in Germany, King Lewis set out to assert his rights in Italy and to humble the King of Naples. In 1327, he was received at Milan by Galeazzo Visconti, and was crowned with the iron crown. He might have firmly established an Imperial party in Italy. He failed through his deceit and treachery. He seized, and for a short time imprisoned, his host Galeazzo. Then he went on

to Tuscany and was entertained by Castruccio at Lucca. He heavily fined the Pisans, who were afraid to open their gates to him because he was with their enemy, Castruccio. He went to Rome and was crowned Emperor, but the rite was performed by two excommunicated Bishops instead of by the Pope. At Rome the Emperor declared his enemy John the Twenty-Second deposed from the Papal throne, and set up an Antipope. For a while the Romans were pleased at having an Emperor and a Pope of any kind in the city, but they soon changed their minds, especially when they saw the fleet of King Robert at the mouth of the Tiber, and the Emperor was forced to go away. Castruccio had been the chief adviser of the Emperor, and had been made *Duke* of Lucca, Imperial Vicar, and Senator of Rome. During his absence Pistoia revolted, but he retook it, and also made himself master of Pisa. Florence was in great danger, but she was delivered, in 1328, by the death of Castruccio. Lewis immediately seized on Pisa, and sold Lucca, and thus despoiled the son of his former friend and ally. The Emperor released Galeazzo Visconti, who shortly afterwards died. He then offered to sell the lordship of Milan to *Azzo*, but he had not left the Visconti enough money to buy it. At last, in 1329, Lewis left Italy, having almost ruined his party by his treachery and covetousness. About the same time died Can Grande della Scala; so the Ghibelins were left without a head.

3. **John of Bohemia.**—Before long, *John of Bohemia* offered himself as leader of the Ghibelin party. He was son of the Emperor Henry, and was a brave and gallant man, and had acted wisely in Germany. A number of the Lombard cities received him gladly, but the Ghibelin lords were angry at his coming because it endangered their power. An alliance was therefore made against him by Mastino della Scala and Azzo Visconti. They were joined by Guelfic Florence and by King Robert, who feared, not without

reason, that the foreigner would betray Italy to the Emperor. John soon became tired of Italy when he found difficulties arise, and, in 1333, he left it in a state of confusion. The Ghibelin lords seized on the cities which he forsook, and thus became all the more powerful, for Robert of Naples had now grown old, and could not lead the Guelfs as he used to do.

4. **The Duke of Athens.**—The Ghibelin lords did not divide between themselves the cities which King John had forsaken without dispute. Mastino della Scala had seized on Lucca, and promised to yield it to the Florentines. He did not keep his word, and, in 1336, he declared war against the republic. Florence was unsuccessful, and was obliged to make peace. Again, in 1341, he offered to sell Lucca, and Pisa was anxious to buy it; for, if Lucca had become Florentine, the independence of Pisa would have been endangered. Pisa made alliance with *Luchino Visconti* of Milan, and with other lords, and the Florentines were utterly defeated before Lucca. In their distress they laid the blame of their defeat upon their rulers. The government had gradually fallen into the hands of a kind of plebeian aristocracy, who kept all the offices to themselves. They were called the *Popolani Grossi*, and were much hated. The Florentines looked to King Robert for help, but he only sent them *Walter of Brienne, Duke of Athens*. When the Eastern Empire was conquered by the Latins, the lordship of Athens was given to one of the followers of the Marquess of Montferrat. It passed by marriage to Walter of Brienne. He was slain and his family were turned out of the Duchy by a company of *Catalan* mercenaries. His son Walter thus became a soldier of fortune, and had been lieutenant of Charles of Calabria. He was a crafty, clever, and unscrupulous man. He made himself very popular in Florence by flattering the lowest class, and by treating the great plebeian families with severity. His flattering promises so pleased the people, that on September 8, 1342,

they gave him the lordship of the city for life. In other cases the Florentines had only conferred this great power for a certain number of years. They now endangered their liberty by setting up a Tyrant. The Duke of Athens cared only for his own interests, not for the safety or honour of the city. He sent for French horsemen, and kept down all insurrections by their help. The nobles found that the depression of the great burghers did not give them any more share in the government than they had before. Even the lowest class found that they had chosen for their master a cruel judge and a licentious despot. All Florence suffered alike, and, after a year of tyranny, the Duke was driven from the city by a general rising of the people. He carried off much spoil, the fruit of his evil rule. Thus Florence continued free and the champion of freedom. Guelf and Ghibelin had ceased to mean simply Imperialist or anti-Imperialist. Neither Pope nor Emperor was at this period of any great importance in Italy. The Guelfic cause was now the cause of freedom, the Ghibelin was the cause of tyranny.

5. **Naples and the Free Companies.**—In 1343, King Robert of Naples ended his long reign. He was succeeded by his grand-daughter *Joanna*, who had married her cousin *Andrew*, son of Carobert, King of *Hungary*. For the Hungarian crown had come to the Angevin house by the marriage of *Charles the Second* of Naples to the sister of *Ladislaus the Third*. Andrew offended his Neapolitan subjects by allowing his Hungarian followers to usurp all political power. He and Joanna lived unhappily together, and after a while he was murdered, perhaps by her orders. Then *Charles of Durazzo*, a cousin of Joanna and the murdered King, roused the citizens of Naples against the Queen. Joanna and her guilty lover, Lewis of Tarento, fled. *Lewis the Great*, the brother of Andrew, was king of Hungary. In 1347, he invaded the kingdom of Naples. Joanna fled to *Pope Clement the Sixth*

at Avignon, and there married Lewis of Tarento. Naples was desolated by war, which was especially terrible because it was carried on by *Free Companies*. These were bodies of soldiers who hired themselves out to the highest bidder, and, when the term of their engagement was over, often made war on their own account. They were a great curse to Italy for many years, for they felt no sort of respect either for God or man; they were licentious, cruel, and treacherous. The greatest leader of these freebooters in Naples was one *Werner*, a German, who boasted that he was "the enemy of God, of pity, and of mercy." When peace was made, in 1351, between Joanna and Lewis of Hungary, these Companies came northwards. The most famous, called *The Great Company*, was led first by a knight of St. John, called "*Fra Moriale*," and then by *Count Lando*. The armies of the Italian cities were no longer composed simply of citizens, for the different lords chose rather to hire heavy-armed cavalry who were entirely dependent upon themselves, than to trust arms to their subjects which might be used to regain their freedom. Accordingly these Companies were paid on all sides, sometimes to make war upon a state, sometimes to leave it in peace. The Italians suffered greatly from these men. If they fought for a state, they betrayed it, if it seemed to their advantage. If they fought against a state, they fought without honour and without mercy. If they left a state in peace, they often left it impoverished by their demands. The Tyrants used them to secure and extend their power, and the cities hired them to take vengeance upon each other. In 1359, the Great Company was broken up by the steady resistance of Florence, but the evil habit of employing mercenary soldiers was still kept up. The *Peace of Bretigny*, in 1360, between England and France, threw a great number of fighting-men out of employment, and many came over to seek service in Italy. An army of English mercenaries, called *The White Company*, led by *Sir John Hawkwood*, was for a time in the service of Pisa, and did much damage to the Florentines and the rest of Tuscany.

6. **The Plague.**—In the middle of this century Italy was also wasted by natural evils. In 1345, there were very heavy rains, which were followed by a great scarcity of grain, and an utter failure of the vintage, so that many died of hunger. Meanwhile, a fearful plague, which had already laid the Eastern part of the world waste, was rapidly advancing westwards. It reached Italy in 1348, and fell upon the country with great violence. It is said that Naples alone lost 60,000 inhabitants, and that in Pisa seven died out of every ten. Siena never again recovered her former prosperity. It is often called the *Plague of Florence*, because the Florentine *Giovanni Boccaccio* has given us a wonderfully vivid account of the sufferings of his native city. Under this terrible scourge men became selfish and lawless, and all the bonds of society, and even of natural affection, seemed unloosed by the nearness of death. Although the violence of the plague soon abated, yet for many years it occasionally broke out again.

7. **The Babylonish Captivity. Rienzi.**—Ever since 1305, there had been no Pope in Rome or in Italy. Philip the Fourth of France, by the overthrow of Boniface the Eighth, and by bringing about the election of the French Clement the Fifth, made the Popes the servants of the French Kings. From 1305 to 1377, they dwelt almost entirely at *Avignon* in Provence, just outside the boundary of France. This city belonged to the French reigning house of Naples through Beatrix of Provence, wife of Charles of Anjou; and Queen Joanna sold it to *Clement the Sixth*. Meanwhile Rome was a scene of great disorder. There were indeed magistrates, called *Caporioni*, (*Headmen*), chosen by the different quarters of the city, but they had little real power. The Pope sent a *Senator*, but as he was

a noble, he added to the confusion. The families of *Orsini*, *Colonna*, and *Savelli* filled the city with their feuds, and made strongholds out of the old ruins. At length, in 1347, the Roman people made an attempt to govern themselves. They were stirred up by *Niccola di Rienzi*, a young man of low birth, and of great talents. He appealed to their pride in the old greatness of their city, and called upon them to restore liberty, and what he called *the Good Estate*. He was chosen *Tribune*, and brought the nobles to obedience by strong measures, in which he was upheld by the people. At first, Pope Clement seemed to favour the movement, and the Tribune gained a great deal of influence in Italy. Rienzi, however, was not able to carry on the work which he had begun. His head was turned with success. He showed a childish vanity and an unyielding resentment of former injuries. Clement was alarmed at his success and at his threats. The Pope and the Cardinals joined with the nobles against him. The people were tired of his rule, and he was forced to flee. He was taken and imprisoned at Avignon. In 1354, he was released and sent back to Rome. He now came as a Senator appointed by Pope *Innocent the Sixth;* he was therefore no longer the champion of independence; his rule was distasteful, and he was slain in a tumult of the people. After his death Cardinal *Albornoz* succeeded in bringing the city to submit to her absent Bishop. All attempts at independence was sure to fail in Rome, for the presence of the Pope was the one great source of the wealth of the city. The Romans, and indeed all the Italians, were most anxious to get the Pope back again, and to take the Papacy away from the power of France. At last, in 1377, *Gregory the Eleventh* came back, and the absence of the Popes from Italy ended. This exile lasted seventy years, and so it is called the *Babylonish Captivity*.

8. **Charles the Fourth and the Visconti.**—Throughout

the latter half of the fourteenth century, the great danger of Italy was from the power of the Visconti of Milan. *Azzo* and his nephew *Luchino* raised the family from the low estate to which it had been brought by the Emperor Lewis. Luchino was killed by his wife, whom he meant to have killed. He was succeeded by his brother *Gian Visconti*, Archbishop of Milan. This new lord of Milan took advantage of an attempt of Pope Clement the Sixth to bring the cities of Romagna under his power; he gained Bologna for himself, and held it in spite of the Pope's wrath. The Archbishop was now lord of more than twenty cities, and the death of Mastino della Scala, and the feebleness of his successor, made him all the more powerful in the North. He next invaded Tuscany, but was kept in check by the Florentines. In 1353, the Genoese were defeated in a sea-fight by the Venetians, and were so disheartened that they delivered over their city to the lord of Milan. This made the Venetians enemies of Gian Visconti, and, as the Florentines had now made peace with him, they looked outside Italy for an ally. *Charles*, King of *Bohemia*, the son of King John, who for a time had tried to head the Italian Ghibelins, had been chosen King of the Romans by the German Electors. This was in the lifetime of the Emperor Lewis, who died soon afterwards. The Venetians sent to King Charles to come into Italy, hoping that he would be able to check the Visconti. Charles unfortunately was poor, and, though he bore such a great title, he was really weaker than the lord of Milan. He came into Italy with only three hundred followers, and tried in vain to make peace between Venice and the Visconti. Charles received the crown of Italy. He was crowned at Milan in 1355, and the same year was crowned Emperor at Rome. The Florentines were somewhat uneasy at his coming into Tuscany, but he rather courted them, and received a large sum for his favour.

The *Lucchese* hoped that the Emperor would have restored their freedom. Since the death of Castruccio their unhappy city had been four times offered for sale, rejected, bought, besieged; at last it had surrendered to the Pisans. The Emperor encouraged the hopes of the inhabitants, and so offended the Pisans. He then went off to Germany, and left Lucca at the mercy of her offended masters. The visit of Charles marks the great decline of the Imperial power in Italy. He did some small amount both of good and of evil, but in no way changed the general state of affairs. Meanwhile Gian the Archbishop died, and was succeeded by his three nephews, the brothers *Matteo*, *Bernabo*, and *Galeazzo*. Matteo soon died and his death is said to have been from poison given him by his brothers, who now divided nearly all Lombardy between themselves. They were attacked, though without vigour or success, by several of the lords of the North, and especially by the *Marquess of Montferrat*, in alliance with the *Beccarias*, who were almost lords of *Pavia*. In revenge the Visconti laid siege to Pavia. A resolute resistance was made, headed by *Jacopo Bussolari*, a patriot monk. The city was taken in 1359, and Jacopo died in prison. The Visconti now strengthened themselves by foreign alliances. The son of Galeazzo, *Gian-Galeazzo*, married *Isabella*, daughter of *John*, King of France; and his daughter *Violante* married *Lionel, Duke of Clarence*, son of our King *Edward the Third*. Bernabo waged a successful war against the Papal troops in Romagna. He employed a famous English Free Company, under Sir John Hawkwood, to help the Pisans in a war with Florence. The great number of these Free Companies enabled the Visconti, who were very rich, always to have a large trained army at their command. Charles again came into Italy, in 1368, to check their power, but instead of doing this made alliance with them. Pisa was now in the hands of one *Agnello*, who had been chosen Doge.

Agnello was little more than a servant of Bernabo. To gain the confirmation of his title he allowed Charles to give freedom to Lucca.

9. **Florence. The Eight Saints of War.**—In 1369 Bernabo began actively to make war on Florence. The Florentines were supported by Pope Urban the Fifth. They upheld a revolt in the Papal States against the French governors appointed by Gregory XI., his successor. Pope Gregory sent Sir John Hawkwood to overrun their land. The Florentines accordingly made alliance with Pisa, which had shaken off the yoke of Agnello, and with the other Ghibelin powers, and even for a short time with Bernabo. It was the cause of liberty against the Pope and the French. Some of the *Parte Guelfa* would have submitted the conduct of their affairs to the Pope. Nobler counsels prevailed, and the Florentines gave the management of the war to eight Commissioners, called "*The Eight of War.*" These Commissioners won great popularity by their able conduct, and received at a later date the curious nickname of "*The Eight Saints of the War.*" The general revolt of the States of the Church, and finally the engagement in their turn of the famous Sir John Hawkwood, enabled the Florentines to carry on the war with success until the death of the Pope, in 1378. This war with the Pope, and the appointment of the "Eight of War," were movements of the moderate Guelfs, who now gained great influence in the city. For a long time all except the most violent Guelfs had been admonished (*ammoniti*) that they were not to take office, so the Parte Guelfa kept itself at the head of affairs. Now, in 1378, *Salvestro de' Medici* was chosen Gonfaloniere, in spite of the efforts of the extreme Guelfs. The city was divided into two parties. On one side were the heads of the old Parte Guelfa, the *Albizzi*, *Soderini*, and others, a large number of the old nobility, and some of the rich *popolani,* or men of the people. The other party consisted of the

Eight of War, the *Medici*, the *Ricci*, and the great number who had so long been deprived of a share in the government of the Republic, because their politics were not satisfactory to the ruling faction. Salvestro determined to strike a blow at the oligarchy which shut out so many citizens from their political rights. He revived the law which forbade the nobles to take any share in the government, and restored the rights of the *ammoniti*. He failed in the Council of the Arts, but he appealed to the larger Council of the People, and carried his measure in the midst of tumultuous shouting. He was thus able, by courting the lower classes, to force the governing faction to give up some of the power which they had wrongfully seized.

10. **The Ciompi.**—The storm which Salvestro de' Medici raised was not easily stilled. The lower classes wished that the political equality which he had begun to enforce should be thoroughly carried out. The Arts, with whom lay the government of the city, had been increased in number to twenty-one, and were divided into seven *greater* and fourteen *lesser Arts*. A large number of the citizens did not belong to any Art, and so had no share in the government, except when all were called together to a *Parliament* in the public square by the tolling of the great bell, and this was done only on rare occasions. These men were handicraftsmen, and their position was a hard one, because, when there was any dispute between them and the masters, they had only the masters' court to go to for redress. The wool trade employed the largest number of these labourers, and they and the rest of their class were called *Ciompi*, which was perhaps a corruption of the French *compère*, or "mate." If this is the real meaning of the name, it was probably a word brought into use by the French soldiers of the Duke of Athens. The populace now demanded that the lesser Arts should be put on an equality with the greater, and that the workmen should have Arts of their own, so that they might be judged by men of their own

class, and that they might have a share in ruling the city. The plans of the Ciompi came to the ears of the Signoria, and, when they knew that they were discovered, partly in hope, partly in fear, they began a wild insurrection. On July 22, the Priors fled, and the people took the Palace of the Signoria. As they rushed in, the standard of the Gonfaloniere was in the hands of a wool-carder, named *Michele di Lando*. Barefoot, and with scanty clothing, he headed the mob, as the rioters ascended the staircase. He entered the audience-chamber of the Signoria, and there turned to those who followed him, and said, "The palace is yours, and the city is in your power : what, think you, ought to be done?" They answered that they would have him for their Gonfaloniere and their lord; and that he should govern them as he thought best. Michele accepted the command, and began to govern as if he was quite used to the work. The Eight of War were glad to see their old enemies overthrown. They wished to take advantage of the popular movement, and to appoint the *Priors* who were to form the new Signoria. Michele, however, made his own choice. He made up his Signoria of eight Priors, two from the greater Arts, and two from the lesser, and four from four new Arts which he made for the workpeople. The Ciompi soon became dissatisfied, and said that Michele favoured the great people too much; and in truth he was forced to keep friends with Salvestro de' Medici and his party. Nevertheless Michele kept the workmen quiet with great skill till he went out of office. The next Gonfaloniere, a man of the same class, was of far lower talents. After a short time of disturbance, the government was divided between the seven greater and sixteen lesser Arts; so the working people were none the better off, and the only advantage was gained by the smaller tradespeople. The party of Salvestro de' Medici was placed at the head of the government, but in a short time it split up. In January, 1382, a *Balia* was demanded by the Guelfic aristocracy. A Balia was a Committee chosen by the people with full power to change the constitution; it was in fact a revolutionary appeal to the people. This Committee repealed all the measures passed during the late troubles, and the *nobili popolani* again came into power.

11. **The Great Schism.**—When Gregory the Eleventh, who had restored the Papal presence to Rome, died in 1378, the Romans loudly demanded a Pope who would dwell in the city, and after some tumult *Bartolommeo, Archbishop of Bari,* was chosen. The new Pope, who took the name of *Urban the Sixth,* was a violent and savage man. He soon made the Cardinals hate him, and deeply offended Queen Joanna of Naples. His enemies chose *Robert of Geneva* for Pope, who took the name of *Clement the Seventh.* Urban lived at Rome and Clement at Avignon. All Christendom was divided by their rivalry. Thus, nearly as soon as the Papacy was restored to Rome, the *Great Schism* began, which lasted until the Council held at *Constanz* in 1414. During this time there were two, and sometimes three Popes at the same time, each claiming to be the rightful Head of the Church. Pope Urban was upheld by *Charles of Durazzo*, the cousin and heir of the childless Queen *Joanna of Naples,* who upheld Clement. The Queen married a fourth husband, *Otto of Brunswick.* In order to thwart Charles, she adopted *Lewis of Anjou,* the son of *John,* King of France, as her heir. Pope Urban crowned Charles as King of Naples, and *Lewis the Great,* King of Hungary, who was his cousin, sent over an army to help him, for he had not forgotten the murder of his brother *Andrew.* Charles took the Queen prisoner, and had her put to death. After the death of Lewis of Anjou in 1384, Charles had entire possession of the kingdom. After the death of Lewis of Hungary, Charles went over to that country to claim the crown, and there

was murdered. By the death of Charles Naples was again made the scene of war. The adherents of the old Angevin line upheld *Ladislas*, the infant son of King Charles, and the French, or new Angevin party, wanted to set up *Lewis the Second*, who was also a child. After a long struggle Ladislas was able to drive out the French.

12. **The War of Chioggia.**—While the Visconti were rapidly increasing their power in North Italy, Venice and Genoa stood somewhat apart from general Italian politics. They waged a constant war against each other, the chief scene of which was the Levant. The Genoese had helped the Greeks to regain the Empire from the Latins. They received in return the suburb of Galata, and exercised great influence over the politics of Constantinople. In 1348, they were at war with the Emperor *John Cantacuzene*, and defeated the allied fleets of the Greeks and Venetians. In every dispute in the East the two republics took opposite sides, and, in 1378, a fierce war was begun about the possession of Cyprus. The Genoese made alliance with Lewis the Great, who wanted to get back the *Dalmatian* coast, which the Venetians had conquered, and with *Francesco da Carrara*, lord of Padua, who feared the power of the great republic. The Venetian fleet was destroyed, and its commander *Vittorio Pisani* was put in prison for the disaster. The war was then carried on against the city itself. The great Lagune, or expanse of water formed by the outflow of different rivers, is defended from the Adriatic by a long line of narrow islands. Between these are narrow channels which lead to the city, and to the different islands in the Lagune. The most southern of these channels is one which leads to the town called *Chioggia*, twenty-five miles to the south of Venice. This channel was occupied by the Genoese fleet, and the little town was taken. The Genoese had the greater share in the taking of Chioggia; but, according to the terms of the treaty, it was given up to the lord of

Padua. Francesco came to view his new possession, and was received by his soldiers with wild delight. He was borne along the ranks upon the shoulders of his men, and, it is said, was hailed with the strange shout of *Carro, carro, Osanna, Benedictus qui venit* (Blessed be he that cometh), for the cognizance of his family seems to have been a red chariot (*un carro rosso*). The way to Venice lay open. The republic was in the greatest danger. The Genoese leader *Luciano Doria* already boasted that he would bridle the bronze horses which stand on the front of the Church of St. Mark. In this extremity the Venetians released Vittorio Pisani, and begged him to save his ungrateful country. He immediately began vigorous measures for defence, and was upheld by the great naval commander *Carlo Zeno*, who heard in the Levant of the danger of his city. He gathered some ships together, and on January 1, 1380, brought them to her aid. The Genoese were in their turn blockaded in the port which they had seized, and all attempts to relieve them failed. Carlo Zeno drew his force closely round them, and at the end of six months forced them to surrender. The war still went on until the *Treaty of Turin*, in 1381. Venice lost her Dalmatian territory, which was taken by the King of Hungary, and was obliged to give up *Treviso*, as yet her only conquest on the mainland of Italy. During this war Trieste revolted from Venice. In 1382, she commended herself to Leopold of Austria. Though Venice lost territory, she soon became as powerful as ever. Genoa, on the other hand, never recovered the effects of the war. She wasted her strength in civil discord; she was exposed to the intrigues of the Visconti, and, to defend herself, in 1396, she conferred the *Signoria* on *Charles the Sixth* of France.

13. **Gian-Galeazzo Visconti.**—On the death of Galeazzo Visconti his son *Gian-Galeazzo* succeeded him, and, in 1385, he slew his uncle Bernabo, and reigned alone. The disputes

of his neighbours gave him an opportunity of spreading his power. Venice, in revenge for the evils she had borne from Francesco da Carrara, set *Antonio della Scala*, lord of Verona, to attack him. The lord of Padua turned for help to Gian-Galeazzo. He defeated Antonio, and took Verona for himself. He refused to give Vicenza to his ally as he had promised, and turned against him, and made alliance with Venice. The Venetians were so anxious to crush Francesco that they agreed to the alliance of Gian-Galeazzo, and he soon spread his power over the *Trevisan March*, and up to the Lagunes of Venice. Both Francesco da Carrara and Antonio della Scala were now exiles. Gian-Galeazzo next made an attack on Tuscany. Florence boldly prepared for war; her army was again commanded by Sir John Hawkwood. He was opposed by *Jacopo del Verme*, a captain in the pay of the lord of Milan. The old Francesco da Carrara gave up his rights to his son *Francesco Novello*, who retook Padua, and thus made a diversion in the North in favour of Florence. The Florentines engaged the *Count of Armagnac* to invade Lombardy, but he was defeated at *Alessandria*, and died soon afterwards. The Florentine army was only saved by the skill of Sir John Hawkwood. During an interval of peace which followed this campaign Gian-Galeazzo made constant intrigues in Tuscany. *Wenzel*, the King of the Romans, offered to help the Guelfs, but they knew his worthlessness and his weakness too well to make any engagement with him. Wenzel then, for an hundred thousand florins, made Milan and its diocese into a *Duchy*, and gave Gian-Galeazzo the *Dukedom*. All the new Duke's territory was included in the Duchy except Pavia, which, as the old capital of Italy and the ancient enemy of Milan, was allowed to remain separate from the rest. This investiture fixed and legalized the dominion of the Visconti. They were no longer simply a great Milanese family which had won a certain power over their fellow-citizens and their neighbours. They were now placed above them by a recognized and hereditary title. The power of Gian-Galeazzo increased continually, and he made use of others to forward his own purposes; some cities were taken by force, and others in great fear gave up their freedom, and received him as lord. The Guelfs made an alliance with *Charles the Sixth* of France. King Charles had been chosen lord by the Genoese, and the town of *Asti* belonged to the family of Orleans by the marriage of Violante with the Duke. In this way France became interested in Italian politics. The madness of the King, the disputes in his kingdom, and the great loss of the French at the battle of *Nikopolis*, against the *Sultan Bajazet*, in 1396, caused the alliance to be fruitless. The Guelfs next found an ally in a claimant for the Empire. In 1400, the Electors deposed Wenzel and chose *Rupert*, the *Count Palatine*. The new King of the Romans made alliance with the Florentines and with Francesco da Carrara against the Duke of Milan. His German army was defeated by the Duke near Brescia. Pisa, Lucca, Perugia, and Siena had all been brought under the dominion of Gian-Galeazzo, and the communication between Florence and the sea was cut off. Her trade was at a stand, even her liberty was in the greatest danger. But the Plague, which had carried off so many wise and noble men, now broke out again, and, in 1402, Gian-Galeazzo died of it when at the height of his power.

14. **Italian Mercenaries.**—In spite of the wars of the fourteenth century, wealth and luxury rapidly increased in Italy. The vast sums which the long war between France and England cost, made the help of the Italian bankers very useful. They made loans to these and to other states, and were often allowed to farm the customs as security for repayment. As men grew richer, they became more luxurious, and this spirit grew stronger as they became more used to tyranny.

Foreign food, and wine, and dress, and manners were fashionable at the courts of the Tyrants, and were adopted by their subjects. Simplicity and warlike spirit disappeared from cities which had ceased to belong to their people, and had become the property of some one man. Italian armies were now no longer composed of the militia of a state, in which each man fought for his home and his city. The different Tyrants knew that it was safer for them to employ mercenaries, who were wholly at their disposal, and who cared not for the cause for which they fought, but only for the man who paid them. This change was liked by the people, for campaigns now lasted a much longer time than formerly. Before the fourteenth century a campaign lasted only a few days. A pitched battle was fought, or a town was attacked, and then the citizen soldiers went back, every man to his own affairs, until they were called out again. In the latter half of the century war became an art. Campaigns and sieges lasted for months, and the citizen soldier would have been ruined, because his shop or his office would have been shut while he was at the wars. The mercenaries were soldiers by profession, and thus were far better fitted for war than the militia, who went to war only when some need arose. In order to pay these troops, the states contracted heavy debts to different private persons; these debts were *funded*, or placed in one stock with the same security for payment and the same rate of interest. From these funds the present system of national debts and securities arose. At first the mercenaries were foreigners, but towards the end of the century a famous school of generalship arose in Italy. This was the *Company of St. George*, founded by *Alberigo, Count of Barbiano*, and from that time the great tacticians in the Italian wars were themselves Italians, as *Jacopo del Verme* and others. These mercenary troops often gave a Tyrant power to extend his territories; but sometimes they enabled a free state, like

Florence, to defend herself against those who wished to enslave her. The use of gunpowder began to change the mode of warfare. Gian-Galeazzo had a great number of large and small field-pieces. It was not however until some years later that muskets began to be used in the Italian wars, and then the length of time which was taken up in loading and firing off these new weapons much hindered their usefulness.

15. **Literature of the Fourteenth Century.**—The danger and distress of Constantinople during the fourteenth century, from the invasions of the Empire by the Turks, led many of her wise men to seek some active ally and often to find a permanent refuge in the West. Their coming caused the revival of Greek literature in Italy, a movement which began in the middle of the century, and was especially taken up by the Florentine *Francesco Petrarca*. This poet is now chiefly famous for the Italian sonnets which preserve the tenderness of his passion for *Laura*. A little later the study of Greek was followed more seriously by another Florentine, *Giovanni Boccaccio*. As Dante may be called the father of Italian poetry, so Giovanni Boccaccio deserves the like title as regards Italian prose, which he wrote in its purest form, in his own native *Tuscan*. His great work is his collection of novels, in which he discloses the wickedness of the time with reckless pleasantry. The two *Malaspini*, the earliest Italian Chroniclers, and *Giovanni*, *Matteo*, and *Filippo Villani*, who wrote in Italian a work which deserves the name of a philosophic history, were also Florentines. The study of Greek letters revived with greater vigour at the close of the century, when *Manuel Chrysoloras* taught at Florence, Pavia, and Rome. Before long this learning found a fixed home in Florence, under the magnificent patronage of the Medici.

CHAPTER VI.

THE GREAT STATES.

Italy at the death of Gian-Galeazzo (1)—great power of Ladislas; end of the Schism (2)—Filippo Maria Visconti wins back the territory which had been lost at his father's death (3)—the disputed succession in Naples, and the wars which arose from it (4)—rise of Cosimo de' Medici (5)—Alfonso of Aragon gains Naples and Sicily; end of the Visconti; Francesco Sforza, Duke of Milan (6)—political power of the Papacy begins: Pope Nicolas the Fifth; Constantinople taken by the Turks; revival of Greek learning (7)—danger from the Turks (8)—the French party in Italy (9)—Cosimo and Piero de' Medici (10)—Conspiracies against Tyrants (11)—assassination of Giuliano de' Medici (12)—Papal wars (13)—time of peace in Italy (14)—change in Italian politics; the French invited into Italy (15).

1. **Petty Tyrants of North Italy.** — Gian-Galeazzo divided his dominions by will between his two sons *Gian-Maria* and *Filippo Maria*. They were both very young at their father's death, and were left by him under the care of their mother *Caterina*, the daughter of Bernabo Visconti, of his low-born favourite *Francesco Barbavara*, and of a Council of Regency made up for the most part of the soldiers of fortune who had led his armies. This Council soon split up, for Francesco had been the Duke's valet, and the generals withstood him and the widowed Duchess, who was said to be in love with him. Caterina ruled with great cruelty, and without ability. She was taken and put in prison and there died; Francesco was forced to flee. The Duchy of Milan was divided between a number of petty Tyrants, who shared the dominions of their former master. The little states of Romagna, which had for the most part been conquered by

Gian-Galeazzo, were at his death overrun by the Count of Barbiano, who with his famous company entered the service of Pope *Boniface the Ninth*. The petty sovereignties of Lombardy and Romagna were in most cases the abodes of the foulest vices. The Tyrant lived only for his own gratification, and for this he readily sacrificed humanity, decency, and natural affection. The vices of the court spread to the families of private citizens, who saw that men gained power and wealth by treachery, murder, and fratricide, that they kept them by cruelty, and used them to gratify their loathsome passions. The Count of *Savoy*, the Marquess of *Montferrat*, and the lords of Padua, Ferrara, and Mantua, were the only independent Sovereigns in North Italy in 1402. Of these Francesco, lord of Padua, was soon to fall. On the death of Gian-Galeazzo he seized on *Verona*. Venice would not allow her old enemy to gain this advantage. She made alliance with *Francesco di Gonzaga*, lord of Mantua, and with his help took Verona and closely besieged Padua. After a gallant resistance Francesco da Carrara was forced to yield. He and his two sons were taken prisoners to Venice, and were there strangled by order of the Council of Ten. This war gave the Venetians great power on the mainland. They reconquered Treviso, and gained Feltro, Verona, Vicenza, and Padua. From this time Venice had a distinctly Italian policy. In Tuscany, the death of her great enemy delivered Florence from her distress, and Siena, which now regained her liberty, placed herself under her protection. Pisa was left to *Gabriello Visconti*, a bastard son of the late Duke. He put himself under the protection of *Jean Boucicault*, who governed Genoa for Charles the Sixth, King of France, and with his consent he sold Pisa to the Florentines. The Pisans resisted this sacrifice of their freedom, and the war lasted a year, until, in 1406, the city was forced to surrender. Many of the people left their homes; for, though

Florence acted fairly towards her old enemy and new subject, yet the Pisans could not bear the yoke, and the greatness of the city, its trade and its wealth, vanished away. The Schism still distracted the Church and the city of Rome, and the rival Popes were treated as puppets by rival Princes. The kingdom of Naples and the island of Sicily were still divided; and as the King who reigned at Naples would not give up his right to Sicily, which had been lost, as well as gained by Charles of Anjou, his kingdom as well as the Island kingdom is often called *Sicily*. When therefore the two kingdoms at last became one, the strange name of the Kingdom of the *Two Sicilies* arose. The contest between Ladislas of Naples and Lewis was the principal question which affected the fortunes of the claimants for the Papacy. In the end Ladislas drove out his rival, and became the head of the Ghibelin or anti-French party in Italy. The island of Sicily had sunk into obscurity under the successors of King Frederic. In 1409, *Mary* Queen of Sicily married *Martin*, son of *Martin* of Aragon, and by this marriage the island again became joined to the crown of Aragon. Early in the fourteenth century the King of Aragon gained Sardinia from Pisa, but the Pisans on the island made frequent revolts, and were not finally subdued till about the same time as Pisa herself fell.

2. **King Ladislas and the Schism.**—The schism in the Papacy gave Ladislas an opportunity of greatly strengthening himself, and he took care to prevent its coming to an end too quickly. He wished above all things to keep out a French Pope, for, if a Frenchman had been acknowledged in Rome, there would have been little chance of keeping the French out of Naples. While *Benedict the Thirteenth*, the Avignonese Pope candidate, disputed the Papacy, first with *Innocent the Seventh* and then with *Gregory the Twelfth*, Ladislas confirmed his power, matured his plans, and even entered Rome. A Council was held at Pisa, in 1409, to end the

Schism, but it only added a third claimant, *Alexander the Fifth,* and so made matters worse. The power of Ladislas grew so great as to become dangerous to the liberty of Florence, and indeed of all Italy. The Florentines hired against him *Braccio,* a famous leader, who had formerly fought for the King, and whom they lured by higher pay. After a little time Braccio was opposed by *Sforza Attendolo,* who had risen from being a peasant of Romagna to lead the army of Naples. These two men were the greatest of all the Italian generals. Florence also had on her side Lewis of Anjou, who was upheld by Jean Boucicault in Genoa. When the Genoese revolted from the French, and went over to Ladislas, Lewis was afraid lest he should be cut off from France, and so he retreated while he could. Nevertheless, the army of the allies had considerable success, and, in 1410, entered Rome and made the Romans accept Pope Alexander. Florence was anxious to put an end to the Schism, knowing that an universally acknowledged Pope would be the most effectual check to the ambition of King Ladislas. On the death of Alexander, the Angevin and Florentine party set up Pope *John the Twenty-Third,* and, in 1411, Lewis of Anjou defeated Ladislas in a great battle at *Rocca secca.* But Ladislas now took into his pay Sforza, who had before this been in the pay of Pope John. Lewis did not follow up his victory, and the King, notwithstanding his defeat, was able to enter Rome. Pope John was much hated for his wickedness and exactions, and was forced to flee from the city. He appealed for help beyond the Alps. After a short schism in the Empire, *Sigismund,* brother of the deposed Wenzel, became sole King of the Romans. Sigismund was the enemy of Ladislas, for the King of Naples had tried to take from him the crown of *Hungary,* to which he had succeeded in right of his wife, the daughter of Lewis the Great, of the house of Charles of Anjou. Pope John hoped

that King Sigismund would defend him against his enemy
Ladislas, who had scarcely left him a safe resting-place in
Italy. Sigismund, however, was fully determined to put an
end to the scandals which the Schism had brought about in
Christendom, and the death of Ladislas enabled him to do
this the more easily. In 1415, Sigismund held a Council of
the Western Church in the Imperial city of Constanz. In
this Council Gregory gave up his claim. The helpless
but obstinate Benedict and the dissolute John the Twenty-
Third were deposed. *Martin the Fifth* was chosen Pope,
and was everywhere acknowledged; and so the Great
Schism ended.

3. **Filippo Maria Visconti.**—Gian-Maria and his brother
Filippo Maria were left with a small part of the vast dominion
of their father. Even what they had was under the control
of *Facino Cane*, who had been one of his generals, and
who had made himself Tyrant of Alessandria. Duke Gian-
Maria only cared to torture and kill his subjects. He loved to
hunt men to death with his dogs, which he fed on human
flesh to make them keen for the prey. At last, in 1412, the
Milanese and some neighbouring nobles, wearied with his
wickedness, set on him and slew him. Facino Cane died of
disease at the same time. Filippo Maria hastily gathered
together the forces of Facino Cane and seized on Milan. He
married the general's widow, Beatrice Tenda, a woman of
twice his age, with whom he gained Alessandria, Como,
Tortona, and other places. He afterwards had her cruelly
tortured and put to death. Filippo Maria, like his father,
was a man of restless ambition, but was kept in check by his
own timidity and indecision. He ruled over his Duchy without ever showing himself, nor would he willingly allow anyone to look upon his face, which was very loathly. He was
served by a great general called *Francesco Carmagnola*, a
Piedmontese, who, in the course of ten years, won back for

him all the small sovereignties which had been lost at the death of Gian-Galeazzo, and gained for him the same power over Genoa which the French had had. The *Val Levantina* and the *Val d' Ossola* had been taken from Gian-Maria by the *Confederates of the Old League of High Germany*, whom we now call the *Swiss*, after the name of the land of Schwyz. In 1422, Filippo Maria tried to gain *Bellinzona*, which was the key to the Pass and the surrounding country. Uri and Unterwalden bought the city from its lord, but *Agnola della Pergola*, one of the Duke's generals, took it from them. The Confederates were divided as to the policy they should pursue. At length part of them determined to fight. An army of 3,000 men advanced against the city, but they were overthrown at *Arvedo* by the cavalry of the Duke.

4. **The Succession to Naples.**—On the death of Ladislas, his elder sister Joanna succeeded to the throne of Naples. She was twice married, but had no children. Her second husband, who was a Frenchman, treated her badly, and was driven away by her people. Sforza, her great general, encouraged Lewis the Third of Anjou, grandson of that Lewis who had been adopted by Joanna the First, to hope for the succession. On the other hand, the Queen's favourite, *Ser Giovanni Caraccioli*, persuaded her to adopt *Alfonso*, King of Aragon and Sicily. After a short time, Joanna revoked this adoption, and adopted Lewis of Anjou instead. The two parties of Anjou and Aragon went to war, and divided all Italy. The Duke of Milan and Sforza upheld the Angevin cause. The Pope and the Florentines, with Braccio and Carlo Malatesta, Lord of Rimini, sided with Alfonso. In this war both Sforza and Braccio died. The place of Sforza was taken by his son, the famous *Francesco*. The Florentines were several times defeated by the army of the Duke of Milan. They sent to Venice for help, and the Doge *Francesco Foscari* persuaded the Republic to make

alliance with them against Milan. The Venetians were encouraged in this by Francesco Carmagnola, who had fallen into disgrace with the Duke, and who offered them his services. Under his leadership the allies took Brescia, and the Duke was glad to agree to a peace in 1426. Meanwhile the affairs of Naples had become settled for a time. The Angevin party, which was generally popular in the kingdom, became so strong that Alfonso could not do anything against it. Lewis the Third remained inactive until his death, and then the Queen adopted his brother René of Anjou in his place. The war which this disputed succession had kindled in North Italy soon broke out again. The Milanese army was constantly worsted by Francesco Carmagnola, until, in 1431, he was defeated by Sforza in a battle at *Soncino*, near Cremona. About the same time Niccolo Piccinino, the Duke's general, was victorious in Tuscany, Lucca revolted from Florence, and Pisa was only kept in subjection by harsh measures. The Allies were much distressed, and Carmagnola, discouraged by defeat, remained inactive. The Signory of Venice began to suspect his loyalty. In 1432, he was called to Venice, and received with every mark of favour. He was suddenly thrown into prison, was tortured, and after three weeks he was led out, with a gag in his mouth, and was beheaded between the Two Columns before the Palace of St. Mark. The secrecy of all the proceedings of the Council of Ten makes it impossible to know whether the sentence was just; it was certainly ungrateful and impolitic, for the Duke no longer cared to make peace when his great enemy was dead. Terms were at last arranged by the King of the Romans. Sigismund had entered Italy, and had been crowned King at Milan. He stayed a twelvemonth at Siena. Florence resented his interference, and barred his progress. Unsupported by the Duke, the Republic easily kept him shut up in Siena, and heavily punished the city for the part it took against her. In 1433 a peace was made at Ferrara between the Duke of Milan and the Allies; and this was immediately followed by a treaty between Sigismund and Siena and Florence. Sigismund advanced to Rome and was crowned Emperor by Pope *Eugenius the Fourth*. He then went to *Basel*, where a Council was sitting to settle the questions which had given rise to a religious war between the Bohemians and the Germans, and to reform the Church both in its head, the Pope, and in its members.

5. **Rise of Cosimo de' Medici.**—Ever since the insurrection of the Ciompi the old Guelfic families and the new *popolani grossi*, or rich men of the people, had had the chief power in Florence. This oligarchy, in 1433, was under the direction of *Rinaldo degli Albizzi*, who, though a brilliant and eloquent man, was wavering in purpose and disdainful in manner. The head of the opposition was *Cosimo de' Medici*, the son of *Giovanni de' Medici*, who by his ability and attention to commerce had amassed a very large fortune. Cosimo carried on his father's trade. He lived splendidly; he was a great supporter of all literary men, and spent and distributed his wealth amongst his fellow-citizens. He was courteous and liberal, and was looked upon with almost unbounded respect and affection by a large party in the state. Rinaldo was bent upon his ruin, and, in 1433, when he had a Signoria devoted to his party, he cited Cosimo before the Council, and shut him up in the tower of the Public Palace. This violent step caused much excitement, and two days afterwards the Signoria held a Parliament of the people. The great bell of the city was tolled, and the people gathered round the Palace. Then the gates of the Palace were thrown open, and the Signoria, the Colleges of Arts and the Gonfaloniere came forth, and asked the people if they would have a Balia. So a Balia was appointed, the names being proposed by the Signoria, to decide on the fate

of Cosimo. At first it was proposed to kill him, but he was only banished, much against the will of Rinaldo, who knew that, if he lived, he would some day come back again. The next year the Signoria was favourable to him. A new Balia was appointed; the party of the Albizzi was banished, and Cosimo was recalled. He was received with a greeting such as men give to a conqueror, and was hailed as the *Father of his Country*. This triumphant return gave the Medici a power in the Republic which they never afterwards lost. The banished party fled to the court of the Duke of Milan, and stirred him up to war against their city. Filippo Maria was at war with Pope Eugenius. The Pope was forced to flee from Rome, and to take refuge in Florence. His cause was upheld by Florence and Venice. Francesco Sforza now entered the Pope's service, and led the Florentine army. He was opposed by Niccolo Piccinino, and the war between these two great generals was carried on with wonderful military skill. On the whole the Duke was worsted, the hopes of the Florentine exiles failed, and Cosimo and his party were strengthened.

6. **Francesco Sforza.**—When Filippo Maria found himself worsted, he enticed Francesco Sforza over to his side. He gave him his natural daughter *Bianca* in marriage, with Cremona and Pontremoli for her dowry. By his means a peace was made between Florence and Venice and the Duke. Meanwhile the crown of Naples passed to the Aragonese. In 1435, Queen Joanna the Second died, and Alfonso claimed the kingdom. The claim of René of Anjou, the Queen's adopted son, was upheld by the fleet of the Republic of Genoa, which was under the Duke of Milan, and Alfonso was defeated and taken prisoner off the island of *Ponza*. The Duke, however, soon changed sides, for he feared lest the French party should grow too strong. King René was besieged in his capital, and fled out of the kingdom.

He went back to France, tarrying for a while at Florence to receive from the Pope the crown which he had already lost. Then Alfonso, King of Aragon, Naples, and Sicily, established himself at Naples, and won the hearts of his subjects by his liberality and literary taste. Throughout his reign he remained constant to the alliance with Milan, which had gained him the throne. Although Francesco Sforza had married the Duke's daughter, yet he was too powerful and too ambitious to be looked on with favour by the jealous Tyrant, and there were constant feuds between them. In 1447, died Filippo Maria, the last of the great Visconti line. He left no legitimate children, and, as Milan was a fief which could descend only to males, neither his natural daughter *Bianca*, nor *Valentina* his sister, who had married the *Duke of Orleans*, brother of *Charles the Sixth* of France, had any lawful claim. One party in Milan upheld Francesco Sforza in right of his wife; while another put forward the claim of Alfonso of Naples, to whom the late Duke had left his dominions. But the greater number of the citizens declared that they would not have another Duke, but would rule themselves as in old times. Their example was followed by Pavia, Como, Alessandria, and other cities, which had long been subject to the Visconti. The Milanese were at war with Venice, and the Venetians would not agree to a peace with them. They were therefore obliged to employ Francesco. This employment gave him the power of making himself master of the city. Thus Venice was really the means of setting up a house which afterward became her greatest enemy. Francesco and the Milanese defeated the Venetians at *Caravaggio*, between the Adda and the Oglio. After this battle he treated with Venice on his own account. The Milanese, when they knew his treachery, tried to get foreign help against him. They sent to Frederic the King of the Romans, who claimed the Duchy as a lapsed fief; to the Duke of

Orleans, who claimed it through Valentina; and to the Duke of Savoy and others, who were related to the Visconti. But they gained very little help from any of these princes. Venice was on the side of their enemy, and Florence was under the influence of Cosimo de' Medici, who had no sympathy with the cause of freedom. Francesco Sforza gained several cities in Lombardy, and advanced to Milan. The city received some help from the Duke of Savoy, and refused to admit its victorious general. The Venetians became conscious of the short-sightedness of their policy, and made peace. But it was too late, and the Milanese were brought down to the greatest straits. In their distress some proposed to become the subjects of Venice, rather than fall into the hands of Francesco Sforza. The greater part of the people, however, would not hear of this, and on February 26, 1450, they admitted Sforza into the city as their Lord and Duke. Thus, in the middle of the fifteenth century, the four great temporal powers in Italy were the King of Naples, the Duke of Milan, and the two Republics of Venice and Florence. Venice was governed by a strict though as yet a patriotic oligarchy, Florence by a vigorous democracy. In Florence, however, for the first time one family began to exercise an undue influence over their fellow-citizens, though as yet the democratic form of government was undisturbed. A fifth power also now began to be conspicuous in Italy, the temporal power of the Popes.

7. **Pope Nicolas the Fifth.**—The *Captivity* at Avignon and the *Schism* weakened the position of the Popes in Italy and in the world. The Church at large had in the Council of Constanz assumed and exercised authority over the Popes. This Council was followed by another held at Basel in 1431. The Council of Basel came to nought. *Æneas Sylvius*, its Secretary, went over to the side of the Pope. By this desertion Pope Eugenius was enabled to triumph over the Council.

After a short schism Nicolas V., the successor of Eugenius, was universally acknowledged. The failure of the Council of Basel restored the position of the Papacy, and set it free from control. The character and ability of Pope Nicolas made him respected, and the part which he took in politics made him rank amongst the great temporal powers in Italy. From this time onwards to the end of our history we shall see the Popes the undisputed Princes of Rome, and the lords of all that part of Italy which they claimed by the gift of Kings and Emperors, and not least by the will of the Countess Matilda. Pope Nicolas used this power better than any of those who came after him, for he used it in the cause of peace, and to forward learning and artistic taste. He applied himself to the general pacification of Italy, and, in 1454, brought about the *Peace of Lodi*, which was signed by Venice and Milan and by King Alfonso. Christendom had great need of peace, for, in 1453, Constantinople had been taken by the Infidels, and *Mahomet the Second* was spreading his conquests over the East of Europe. Before the fall of the city a great many Greeks had come to Italy, on different missions, and especially to attend a Council at Florence, where terms of union were made between the Greek and Latin Churches. Their coming revived the taste for Greek learning, which had been so powerfully felt by Petrarca and Boccaccio. Pope Nicolas made Rome the centre of this literature, and others followed his example. *Theodore of Gaza, George of Trebizond*, and many more, found enlightened patrons in the Pope, the King of Naples, Cosimo de' Medici, and Federigo, Count of Urbino. The Pope was a lover and patron of art as well as of literature. He rebuilt the churches, palaces, and fortifications of Rome and the Roman States. He formed the scheme of raising a church worthy of the memory of St. Peter, and left behind him the Vatican Palace as a worthy residence for the Apostle's successors. The Papal Library had been scattered during the Captivity and the Schism. Pope Nicolas made a large collection of manuscripts, and thus founded the Library of the Vatican. The introduction of printing into Italy about this time gave great strength to the revival of learning. In 1452, the Pope crowned *Frederic the Third* Emperor at Rome with great magnificence. Nicolas, however, was in danger in his city, for the next year a wild plot was made against him. A large number of Romans were displeased at the rapid growth of the power of the Pope. They were headed by *Stefano Porcaro*, who declared that he would free the city which had once been mistress of the world from the yoke of priests. The rising was to be ushered in by the slaughter of the Papal Court and the plunder of its treasures. The plot was discovered, and was crushed with considerable severity. This was the last and most unworthy of the various attempts of the Romans to set up self-government.

8. **Danger from the Turks.**—The advance of the Ottoman Turks during the latter part of the fifteenth century caused the utmost alarm in Italy. Venice, from her possessions and her trade in the Levant, was most exposed to the attacks of the Infidels, and she became the great champion against them. The learned *Æneas Sylvius* was chosen Pope, in 1458, and took the title of *Pius the Second*. He caused a Crusade to be preached against the Turks, but he died in 1464, while the forces were gathering. The Venetians were constantly defeated in the Archipelago, and lost Eubœa, Lesbos, and other islands. In 1477, a large Turkish army entered Italy by Friuli, defeated the Venetians, and crossed the *Tagliamento*. They laid waste the country as far as the *Piave*, and their destroying fires could be seen from the campanile of St. Mark's. In 1480, Mahomet's general, *Ahmed Keduk*, took the strong city of Otranto, and massacred its inhabitants. This expedition was secretly favoured

by the Venetians to spite the King of Naples. The danger to all Italy was very great, for the Sultan eagerly longed to conquer the older Rome. The death of Mahomet the Second, and a disputed succession to his throne, fortunately checked the further advance of the invaders.

9. **The French Party in Italy.**—When Alfonso, King of Aragon, Naples, and Sicily, died in 1458, he left Aragon and Sicily, which he had inherited, to his legitimate son *John;* the crown of Naples, which he had won for himself, he left to Ferdinand, his illegitimate son. Ferdinand was a cruel and suspicious man, and the barons invited *John of Calabria* to come and help them against him. John of Calabria was the son of René, who had been adopted by Queen Johanna, and who called himself King. He was the French Governor of Genoa, and so already had a footing in Italy. He applied to Sforza to help him, but the Duke of Milan was firmly attached to the Peace of Lodi, and was too justly fearful of the French power to do so. *Lewis the Eleventh,* King of France, was too wise to meddle in Italian politics. Florence, which was usually on the French side, was now under the influence of Cosimo de' Medici, and Cosimo was under the influence of Francesco Sforza, so that the Duke of Calabria found no allies. The Archbishop of Genoa, *Paolo Fregoso,* excited the people to drive out the French and the Doge, *Prospero Adorno,* who belonged to their party. He then defeated King René, and the Duke of Calabria was forced to give up his attempt on Naples. The new government of Genoa was so oppressive that the Genoese put themselves under the protection of Francesco. Lewis the Eleventh ceded all his rights to him, and the city thus became part of the Duchy of Milan. The hopes of the French party in Italy were for the present entirely crushed.

10. **Cosimo and Piero de' Medici.**—After the return of

Cosimo de' Medici, his great wealth gave him the chief power in the republic. He was upheld by *Neri Capponi*, who was an able statesman, and the stay of the popular or Medicean party. Cosimo and Neri, when they were in any fear lest elections should be made which would hurt their power, used to appeal to the will of the mass of the people. They called a Parliament and had a Balia appointed, and, by the extraordinary power they gained in this way, they were always able to secure the election of men of their own party. This was a great abuse of the Constitution, and, when Neri Capponi died, a Balia was refused. Then the lesser citizens came into power, and immediately set about to revise the *catasto* or old assessment of taxes, so that they might be levied more fairly. This much annoyed the great men, who were used to see the taxes assessed very much as they liked, and for this and other reasons they began to repent of having overturned the power of Cosimo. But he would not help them until he had made them thoroughly humble. At last he condescended to manage the affairs of the Republic again, and arranged with *Luca Pitti*, the Gonfaloniere of justice, as to the way in which he should again take the reins. In 1458, the Parliament was assembled in the *piazza*, or public place, in front of the Palace. Armed men filled the Palace, and a Balia was granted by the people. All the power was thrown into the hands of Cosimo, and his enemies were banished. Luca Pitti received an ample reward, and, as Cosimo grew old, became very ambitious. The magnificent palace which bears his name remains as a proof of his pride and arrogance. In 1464, Cosimo de' Medici died. He had gained and used too absolute a power for the safety of a free state, but he had used it with moderation and magnificence. He was a great lover of literature and the arts, and they owed much to his encouragement. Under his patronage *Filippo Brunelleschi* raised the wonderful dome of the cathedral church of

Florence, and *Tommaso Guidi*, commonly called *Masaccio*, painted in a style so true to nature that, in after-times, young artists, and among them *Michel-Angelo*, went to learn in the chapel of the *Brancacci*, in the church of the *Carmelites*, which he adorned. Cosimo helped forward the revival of classic taste and study, and *Poggio Bracciolini* and many other scholars searched through Western and Eastern Europe for manuscripts to adorn his library. The splendour and refinement of his taste enriched the Republic; and, though his ambition robbed it of some real freedom, the wisdom of his administration respected the form of its government and upheld its external greatness. Cosimo's only surviving son *Piero* was crippled by gout, and was thus unfit to take his father's place. He became very unpopular, because he called in the outstanding debts due to his house, and thus ruined a great number of persons, not only in Florence but throughout all Italy. He was engaged in constant disputes with Luca Pitti, until Luca was ruined by his own extravagance. Though Piero's body was infirm, his mind was active. His enemies found him more formidable than they looked for; several of them were banished, and sought help from Venice. The Venetians took up their cause and went to war with the Florentines. No important action was fought, and peace was soon made. Piero was left with undiminished power, but his health became worse, he was forced to employ others to carry out his plans, and the state suffered much in consequence, for he was not able to make his party act as he wished. At his death, in 1469, he left two sons, *Lorenzo* and *Giuliano*. They were both very young men, and for a time the headship of the state was taken by *Tommaso Soderini*, and others who had acted for Piero.

11. **Conspiracies against Tyrants.**—The success of Francesco Sforza, Duke of Milan, exercised an evil influence throughout Italy, for it encouraged men to enslave free

states. Milan and Genoa were the victims of the wanton outrages of *Galeazzo Sforza*, who succeeded to the Duchy in 1466. Bologna had fallen under the family of *Bentivoglio*, and a crowd of smaller cities, especially in the Papal States, were governed each by its own Tyrant. Pope *Paul the Second* cared only to enlarge his dominions, and especially to get Rimini from the *Malatesti*, and ruled and intrigued like any other prince. Florence still remained free, but her freedom had suffered some damage. The Medici had not become tyrants like the Visconti, but they were no longer simply a great family in a free state, as they had been in the time of Salvestro. Without hereditary title or office, they passed on the management of the state from father to son. They had entire command of the public treasury, and sometimes used it to uphold the commercial credit of their house. As yet they had used their power on the whole for the good of their city, but for its true welfare no such power should have existed at all. The study of the older writers of Greece and of Rome, which had lately become the fashion in Italy, taught men a short method of dealing with Tyrants, and led them to hold that nothing was to be counted as a crime which might rid them of a master. Conspiracies broke out constantly. *Bernardo Nardi*, one of the Florentine exiles, attempted to seize the little town of Prato, hoping from thence to make an attack on Florence, and overturn the Medici. He failed, and was put to death. Unsuccessful conspiracies were also made in Ferrara and Genoa. In Milan men could no longer bear the cruelties and insults of Duke Galeazzo. He was stabbed, in December 1476, by three young men as he entered St. Stephen's church. Two of the conspirators were killed on the spot; the third, *Girolamo Olgiato*, was put to death with fearful tortures. Galeazzo left an infant son, *Gian-Galeazzo Maria*, and a widow, *Bona of Savoy*, sister-in-law of Lewis the Eleventh of France. The Duchess governed for her son. *Lodovico Sforza*, the brother of the murdered Duke, tried to take the power from her, and after a time he succeeded. A more widely-spread conspiracy was made against the two young Medici. The scheme of assassination was at least defended, and was almost certainly planned, by Pope *Sixtus the Fourth;* it was aided by his nephew *Count Riario*, by his great-nephew *Cardinal Riario*, by *Francesco Salviati* the Archbishop of Pisa, and by the family of the *Pazzi*, from whom the conspiracy has taken its name. The aim of all the policy of Pope Sixtus was to establish his nephews in Romagna. His reign marks the beginning of a new Papal policy. Before this time many Popes had striven for temporal dominion, that so they might increase the greatness of the Holy See. Now for the first time the Popes began to strive to gain dominion for their own families, and to make their nephews or sons Italian Princes. Pope Sixtus gained Imola and Forli, and sent Cardinal *Giuliano della Rovere*, who was afterwards Pope *Julius the Second*, to take Castello from Niccolo Vitelli. This expedition came to nought, for Lorenzo de' Medici helped Vitelli and the other lords of Romagna against him. This interference made the Pope and his nephews anxious for the overthrow of the Medici. The family of the Pazzi was one of the noblest and richest in Florence, but had been shut out from office by Lorenzo. The conspirators took counsel with King Ferdinand, who seems to have favoured their designs.

12. **Conspiracy of the Pazzi.**—The young Cardinal Riario, who was studying at the University of Pisa, was bidden to make a visit to Florence, for the conspirators thought that, during the time of feasting which his visit would occasion, they would be able to kill the two brothers Giuliano and Lorenzo together. The Cardinal was entertained by *Giacopo de' Pazzi*. The two Medici were asked to meet

him at a feast to be given on Sunday, April 26, 1478, and it was determined to assassinate them while they sat at the table. On Saturday evening the conspirators met to make their final arrangements. The next morning they were told that Giuliano would not come. They met again without delay, and as the design was known to so many people they did not dare to put off the deed. Accordingly they determined that it should be done that day while the brothers were in the cathedral church. Francesco de' Pazzi and Bernardo Bandini promised to murder Giuliano, and the conspirators asked one Giovanbattista Montesicco to murder Lorenzo. Giovanbattista refused to do this because he was afraid to commit sacrilege; so Antonio and Stefano, two priests who had more familiarity with sacred things, undertook to do it instead of him. When the conspirators came to the church they found that Giuliano was not there. Giacopo de' Pazzi and Bernardo went to his house, and, taking hold of him on each side in a playful manner, they persuaded him to come with them, and managed at the same time to find out that he was unarmed. The church was very full of people, so that each of the assassins was able to stand close to his intended victim without being noticed. As the little bell sounded from the altar and the Host was lifted up, as all knelt in the presence of their God, Bernardo stabbed Giuliano de' Medici to the heart. Francesco rushed upon him and pierced him in several places: striking so wildly that he even wounded himself in his rage. But the two priests, who were to have killed Lorenzo, failed in the attempt, and fled and hid themselves, until they were found and put to death. The other assassins forced their way out of the church, leaving their work half done, for Lorenzo was only slightly wounded. Then the Archbishop and some of the others ran to the Palace to overpower the Priors. They faltered and were made prisoners. Francesco de' Pazzi was disabled by his wound, but the aged

Giacopo gathered a few followers together and rode to the Piazza before the Palace crying out "Liberty and the People." No one answered to the cry. The people had become too well accustomed to the Medicean gold, and they would not see how much their liberty had been damaged by the over-great influence of that family. The citizens rose against the conspirators, crying *"Palle, Palle"* (*the Balls*, the cognizance of the Medici): they slew several in the streets, and dragged off others to put them to death in a more formal way. The Archbishop of Pisa, still wearing the robes of his office, and Francesco de' Pazzi, were hanged side by side from the windows of the Palace. More than two hundred were put to death for real or pretended participation in the plot, and amongst them was one of the captains of the Pope's troops.

13. **Papal Wars.**—The conspiracy of the Pazzi strengthened the power of Lorenzo in Florence. The murder of his brother and the attempt on his own life roused the feelings of the citizens on his behalf, and they appointed him a guard to watch over his safety. He took upon himself a greater state than any of his family had assumed before him. He gathered round him a crowd of men of letters, who lived on his bounty, and were devoted to his cause. The title of *Magnificent*, which is still joined to his name, marks the foremost feature of his character. This magnificence was selfish; it was upheld by the public purse, and only ministered to his private pleasure. The splendour of the Medicean court was the sign and the cause of the decay of liberty and of true greatness. Pope Sixtus was very angry at the failure of the conspiracy. He first excommunicated the Florentines, and then went to war with them. Ferdinand, King of Naples, was on his side. The widowed Duchess of Milan remained steadfast to the Medicean cause, and her brother-in-law Lewis the Eleventh assured Lorenzo of his support. Milan how-

ever had enough to do with her own affairs; for King Ferdinand persuaded Genoa to revolt again from her, and the Pope brought the men of Uri down again upon Bellinzona. After a while Lodovico Sforza, who had been exiled by the Duchess, came back to Milan, and declared that his nephew was of age, though he was only twelve years old, and took all the power himself. Then Lodovico and the King made peace with Lorenzo, and, in 1480, the Pope did the same, for the presence of the Ottomans in Otranto threatened the safety of Rome. After the Turks had gone away, Pope Sixtus again disturbed the general peace by trying to get Ferrara for his nephew. His great captain in these wars was *Federigo, Duke of Urbino*, who died in 1482. He deserves to be remembered, for, unlike other Italian princes, he was distinguished, not only for his skill in warfare, and for the refinement of his taste, but for the justice of his rule and the uprightness of his life. The next Pope, *Innocent the Eighth*, engaged in a short war with the King of Naples. The barons of the kingdom revolted against King Ferdinand, because he was cruel and fond of oppression. They sent to the Pope to help them, reminding him that Naples was a fief of the Holy See. Lorenzo helped the King. The Pope and the nobles sent to *René the Second, Duke of Lorraine*, the grandson of René the First, and offered to make him King, but the Duke delayed so long in France that the opportunity passed by. At last Lorenzo arranged terms of peace. Then the King broke his word to the nobles, and revenged himself upon some of them with great cruelty.

14. **The Twelve Years of Rest.**—In spite of little wars, the twelve years from 1480 to 1492 were a time of great quietness and prosperity in Italy. King Ferdinand, Lodovico Sforza, and Lorenzo de' Medici were all anxious to be at peace. They were determined to check the future growth of the power of the Venetians, who were far stronger than any one of them.

The Venetians would have been glad of any Italian war, because it could not fail, in some way or other, to give them an opportunity for interfering, and enriching themselves at the expense of other powers. Besides this common motive, King Ferdinand feared the strong French party in his kingdom, and war would have given a French pretender a chance of success. Lodovico Sforza wished for peace, for his nephew Gian-Galeazzo had married the daughter of Alfonso, the son of King Ferdinand, and he was fearful lest, if there should be a war, he should be forced to give up the power which he had unjustly seized. He was also afraid lest the French should take up the cause of the young Duke, for Gian-Galeazzo was cousin to *Charles the Eighth*, King of France, through his mother Bona, the daughter of the Duke of Savoy. Lorenzo de' Medici, who had gained great influence in Italy by his alliance with Pope Innocent, wished to maintain an even balance of power between the different States. He carefully managed to keep Italy in peace, and thus upheld the power of Lodovico, which would have been endangered by war. He held that the alliance of Milan was most important to the well-being of Florence. He looked on Milan as the key of North Italy to a foreign invader. It formed a bulwark against Venetian aggression, and a counterpoise to the power of the King of Naples.

During this time of peace the Italian people enjoyed great prosperity. Much land was brought for the first time into cultivation, and this marks an increase in population, in wealth, and in the feeling of public security. Unlike the Northern "*villein*," the Italian peasant shared the fruit of his labour with the owner of the soil, and, in spite of the constant state of warfare, which had now only ceased for a season in Italy, he was on the whole better lodged, clothed, and fed than men of the same rank in other lands. The cities of Italy had grown richer than ever; wool and silk were manufactured in great quantities, and the trade in money yielded an enormous profit. Long wars and some fearful floods had damaged the fruitful plains of Pisa, but in general the land brought forth abundantly. Lorenzo de' Medici encouraged architecture and the other arts, and was a patron of literary men. At this period Italian art and literature were too often engaged in copying classic models, and not in expressing the thoughts of living people. Tyranny had lessened the virtue of the people, and the Italians of the fifteenth century were learning to be idle and dissolute. Sensuality was the natural result of absolute rule over rich and prosperous states, for men had no scope for lawful political ambition. The mock philosophy of the *Academy*, which met in the *Rucellai* gardens, could not supply those motives of virtue which were fast dying out in Florence under the influence of the Medici. A strong protest was raised in Florence against tyranny, vice, and luxury by *Girolamo Savonarola*, a Dominican friar, who began to preach in 1489. The worldliness of the Church, the usurpations of the few, and the vices of society, gave him plenty of subjects for his sermons. His followers, who professed repentance, were called *Piagnoni*, the "Weepers." Like some other reformers, he was of an highly nervous temperament, and thought that he had special revelations. In the smaller sovereignties which existed throughout Italy, and especially in Romagna, tyranny and vice assumed their worst forms, and crimes too foul even to name needlessly were daily practised by Tyrants who held themselves above public opinion.

15. **The French invited into Italy.**—Lorenzo de' Medici died in 1492. He left three sons—*Piero*, who succeeded to his power in Florence; *Giovanni*, who had been made a Cardinal at the age of fourteen, and who became *Leo the Tenth*; and *Giuliano*. The next year Pope Innocent the

Eighth was succeeded by *Roderigo Borgia*, who took the name of *Alexander the Sixth*. This Pope gained his election by open bribery, and used his power to forward the ambitious schemes of his children; of whom the two most celebrated were called *Cesare* and *Lucrezia*. He was shameless in his vices and greedy in his ambition; false in his friendship and cruel in his hatred. His industry and political ability, and the wealth, beauty, and utter want of conscience of his children, made the Borgias powerful to work wickedness. *Piero de' Medici*, instead of following his father's politics and trying to keep an even balance of power in Italy, threw himself into the hands of King Ferdinand. In alliance with the King he thwarted the plans both of Lodovico Sforza and the Pope. This alliance alarmed Lodovico, for the friendship of the Medici had hitherto upheld him in his schemes. He was afraid lest Alfonso should take up the cause of his son-in-law the dispossessed Duke. He therefore made alliance with the Pope and the Venetians for their mutual support. At the same time Lodovico was well aware that the interests of both his allies were different from his own, and was not satisfied with their promises. In order to make himself safe he sent to *Charles the Eighth* of France, and invited him to invade the kingdom of Naples. The claim which King Charles put forward to that throne was derived, such as it was, from the House of Anjou. *René the First* had left the County of Provence, his dominions in France, and his claim on Naples, to his nephew Charles of Maine, and Charles, dying without children, left them to Lewis the Eleventh, King of France. When Charles succeeded his father Lewis, *René the Second, Duke of Lorraine*, the grandson of René the First claimed to succeed to his grandfather's dominions and titles. His claim to Provence, which Beatrice had brought to her husband Charles of Anjou, was disallowed. It was also declared that both Charles the First and his son had laid down by will that the kingdom of Sicily should not be parted from the county of Provence. The island of Sicily had been lost by Charles the First to the Aragonese; the rest of the kingdom of Sicily, Sicily on this side the *Faro*, or the kingdom of Naples, remained under his family for two hundred years. It was then won by Alfonso of Aragon, who left it to his son Ferdinand. Charles the Eighth therefore claimed Naples as the representative of the Angevin house. Lewis the Eleventh had always kept aloof from Italian affairs, and had parted with his rights over Genoa to Francesco Sforza. Unhappily Charles was dazzled by the brilliant hopes which Lodovico held out to him. He was to conquer Naples with ease, he was thence to cross to Greece, to drive the Turks before him, to retake New Rome from the Infidels, and win back the Holy Sepulchre. He was to be a second Charles the Great, and to perform exploits which would be glorious to God as well as to himself. Many of his wisest counsellors tried to dissuade him from engaging in such a costly enterprise, but he would not hear them.

CHAPTER VII.

ITALY INVADED.

Preparations for the invasion of Italy (1)—difference between French and Italian warfare (2)—Charles enters Italy; the death of the Duke of Milan (3)—Piero de' Medici gives up Pisa and other strong places to Charles, and flees from Florence (4)—King Alfonso abdicates; Naples conquered (5)—Lodovico, Duke of Milan, turns against the French and forms a league against them; Charles leaves Naples (6) — the battle of Fornovo; his plans end in failure (7) — the Florentines alienated from France by the refusal of Charles to give up Pisa; war with Pisa; preaching of Fra Girolamo Savonarola (8)—his ordeal and death (9)—Lewis XII. conquers Milan (10)—is outwitted by the Spaniards, who conquer Naples (11)—the exploits of Cesare Borgia (12)—the fall of Genoa and Pisa (13)—the League of Cambray against Venice (14)—Pope Julius deserts the League and forms the Holy League to drive the French out of Italy (15)—the return of the Medici to Florence (16)—summary (17).

1. **Preparations for Invasion.**—The coming of the French into Italy was the beginning of great changes. From that time Italy became first the victim of the attacks of foreign powers—then the battle-field on which foreign sovereigns fought out their quarrels—then the slave of foreign conquerors—until in our own day she regained her unity and her freedom. When King Ferdinand knew that Lodovico had invited the French to invade his kingdom, he was much frightened; for his people hated him, and were strongly inclined to welcome the French. He therefore made an alliance with the Pope, and promised that he would forward his plans for his children's aggrandizement. He also tried to make terms with Lodovico, but he was not successful. Lodovico deceived him and the Pope and Piero de' Medici, his allies, for he was anxious not to come to an open

quarrel until he was quite sure of the French king's help. The aim of Lodovico was to become Duke of Milan, and it was for this reason that he had invited the French; for he knew that the King of Naples would not willingly allow his grandson to be deposed. He was already Duke in all save the title. He now purchased that title from *Maximilian* the King of the Romans, for Milan was a fief of the Empire. He did not as yet call himself Duke, because he was afraid to provoke the King of Naples, and because he knew that he was much disliked by the Milanese. The Duchy of Milan was a rich and powerful State, but was heavily burthened by taxation. The ambitious schemes of Lodovico made the burthen heavier than it had been before, so that the people were ready to revolt. Meanwhile King Charles made treaties of peace with King *Henry the Eighth* of England, with *Ferdinand* and *Isabella* of Spain, and with the *King of the Romans* and his son the *Archduke Philip*, so that he might leave peace behind him when he crossed the Alps. He delayed the expedition, and seemed for a long time unable to make up his mind. Many of his advisers opposed his plans, some because they knew how unwise they were, and some because they wished to please *Lewis, Duke of Orleans*. The Duke claimed the Duchy of Milan as the representative of the Visconti in right of his grandmother *Valentina*, and he was therefore anxious to thwart the hopes of Lodovico. In the beginning of 1494, King Ferdinand died, and was succeeded by his son Alfonso. This was a great misfortune for Italy, for Ferdinand would have done anything to avoid the war. Alfonso was more haughty and obstinate, and was more hated than his father had been, and some of Ferdinand's worst deeds were put down to his son's advice. The new King made alliance with the Pope, and they both joined in inviting the Sultan *Bajazet the Second* to attack the French. They told him of the King's design against

Constantinople; but the Sultan did not think much of such a far-off danger, and would not help them. Meanwhile Charles spent large sums of money in building a fleet at Genoa, in hiring troops from the *Confederates* or *Swiss*, and other German mercenaries, and in fitting out his army in Dauphiny. These expenses quite emptied his treasury, and his courtiers borrowed largely from the Bank of Genoa and from Lodovico to enable them to carry on their preparations.

2. **Italian and French Warfare.**—The French army which was gathering together at Vienne was very different in its strength, its order, and its mode of warfare to any of the armies of Italy. The French cavalry was made up of *Lances*, each composed of a man-at-arms who was fully armed, and his four or five attendants. These men-at-arms were all Frenchmen, and their officers were for the most part of noble birth. The troops belonged to the King and not to their officers, and were paid by him. They and their horses were splendidly equipped; they were well paid and under good discipline. The infantry consisted of Frenchmen armed with bows and arbalists, and of Swiss and German mercenaries. The Italian troops were subjects of different states; they followed their own captains, and were paid by them. An Italian state when at war engaged different captains, and only had power over their men through them, so that there was a total lack of union and order in their armies. The Italian infantry fought in small detached bodies, while the Swiss of the French army formed solid squares, against which heavy cavalry charged in vain. The Italian foot-soldiers were quite equal to the native French, but were far inferior to the Swiss, who were held to be the first foot-soldiers in the world. The chief strength of the King's army lay in his artillery. The Italians used great guns called *bombards*, which threw stone balls. They were drawn by oxen, and were so heavy that they were for the most part

only used in sieges, and a long time was spent between each discharge in loading and pointing the gun. The French brought with them much lighter guns, called *cannons*, made of brass, which threw iron balls. These cannons were drawn by horses, and could be used in the field, and the French artillerymen pointed and fired them off with great speed. The loss of life in the Italian wars of the fifteenth century was usually very small. No great interests were at stake. The leaders and the troops in their pay fought for foreign states, and might soon be in the pay of the very state with which they were at the time at war. The Italian leaders treated war as a game; they played it with wonderful skill, with much profit and with but little loss, even to the lowest of their troops. The armour of defence was so massive that it was hard to kill a man, though it was easy to unhorse him, and sometimes two armies fought together for hours without one being slain on either side. At the close of the century light irregular horse were used in Italy. The most formidable troops of this sort were the *Estradiots;* they were formed by the Venetians from the natives of their Greek and Albanian dominions, and were looked upon by other troops as objects of wonder and fear, for they were fierce and active. The fierceness of these Estradiots was matched by the German *Lanzknects* in the French army. The Italians, who had long been used to see their wars carried on with little bloodshed, were frightened at the sternness and cruelty of the northern invaders of their land, who fought with passion and revenge. They saw with horror soldiers, and even citizens, slaughtered after the storming of cities, buildings set on fire, and the fruits of the earth destroyed.

3. **Charles enters Italy.**—Charles was still delaying his march when the war began in Italy. *Don Frederic*, the son of King Alfonso, made an attempt upon Genoa, but he was defeated at *Rapallo* by the Swiss under the Duke

of Orleans. In this battle the country-people helped the French, out of love for the *Adorni*, who were on the French side, while their rivals the *Fregosi* were on the side of the King of Naples. At last, Aug. 23, 1494, Charles left Vienne, and marched across the Alps to Asti. The *Duke of Savoy* and the *Marquess of Montferrat* were both children, and their mothers were afraid of the French King, who begged for, received, and pawned, the jewels of the two widows, for he was very short of money. Asti belonged to the Duke of Orleans in right of his grandmother Valentina. There the King fell ill for a time. When he was well, he visited his cousin, the dispossessed Duke of Milan, and his young wife, who were kept by Lodovico in the Castle of Pavia. The Duchess pleaded very hard for her husband and her infant son. She threw herself at the feet of Charles before all the court, and prayed him to have pity upon them, and upon her father and her family, against whom he was marching. The King was much moved, but he had gone too far to stop. Soon after this visit the unhappy Duke died, and it was generally believed that he was poisoned by his uncle, who now openly took his title. This suspicion caused all men to hate the new Duke, but the presence of the French army made him safe.

4. **Flight of Piero de' Medici.**—King Charles had sent as his ambassador to Venice *Philip de Comines, Lord of Argenton*, who wrote a very able history of his own time. As yet, however, the Venetians held aloof from either side. It was needful that the French should secure Florence before they advanced into the kingdom. Charles accordingly determined to march through Tuscany. This met the wishes of the Duke of Milan, who was set on making himself *Lord of Pisa*. He now hoped to be able to do this by the help of the French. Florence from very old times had been a Guelfic city, and well inclined to the French;

and this was more than ever the case now, for the Florentines hoped that the French would rid them of Piero de' Medici, who ruled over them as a *Tyrant*. Piero would not desert his ally the King of Naples, and the French accordingly entered Tuscany by Pontremoli and besieged *Sarzana*. Then the heart of Piero suddenly failed him, and he went away secretly to the French to make terms on his own account. On his way he became frightened, for he heard that the French had cut to pieces a body of horse who were sent to relieve Sarzana, so that when he came before Charles he was ready to agree to almost any terms. He surrendered Sarzana, and promised to give up to the King *Pisa, Leghorn, Pietra Santa*, and *Librafatta*, and engaged that the Republic should advance him a large sum of money. When the Florentines found out how they had been outwitted, and what a disgraceful agreement Piero had made, they were very angry. Piero tried to make himself master of the city, and came armed to the Palace of the Signory with his guards crying, "*Palle, Palle!*" Happily a signory had been chosen which was on the side of liberty. The great bell was tolled, and at the sound the citizens poured out from their houses, and left their shops and stalls and gathered together in the Piazza, crying, "*Popolo*," and "*Liberta!*" When Piero heard these cries, he fled out through the gates, and went off to *Giovanni Bentivoglio, Lord of Bologna*, and never came back again. On the same day on which Florence rid herself of Piero, the Pisans came before the French King and pleaded for their liberty. Pisa had been subject to Florence for nearly ninety years, and her citizens recounted with many tears the wrongs she had suffered. The Florentine rule had probably not been hard, as far as life and personal liberty were concerned. Nevertheless it had ruined the commerce of Pisa, and lessened the value of landed property. It was hateful to the citizens of a city which

had once been the rival of Florence, and in older times
had surpassed her in wealth and importance. The French
courtiers were strongly in favour of the Pisans, and the
King granted them their liberty. This greatly vexed the
Florentines, but they still kept steadfast to the French,
for they always sought to be in alliance with them. They
were encouraged to remain friends with the King by the
preaching of Fra Girolamo, who considered Charles as a
messenger of God come to do His work of reformation
in Italy.

5. **The Conquest of Naples.**—After Charles had stayed
a few days at Pisa, he entered Florence. The citizens were
much disturbed, for they had reason to fear that the King
would try to enslave the Republic, and they were fully
determined to defend their liberty. The King declared that,
as he had entered the city in arms, he had the rights of
a conqueror, and even threatened to bring back Piero de'
Medici. One day, while *Piero Capponi* and other Florentine commissioners were in the King's presence, the French
Secretary read over a list of propositions on which the King
insisted. The conditions were so disgraceful to the Republic
that Piero Capponi in a noble rage snatched the paper from
the reader's hand, and tore it in pieces before the King's face,
crying, "Since you demand such shameful terms, sound your
trumpets, and we will ring our bells." By this he meant,
that, as the French men-at-arms would gather at the sound
of the trumpet to attack the liberties of Florence, so the
Florentines were ready to gather at the sound of their common
bell to defend them. The King was fearful of a fight in the
narrow streets of the city, for his men-at-arms would have
been of no service against the barricades of the burghers.
When therefore he heard the bold speech of Piero Copponi,
he agreed to accept the subsidy which the Florentines offered
him, and promised that, when he had taken Naples, he would

restore to them Pisa and the other strong places which Piero de' Medici had given up. After a few days' stay the King went on to Rome. The Neapolitan troops under the Duke of Calabria retreated without making any resistance, and the King entered Rome, as he had entered Florence, with his lance on his thigh, like a conqueror. The Pope was greatly alarmed. He was afraid lest the King should depose him, for a strong party of the cardinals exhorted Charles to free the Church from his tyranny. At last terms were made, though the Pope and the King did not meet. Alexander was obliged to hand over to the King, *Zizim*, the brother of the Sultan Bajazet. Zizim had once tried to gain the Ottoman throne, and had long been kept prisoner at Rome. Charles thought that, if he had him with him, he would be able to raise a party amongst the Ottomans, which might help him in his plans of retaking Constantinople. Zizim, however, died suddenly, and many said that the Pope poisoned him. When King Alfonso heard that Charles had entered Rome, he was quite confounded. He left his kingdom, and took shelter in Sicily, and there did penance, and repented of all his evil deeds. His son *Ferdinand* succeeded him. *Gian Giacopo Trivulzio*, the general of Ferdinand, deserted him, and betrayed Capua to the French; the people of Naples rose against him, and he was forced to seek refuge in the island of Ischia. As Charles advanced, the people everywhere welcomed him as a deliverer. He entered Naples in triumph, and the whole city gladly received him; for Alfonso and his father had reigned with great wickedness and cruelty. .

6. **Charles leaves Naples.**—Although Charles was entirely successful, he soon lost all his conquests, because he made many enemies. The Duke of Milan became angry, because he was refused some requests. When he found that he was no longer necessary to the King, he grew frightened

at the success of the French, and repented that he had called them into Italy. The Florentines were angry, because the King had helped the Pisans to revolt from them, and Girolamo Savonarola, who had now gained the chief influence in the city, alone kept them from breaking with him. The Venetians were jealous of the French power which threatened to overshadow the rest of Italy, and to make their Republic of small importance on the mainland. The Pope wanted the French to leave Italy, because their presence thwarted his schemes for the advancement of his family. Several of the cardinals were disgusted, because the King had made terms with the Pope, whom they hated. The great Roman family of the *Orsini* was angry, because Charles favoured its rival, the house of *Colonna*, which had always been Ghibelin and was therefore the enemy of France. Outside the peninsula, *Ferdinand* of Aragon, who had married *Isabella* of Castile, and had thus united the two kingdoms, was afraid lest the French should attack Sicily and Sardinia. Maximilian King of the Romans also began to be jealous, for he heard that the French King aimed at the Imperial dignity. The Duke of Milan soon became actively hostile, for Lewis of Orleans put forward his claims to the Duchy. He therefore made an alliance against the French with the Pope, the King of the Romans, the King of Spain, and the Venetians. Meanwhile the French army spent their time in riot and excess, and disgusted the Neapolitans by their insolence. King Charles also gave great offence to many of the chief men of the kingdom by making large grants of lands and offices to his own countrymen. Thus everyone was anxious to get the French out of Italy, and Lodovico Sforza most of all, though it was he who had invited them to come in. There was great joy when the League was proclaimed, and Philip of Comines, who was still ambassador at Venice, had the mortification of witnessing the rejoicings which were made at the prospect of his master's defeat. When Charles heard of the League, he determined to go back to France. He left the *Count of Montpensier*, and several captains under him, to rule the kingdom and finish its conquest. In May, 1495, he marched out of Naples.

7. Failure of his hopes.—King Charles on his way back to France again entered Rome, but the Pope left the city, and would not meet him. He avoided Florence, and did not give back Pisa and the other towns, as he had promised to do. Meanwhile the Duke of Orleans, who had taken Novara, was besieged in that city by the Duke of Milan. The King reached Pontremoli, and crossed the Apennines without meeting with any resistance. On the other side of the mountains he found the army of Milan and Venice waiting for him under the command of *Francesco da Gonzaga, Marquess of Mantua*. After a short struggle at *Fornovo*, in which the French were completely victorious, Charles was able to go on his way to Turin. The Duke of Orleans and his army, however, were in great danger, for their provisions failed, and the Duke of Milan besieged them so closely, that no one was able to relieve them. At last Charles made peace with the Duke of Milan, apart from his allies, at *Vercelli*, and by the end of October he entered France again. Lodovico, though he agreed to terms with the King, was all the time fully set upon deceiving him, for he was much frightened by the attempt which the Duke of Orleans had made on his Duchy. When the King of France left the kingdom of Naples, King Ferdinand came back, and began to reconquer his land. He was joined by a small force from Spain under the *Gonsalvo de Cordova*, and was helped by the Pope and the Venetians, and secretly by the Duke of Milan. The French who still remained in Naples were left without pay and without reinforcements, and seemed to be quite forgotten by King Charles. Within a year after Charles had left Italy, King

Ferdinand gained nearly all that his father had lost. He died in 1496, and was succeeded by his uncle Frederic, and so, without counting the French King, there were four Kings of Naples, one after another, in three years. King Charles, who was at war with Spain, made great preparations for a second invasion. The Duke of Orleans formed a league against the Duke of Milan with the *Florentines*, the Duke of *Ferrara*, and with the Marquess of *Mantua*, who was dissatisfied with the allies. The plans of the Duke of Orleans came to nothing, for he changed his mind at the last moment, and would not act without the King. Maximilian, King of the Romans, was brought into Italy by the allies, but he only had a very small number of troops, and returned without glory or gain. The preparations of the King ended in a disastrous expedition against Genoa, and, in 1497, a truce was made between France and Spain, which included the Italian allies of both parties. Thus the French invasion ended in utter failure. Lodovico Sforza brought them into Italy to serve his own ends, and when he had gained the Duchy, he turned against them, and outwitted King Charles, who was no match for him in statecraft.

8. **Pisa and Florence.**—While Charles was on his homeward march through Italy, the Florentines asked him to give back Pisa to them, as he had promised. He was unwilling to give up such an important place. The Pisans besought him not to deliver them up to the Florentines, and their cause was warmly taken up by the French soldiers. He broke his promise, which he had thrice solemnly given, and thus inflicted a heavy loss on his most faithful ally. The citadel of Pisa was given up to the citizens, and the other Florentine fortresses were sold by the French to Genoa and Lucca. The Duke of Milan and the Venetians were both anxious to get hold of Pisa. After the French had left Italy, the Pisans chose the Venetians to protect them against the

Florentines. Their choice made Lodovico very angry, and he even wished to restore Pisa to the Florentines again. The Venetians determined to uphold it as a free state, and helped the Pisans to carry on a war with Florence. The Duke then tried to get Piero brought back to Florence again, in order that through him the Florentines might be inclined to join the League. As a bait he held out hopes that if they would join they should receive Pisa as the price of their alliance. By this plan he hoped to detach Florence from the French, and to get away Pisa from the Venetians. If he had succeeded he would have weakened the two powers which he feared most. The Florentines were too watchful to allow any movement on behalf of Piero to pass unnoticed. He made an attempt to enter the city, but the Signory were aware of it, and he retreated hastily. Ever since he had fled from the city the Florentines had been divided into three parties. The followers of Girolamo Savonarola, who were in favour of the old popular government, and still kept faithful to the French alliance, were called *Piagnoni* (weepers), because they had repented at his preaching. The *Arrabiati* (raving madmen) were the members of the oligarchy who had turned against the Medici, and who tried to take their place. The third party favoured the Medici, but its members were obliged to keep their feelings secret, and so were called *Bigi* (grey), because they had, as it were, to keep out of the light of day. For a time the popular party had the upper hand, and Fra Girolamo had the greatest influence in the new government. He preached to enraptured multitudes that unworldliness, democracy, and the French alliance, would be the means of bringing in an age of peace and glory. Under his direction troops of children, clad in white, and bearing crosses, begged, and carried off in triumph to the flames, the "*anathema*" (or cursed thing), for by this name he called all those things which ministered to luxury. His followers gave themselves up to the wildest religious excitement. Their leader proposed that *Christ* should be proclaimed *King of Florence*. They eagerly applauded the proposal. The streets of Florence were filled with people, who sang and danced in a frantic manner, and who shouted the name of the King whom their leader had chosen, crying "*Viva Cristo!*" But when it became evident that King Charles would not again enter Italy, and the Florentines found themselves deceived by their ally, and left burthened with the Pisan war, the influence of Girolamo began to grow less. The Florentines longed for their old gaieties, and repented of their repentance.

9. **Savonarola's Ordeal and Death.**—Girolamo Savonarola had strongly denounced the vile lives of Pope Alexander and his family. He had been excommunicated, but he had disregarded the sentence, and had been upheld by a large party. But, in 1497, he was no longer so strong as before, and some unwise, though just severities of his party against the *Bigi* added to the distrust which men had begun to feel of his fanaticism. The Pope laboured for his destruction, and was aided by the Franciscans, who were jealous of the great Dominican preacher. The *Arrabiati* began to gain power, and Savonarola and his party were insulted. The next year the Pope threatened to put Florence under an interdict unless Savonarola was silenced, and the Government forbade him to preach any more. His cause was warmly taken up by his brother Dominicans, and was attacked by their rivals the Franciscans. At last a Franciscan declared that he was ready to enter the fire, if Fra Girolamo would do the same, and thus submit his mission to the *judgment of God*. A great many of both sexes and of every rank offered themselves for the *ordeal* on each side. At last a Brother of each Order was chosen as a champion in this appeal to God. On April 7, 1498, a great pile of wood was raised in the Piazza

before the Palace; in the midst was a narrow passage, and through this the champions had to pass while the fire raged all around them. An immense crowd of people had come together to witness the trial. The Franciscans first made an objection, because *Fra Domenico*, the champion of Fra Girolamo, wore his priestly robes. They were accordingly taken off. Then they raised another objection, because Girolamo bade him take the Holy Wafer with him into the fire. Girolamo would not give way. The day was wasted in disputes, and the people grew discontented at waiting in vain for the show. At last a storm of rain came and soaked the pile. This put an end to the hopes of the crowd, and added to their ill-temper. Girolamo in vain tried to explain his reasons; every one declared that he had shirked the test to which he had agreed. His influence with the people was gone. On the next day a riot was made, and Girolamo was seized and shut up in prison. He was put to the torture, and his excitable and nervous constitution could not bear such treatment. He made a confession, in which he declared that his prophecies came not from God, but from his own understanding of the Holy Scriptures. He was condemned as an heretic and a seducer of the people. On May 23, he and two Brothers of his Order were hanged, and their bodies afterwards were burned. He was an upholder of truth and purity in a corrupt age, and there is no reason to doubt his own full belief in his Divine mission. He was ruined because, like many other great reformers, he mixed himself up in politics and party intrigues.

10. **French Conquest of Milan**, 1500.—Charles the Eighth died of an accident in April, 1498. He was succeeded by *Lewis the Twelfth*, who had before been Duke of Orleans. The new King immediately took the title of Duke of Milan, which he claimed on the ground of his descent from his grandmother Valentina, the daughter of Gian-Galeazzo Visconti,

from whom also he inherited Asti. The Pope favoured his plans, because he thought that his son Cesare Borgia was sure to gain by a war. Cesare had been made an Archbishop and a Cardinal, but he cast off his orders, and strove only for secular greatness. King Lewis gave him the city of *Valence* in *Dauphiny*, with the title of Duke of Valentinois, and hence the Italians called him *Duca Valentino*. The Venetians made alliance with King Lewis, for they were deadly enemies of the Duke of Milan, and the Republic and the Duke were both set upon the possession of Pisa. The Venetians had as yet successfully defended Pisa as a free state against the Florentines, but they grew tired of the war and made peace. Pisa was now defended by her own citizens only. She was greedily desired by Florence, Venice, the Duke of Milan, and several smaller powers, and these rival hopes are the key to a great many of the changes, alliances, and wars of this time. King Lewis and Lodovico Sforza both offered to help the Florentines against the Pisans. The Florentines, however, remembered that both King and Duke had caused them to lose the city in the first place, and they stood neutral. The Duke of Milan was left without allies. The generals of King Lewis, *Lewis de Ligni*, *Everard d'Aubigni*, and *Gian Giacopo Trivulzio*, who joined the French service in the reign of Charles, entered the Milanese territory, and advanced almost unopposed. The Duke was hated, because he taxed the people very heavily; and, though he did away with many of the taxes, it was too late to gain their confidence. He fled away into Germany. Milan and Genoa submitted to the French, and Cremona to the Venetians. When the King was in Milan, he made alliance with the Florentines, and promised to help them to reconquer Pisa, for the Pisans defended their city nobly. After a few months the Milanese became tired of the French. A great many were angry, because the King made Gian

Giacopo the governor of the city; for he had many enemies there, and was a proud and cruel man; and the mass of the people were dissatisfied, because they were taxed. So the Duke was recalled, and came back with a body of Swiss mercenaries. He speedily gained back Como, Milan, Pavia, and other places. But neither Venice nor Florence, nor Genoa, would help him. King Lewis sent another army into Italy, and the Duke was betrayed by his Swiss. They made agreement with their fellow-countrymen in the French army, and set out to return to their own land. The Duke in vain tried to make them stay; he then dressed himself like a Swiss, and tried to escape in their midst. He was betrayed as he was marching afoot, and sent off to King Lewis, who was at Lyons. He was kept a prisoner in the castle of Loches, till he died, about ten years afterwards. Thus, in 1500, King Lewis became undisputed master of the Duchy of Milan. Some of the Confederates on their way home seized Bellinzona, which Filippo Maria had retaken from Uri in 1422. This city commanded the entrance from the Cantons into the Duchy. The King took no notice of this cool breach of good faith and peace, and thus lost a valuable outpost.

11. **Spanish Conquest of Naples, 1504.**—King Lewis, having gained Milan so easily, determined to invade the kingdom of Naples. He was afraid lest Ferdinand of Spain should help his kinsman King Frederic, which he could easily do from Sicily. He therefore persuaded Ferdinand to betray his kinsman, and share in despoiling him of his kingdom. King Frederic did not know of this agreement, and had a good hope that, with the help of the Spaniards, he would be able to defeat the French invasion. When, however, the French had passed the Roman territory, Gonsalvo openly declared the alliance of Ferdinand with them. Frederic, when he found himself betrayed and helpless, surrendered his rights to the French King, and embarked for France,

where he died about three years afterwards. The next year, in 1502, the French and Spaniards quarrelled over the partition of their ill-gotten territory. The Pope and Valentino were nominally on the side of Lewis, but as the French were worsted by Gonsalvo, "the Great Captain," they intrigued with the Spaniards. After two victories, in 1503, the Spaniards utterly defeated the French under the Marquess of Mantua, in December 1504, at *Mola* near Gaeta. In the rout, Piero de' Medici, who was with the French army, was drowned in the Garigliano. King Ferdinand became master of the whole kingdom, but the people did not enjoy any of the blessings of peace. The pay of the Spanish soldiers was in arrears. They became mutinous, and in order to keep them quiet the people were heavily taxed. The soldiers were under no discipline, and indulged themselves in robbery and licentiousness.

12. **Exploits of Cesare Borgia.**—The invasions of Italy by the French enabled the Pope and his son Valentino to push forward their schemes. The Romagna, though it nominally belonged to the Holy See, was divided into a great number of small states, under lords who were really independent of the Pope. These petty Tyrants were, for the most part, cruel and wicked men, and their subjects learned to follow their example. Pope Alexander was bent on forming a principality for his son out of these various lordships. When King Lewis prepared to invade Milan he made an alliance with him, and persuaded the King to help him in his plans. Lewis gave the Pope a detachment from his army, and declared himself on his side. Valentino then began the conquest of the Romagna from its different lords. He put to death the heirs of the reigning families in the cities which he gained. He took *Pesaro*, *Rimini*, and *Faenza*, and, in 1501, was made *Duke of Romagna* by the Pope. He threatened Bologna, but King Lewis took *Giovanni Benti-*

voglio, the Tyrant of that city, under his protection, and the Duke was forced to give up his hopes in that quarter. He entered the Florentine territory, and the Signory took him into their pay for fear that he should help the Pisans; but nevertheless he ravaged the country, and seized on *Piombino*. When the war began between the French and Spaniards, King Lewis wanted to have the Florentines on his side, and therefore refused to allow the Duke to annoy the Republic any further. The Duke then, in 1502, surprised *Guidobaldo, Duke of Urbino*, and seized his city. A confederacy was made against him by the lords of Bologna, Perugia, and other places, and the people of Urbino received back their Duke, who was a wise and noble man. The power of Cesare for the moment was shaken. With great address he divided the Confederates. He lured some of the princes to meet him at Sinigaglia, and there treacherously killed them. A certain Ramiro d'Orco, a monster of cruelty, quelled the disorders of Romagna for the Duke, and was afterwards put to death by his master. Valentino retook Urbino, with the help of the French King. He then engaged in a war with the powerful Roman family of *Orsini*, who were allies of the French. Lewis had checked his ambition, and now that the French were losing ground before the Spaniards, the Duke no longer cared to keep on good terms with him. He still further offended Lewis by aspiring to the sovereignty of Pisa, which was offered to him by the citizens. If he had become master of Pisa, he would have established a power in Tuscany which Florence would hardly have been able to withstand. In 1503, his father, Pope Alexander, died suddenly, from having, it is said, drunk of a poison which his son, with whom he was at supper, had mixed for one of the Cardinals. This was the end of the wonderful success of Cesare. The next Pope, *Pius the Third*, lived only a few months, and was succeeded by *Giuliano della Rovere*, who took the name of

Julius the Second. The Orsini attacked and routed the army of Duke Valentino at Rome, and a large number of his towns in Romagna revolted from him. Venice took the opportunity of seizing on twelve of these towns, despite the remonstrance of the Pope, who claimed them for his See. The Pope at first was on friendly terms with the Duke, for he hoped to make use of him against the Venetians, but afterwards he seized and imprisoned him. Valentino was liberated in 1504, and went to Gonsalvo, who received him with much friendliness. After a little while, however, Gonsalvo sent him off to Spain. King Ferdinand was glad to get him into his power, for he had long been the ally of France, and was too powerful for the safety of the Spanish dominions in Italy. For two years he was shut up in the Castle of Medina del Campo. He then escaped, and fled to his brother-in-law, *John*, King of Navarre, and served in his army, until he was shot under the walls of Viana.

13. **Fall of Genoa and Pisa.**—The conquest of the Duchy of Milan gave King Lewis the lordship of Genoa, which had before been under Lodovico Sforza. Although the lordship of the city had belonged, after it had revolted from Filippo Maria, first to the French King and then to the Duke of Milan again, the citizens had enjoyed the right of managing their own internal affairs. After the conquest of the Duchy by King Lewis, the French broke the agreements by which the government had been secured to the citizens; and the Genoese nobles, in order to gain a larger share of power, sided with them. In 1507, the people rose against the nobles, who were thus betraying their liberties, and, in the absence of the French governor, forced a great many of them to leave the city. They appointed new magistrates, whom they called *Tribunes of the People,* and shut out the nobles from all share in the government. The French King, however, came against the city with a large army, and easily

routed the Genoese. He entered the city as a conqueror, and, though he still allowed the Genoese to manage their own affairs, he did away with all the agreements which had been made with them, and granted them privileges instead, so that for the future their constitution was not a matter of right, but the gift of a master. He ordered that for the future the Genoese coins should be stamped with his mark, as a sign of subjection. He fined the city, and beheaded the two chiefs of the late rebellion. Ever since Charles the Eighth had given Pisan her liberty, the Florentines had tried in vain to regain the city. The Pisans defended themselves with great courage, although they were attacked, not only by the Florentines, but by the different forces which the Florentines were able to hire, and at one time by the French. They were chiefly helped by Genoa, Siena, and Lucca, which were all fearful of the power of Florence. This long war brought the Florentines into great difficulties, and caused a change in their constitution. They found that the frequent change of the Signory made it difficult for them to carry on intricate negotiations. It spread the knowledge of State secrets, and gave complicated questions into the hands of men who were quite new to them. The Republic was thus outwitted in treaties, and had no singleness of plan in carrying on a long war. The Florentines therefore adopted the startling change of choosing their Gonfaloniere for life. At the same time they took care to secure a good administration of justice, and to prevent any danger from the too great power of one man, by creating a powerful bench of judges in place of the old Podesta. The unsuccessful revolt of Genoa checked the help which the Pisans received. In 1507, Lewis and Ferdinand held a conference at *Savona*, and agreed to sell Pisa to the Florentines, for Maximilian was expected to come into Italy, and they were afraid lest he should get hold of it. The next year Maximilian came, but was turned back by the

Venetians. The two Kings did not carry out their agreement, and, in order to get a higher price, King Lewis sent a reinforcement to Pisa. At last, in 1509, the Florentines offered a bribe which satisfied even the French King. Lewis and Ferdinand both agreed to give no more help to the Pisans. Lucca was forced to make a three years' truce, and could only supply the Pisans with provisions by stealth, and in small quantities. The city was closely besieged, and was forced to yield after nearly fifteen years of war. The conquerors behaved with moderation, though not with generosity. The Pisans could not bear the yoke, and left their home in great numbers.

14. **The League of Cambray.**—In 1503, the Venetians, after fifty years of war, made a truce with the Turks. They then began to extend their possessions on the mainland. After the death of Pope Alexander, they seized on several of the cities in the States of the Church which Cesare Borgia had taken. They brought upon themselves the hatred of the King of the Romans, for when he tried, in 1508, to enter Italy and to share in the spoils, which as yet had only fallen to his neighbours, and hoped also to gain the Imperial crown, the Venetian army under l'Alviano defeated him in the valley of *Cadoro*, and took from him Trieste and other places. The Venetian territory now stretched from Aquileia to the Adda, and southward to Ravenna and Rimini. It took in Friuli, the coast of Dalmatia, some islands of the Archipelago, Cyprus, Crete, some points of Peloponnêsos, and some towns in the kingdom of Naples, which had been pledged to them by Ferdinand the Second. In 1508, by a secret treaty formed at *Cambray*, a league was formed, against Venice, by the King of the Romans, the Pope, the Kings of France and Spain, the Dukes of Savoy and Ferrara, and the Marquess of Mantua. Each of these was to receive some part of Venetian territory. The King of the Romans claimed Padua, Vicenza, and Verona, as fiefs of the Empire

which had been seized by Venice after the defeat and death of her enemy Francesco da Carrara. As head of the house of Austria, he claimed Treviso and Friuli. The Pope was to have the cities of the Romagna, and the King of Spain the cities which Venice held in his kingdom of Naples. King Lewis was to have the old boundary of the Duchy of Milan restored. Ferrara and Mantua were to be freed from all Venetian sovereignty, and the Duke of Savoy was promised the island of Cyprus. In 1509, war was declared. King Lewis crossed the Adda, and utterly defeated the army of the Republic at *Agnadello*, and soon conquered the dependencies of the old Duchy. Meanwhile the Pope regained the cities of the Romagna; the Duke of Brunswick overran Friuli; and the Italian allies were equally successful. Venice seemed on the point of ruin; she gave up her possessions in North Italy, and ordered her officers to quit Vicenza, Verona, and Padua. The Venetian State in Italy was thus reduced to the islands on which it had first been founded. Within the city, the Senate was in fear of an insurrection, for the people at large were justly angry at being shut out by the nobles from all share in the government. Before long the tide turned. The slothfulness of Maximilian was the first cause of the success of the Venetians. They surprised and took Padua. Maximilian laid siege to the city with a large army. If he had taken it, Venice would have been lost. He was forced to raise the siege, and thus lost all influence for the future in Italy, and all chance of the Imperial crown. The Kings of France and Spain had gained all that they wanted. Pope Julius had attacked the Venetians both with spiritual and carnal weapons, with excommunication and with an army. He now began to fear lest the power of Venice should be brought so low that she would never again be able to check the advance of foreign invaders, as she had done when King Charles had taken Naples.

15. **The Holy League.**—The invasion of the territory of Venice caused fearful suffering in the north and east of Italy. Pope Julius, though he was violent and ambitious, hated to see his country exposed to the fierceness of the French and Spaniards, and to the brutality of the Germans. He formed the noble design of driving the *Barbarians* out of Italy. In 1510, he absolved the Venetians, and began a series of intrigues which broke up the League of Cambray. He determined first of all to attack the French, for he had several causes of quarrel with Lewis. The Pope began the war in alliance with the Swiss and the Venetians. The Swiss invaded the Duchy of Milan, but retreated before the French. Trivulzio forced the army of the Pope and the Venetians to retreat. He took Bologna, and brought back the Bentivogli, who had been overthrown by Cesare Borgia. Thus the Pope was unsuccessful, and King Lewis, in revenge for his attack upon him, prevailed on some of the Cardinals to call a General Council. This Council was to judge of and condemn the Pope's conduct, and the King fixed upon Pisa as the place of meeting. The Council was very thinly attended, and the Florentines did not welcome the few Cardinals and Bishops who came to it. They were angry because King Lewis fixed on a place in their dominions, for they feared that this might bring them into trouble. The clergy of the metropolitan church would not let the Bishops use their church, nor would they lend them any things which they needed for the celebration of the mass. One day a soldier of the French guard grossly insulted a woman in a public place, near to the Church of *San Michele*, where the Council sat. The bystanders began to abuse him, and a number of his comrades and some servants of the Bishops came to help him. Then several of the Pisans and Florentines ran to the place, and a fierce street fight began, one party calling out *France*,' and the other '*Marzocco*,' the name of the bronze

Lion, which sits before the Palazzo of Florence. The Cardinals were so frightened at the noise that they decided to move the Council to Milan. Even in Milan, although the city belonged to the French, the people cursed the Bishops in the streets, because they were bringing schism into the Church, and bloodshed into the land. Pope Julius, to meet this attack upon himself, persuaded Ferdinand of Aragon to join himself with him and the Venetians in a *Holy League*, to maintain the unity of the Church, and to drive the French out of Italy. The Pope also persuaded King Henry the Eighth of England and Ferdinand of Aragon to attack France, and bribed the King of the Romans to make peace with the Venetians. The allied armies closely besieged Bologna; but *Gaston de Foix*, the nephew of King Lewis, relieved the city, and forced the besiegers to retreat. The Venetians meanwhile recovered Brescia and Bergamo, but Gaston retook Brescia by storm. His soldiers pillaged the city for seven days, and slaughtered the inhabitants. In spite of these successes, King Lewis was placed in a great strait by the powers which the Pope had arrayed against him, and he therefore instructed Gaston to force the allies to a pitched battle. The French general brought this about on April 11, 1512, before the walls of *Ravenna*. The Pope's army was led by Fabrizio Colonna, and the Spaniards by Raymond de Cardona, the Viceroy of Naples. The battle was fought with great fierceness on both sides. The French were at last left masters of the field. A large number of the allies were slain, and many of their leaders were taken prisoners. Amongst these prisoners was the Cardinal Giovanni de' Medici, the second son of Lorenzo the Magnificent, who had been given a seat in the Sacred College by Pope Innocent the Eighth. The French bought their victory very dearly, for their general, the young Gaston de Foix, Duke of Nemours, was slain in the battle. With him passed away the vigour of the French army, which had already suffered from the effects of pillage and excess. The position of King Lewis was very critical, for the King of England was making repeated expeditions against the French coast, and Ferdinand had conquered Navarre. Maximilian now joined the League, and allowed twenty thousand Swiss in the pay of the allies to descend on the Duchy of Milan. The French were driven out of the Duchy, and the Swiss poured into Lombardy in great numbers. The Confederates of the Old League seized on Lugano, and the Three Leagues of the Grisons seized on the *Valtellina* and *Chiavenna*. The Swiss soon afterwards made *Massimiliano Sforza*, the son of Lodovico, Duke of Milan. The Pope regained Bologna and Ferrara, and also managed to seize Parma and Piacenza. Genoa revolted, and only two or three castles were left to King Lewis of all the territory which he had conquered so quickly.

16. **The Return of the Medici.**—During the war of the Holy League Florence refused to break with King Lewis, and maintained a strict neutrality. When the French were driven out of Italy, the allies held a Congress at Mantua, and there it was determined to make the Florentines change their policy, depose their Gonfaloniere, *Piero Soderini*, who favoured the French, and receive back the Medici. *Giuliano de' Medici*, the brother of the Cardinal Giovanni, pointed out the advantage it would be to the allies, if Florence were handed over to his family, which had suffered such wrongs from the French. The allies agreed to do as he and the Pope wished, and the Viceroy Raymond de Cardona was sent against the Florentines. When he came near to the city, he sent to propose that the Gonfaloniere should have his office taken from him, and that the Medici should be received back into Florence as private persons. The Great Council determined to agree to admit

the Medici as was proposed. At the same time the people considered that, if the Gonfaloniere were turned out of office, the way would be open for the Medici to become masters of the city, and they therefore refused the Viceroy's first proposal. Then the Viceroy advanced to the little town of Prato, which was defended so feebly that it was easily taken by storm on August 29, 1512. The town was given over to the soldiers. The sack lasted, more or less, for twenty-one days. During that time at least two thousand, and some say more than twice that number, were killed by the conquerors, and many dreadful cruelties and other deeds of wickedness were done by them. The Florentines were much alarmed by this sad disaster, and some young noblemen, who were in favour of the Medici, took advantage of it to forward their schemes. Paolo Vettori, Bartolommeo Valori, Antonfrancesco degli Albizzi, two of the Rucellai, and some others, entered the Palazzo and forced the Gonfaloniere to leave the city. Messengers were sent to Don Raymond. They promised on behalf of the city that the Florentines would join the league against France, and pay a large sum of money to the Viceroy. Giuliano de' Medici, and his nephew Lorenzo, the son of the unlucky Piero, entered the city quietly. The Florentines began to make some changes in their government, but these did not in any way favour the Medici. In a few days, however, the Cardinal Giovanni entered the city with a good many soldiers. The next day Giuliano, at the head of some armed men, interrupted the discussion of the Signoria, took possession of the Palazzo, and seized on the public plate. Then he had the common bell rung out, and the people came together in the Piazza. When they had assembled they found themselves surrounded by armed men, and so they agreed that a Balia should be formed to remodel the government. The old system of *scrutiny* was again brought into use, by which the names of all who were disaffected were withdrawn from the lists for the ballot. Affairs were put in the same position as that in which they were before 1494, and the Medici returned to their former greatness in the city.

17. **Summary.**—The vain ambition of Charles the Eighth was the first cause of the entrance of the *Barbarians* into Italy. His invasion and conquest of the kingdom of Naples brought him no fruit, but he left behind him the seeds of many evils. Lodovico succeeded in his designs. He became Duke of Milan by the help of the French, and, when their rapid success threatened his safety, he got rid of them by making an alliance against them with foreign as well as with Italian powers. The military success of the King of France taught other kings to look on Italy as a tempting and easy prey. The political success of the Duke of Milan taught Italian powers to seek the overwhelming advantages which were to be gained by alliance with one of the great foreign states, and thus the hopes and plans of ambitious kings were forwarded. Through the conquest of Milan by Lewis the Twelfth, and that of Naples by Ferdinand of Aragon, two foreign and unfriendly powers were established in Italy. From that time Italian politics became the means by which foreigners sought their own advancement. The first great question which, though purely Italian, was used by foreign invaders for their own purposes, was the Pisan War of Independence. Lewis and Ferdinand helped sometimes one side and sometimes the other, either openly or by intrigue, just as suited their convenience. In the same way, the greatness of Venice, which had been looked at with suspicion by the other Italian states before the coming of the French, was humbled, not to preserve the balance of power in Italy, which would have been the case in the days of Lorenzo de' Medici, but to gratify the ambition of the Kings of France and Spain, and the spite of the King of the Romans.

The Papacy was the power which most effectually thwarted the designs of the foreign invaders of Italy, for the Popes would have lost most of all, if any one gained a decided predominance. All their greatness depended on their being independent. Their power did not lie for the most part in material strength, but in being able to combine and use the strength which others had; and for this end it was needful that they should not depend on any greater power. An Italian prince or republic might gain by acting for a time as second to some great foreign power. The Pope could only be either the head or the servant of others. This necessity for independence of action threw difficulties in the way of the foreign invaders of Italy, and made the Papacy rank as the most important temporal power in the peninsula. It was counterbalanced by one serious drawback. Each Pope struggled to make his own family a princely house, and for this reason the policy of each Pope died with him. Alexander the Sixth used the French and the Spaniards alike to set his son Cesare at the head of a newly-created Italian state. He thus hindered the advance of the King of Spain, and, towards the end, the cause of King Lewis also. As long as Alexander lived, his policy prospered, and his son became by far the most powerful of all the Italian princes. At the death of Alexander his policy ended, and his son lost his possessions and his liberty. Pope Julius the Second followed a nobler policy; he strove for temporal dominion, not to enrich his family, but to raise the power of the Holy See. He set himself first of all to regain the cities which Venice had seized on the death of Cesare Borgia, and for this purpose he made use of the League of the foreign powers against Venice. He gained his end, and then, because he saw the danger of oppressing the Venetians too far, he took up an independent line and left the League. Then, moved by feelings of ambition and of patriotism, seeing his country oppressed by foreigners, and fearing doubtless lest the

Holy See should be made of secondary importance, he took on himself the task of driving the Barbarians out of Italy. He began with the French. In the first part of the war which followed, the possession of Bologna was the point on which politics turned, as the possession of Pisa had been a few years before. The Pope gained the city, and laid a foundation for fresh Papal intrigues by seizing Parma and Piacenza. He succeeded in driving out the French, but the Spaniards were left all the stronger. "If Heaven allow," he said, "the Neapolitans shall soon have another master." It was not to be. He died in 1513, and his hopes died with him. The Cardinal Giovanni de' Medici was chosen Pope, and took the name of *Leo the Tenth*. His first object was to keep his power over Florence, and he owed that power to the interference of the Spanish Viceroy.

CHAPTER VIII.

ITALY CONQUERED.

Italian art and literature at the beginning of the sixteenth century (1) —*Lewis tries to regain Milan* (2)—*Francis the First defeats the Swiss at Marignano, and regains Milan* (3)—*the schemes of Pope Leo X.* (4)—*the dominions of Charles V.; he is called into Italy by Pope Leo, and becomes master of Milan* (5)—*Francis I. tries to regain Milan* (6)—*is defeated and taken prisoner at Pavia* (7)—*the Duke of Milan tries to shake off the yoke of Spain by a conspiracy with the Marquess of Pescara* (8)—*Francis regains his liberty, and makes the Holy League against Spain, with the Pope, England, Venice, and Milan; the army of the Constable in want of supplies* (9)—*marches southwards; the Florentines desire to defend themselves, and rise against the Medici* (10)—*the sack of Rome by the army of the Constable* (11)—*the French army weakened by excess; Genoa deserts the French cause, which fails in Italy* (12)—*the Medici are turned out of Florence; the different parties in the city* (13).

1. **Art and Literature.**—The early part of the sixteenth century was a time in Italy of wonderful growth in literature and art. The use of the word 'Barbarians' for foreigners marks the fact that Italy was the home of that literary and artistic revival which is called the *Renaissance*. It also seems to shew the pride with which the Italians looked on themselves as a nation. The old influence of the Emperor and the Pope had passed away. There were no longer Guelf or Ghibelin principles to bind Italians together. Pope and Emperor, Guelf and Ghibelin, still went on; but the names now had no longer anything to do with the principles with which they were once associated. Those ties no longer

existed. In their place a national feeling had arisen; and the fact that Italy was the home of literature and art served in no small degree to awaken and encourage the national pride of the people, and the dislike and contempt which they felt towards foreigners. For a long time men had been shaking off the stiffness which marked the art of earlier days, and which arose from their choice of religious subjects. The chapel of Masaccio now became the school of disciples who surpassed their master. Artists were helped in returning to a more faithful following of Nature, by the study of the masterpieces of antiquity. Lorenzo the Magnificent had made a collection of these in Florence, but that which gave the greatest encouragement to this study was the finding of the group of the *Laocoon* in the ruins of the *Baths of Titus* during the reign of Pope Julius. The Popes led the way in the new fashion of art which arose from these discoveries. They had become worldly in their lives and in their plans. They did not now care so much for the things of the Church— the various objects for which Gregory the Seventh and his successors strove for three centuries and a half—as for the things of the world. They were not therefore hindered by any scruples from encouraging in others, or from following themselves, a more secular spirit in art and literature than had ever before been patronized by the head of the Church. Something of this feeling led Pope Julius to pull down the old basilican church of St. Peter at Rome to make way for a more stately building. He employed *Donato Lazzari*, surnamed *Bramante*, as the architect of his new church. Bramante planned a building so noble and great that the church remained unfinished long after he and his patron had died. Many different artists were employed at various times on this great building, and the expense of the work was the cause, or at least was put forward as the cause by Pope Leo, for which a large sum of money was demanded of all Christendom. One of the ways by which Leo raised this money was by the sale of *indulgences*, or pardons for sin. This sale led to a great revolt against the spiritual power of the Pope, which began in Germany. The patronage of Pope Julius brought many artists to Rome, and amongst them *Michel-Angelo Buonarroti*, a Florentine sculptor and painter. Michel-Angelo painted for the Pope the frescoes which adorn the chapel built by Sixtus the Fourth, the uncle of Julius, and called, after him, the *Sistine Chapel*. Though darkened by time and neglect, the sublime figures which he painted still bear testimony to the grandeur of his genius. Michel-Angelo, while he was still at Florence, had met and rivalled the older artist *Lionardo da Vinci* in a trial of skill, in making a design for the Palace of the Republic, of which the subject was a Florentine victory. Lionardo da Vinci was brought to Milan by Lodovico Sforza. He left that city when it was taken by the Swiss. He there painted his great picture of the "Last Supper." Lionardo, however, did not care to give himself exclusively to one art. He sought after beauty, and loved to try different experiments in the hope of bringing to light some form of beauty which yet lay hidden. His finished works are therefore few, but have a peculiar charm. The patronage of art reached its greatest height under Pope Julius the Second. Another famous artist who worked for him was *Raffaello Sanzio* of Urbino. By the orders of the Pope, Raffaello painted the wonderful representations of Theology, Philosophy, Poetry, and Jurisprudence, which adorn the *Camera della Segnatura*, in the *Vatican Palace*. Pope Leo the Tenth also set Raffaello to paint historical scenes for the same Palace. In this work Raffaello employed many young artists who worked under him, and thus he made the Vatican a school of painters. He designed the *loggie* (galleries) which join together the different parts of the Palace, and ornamented them with carvings, paintings, and mouldings. By the Pope's order he made designs from the Acts of the Apostles, for tapestry to be worked by the weavers of Flanders. The tapestry came safely to Rome. The drawings or cartoons for it had been cut into strips by the weavers, and were left in Flanders. They were bought by our King *Charles the First.* After his death they were to have been sold, but *Cromwell* interfered, and caused them to be preserved for the nation. In the reign of *William the Third* they were joined together, and were hung in *Hampton Court.* The works of the *Roman School* of painters, of which Raffaello was the founder, are marked by majesty, but this majesty is often lost by exaggeration, by falseness of conception, and lack of colour. The *Florentine School,* of which the works of Michel-Angelo are the finest examples, are known by vast and bold outlines. The *Venetian School* by the brilliant colouring of three great artists of a little later date, *Tiziano Vecellio,* *Jacopo Robusti,* commonly called *Tintoretto,* and *Paolo Veronese.* *Benvenuto Cellini,* the Florentine goldsmith, engraver, and sculptor, worked mostly in the reign of *Pope Clement the Seventh,* the successor of Leo, and was patronized by him. The reign of Leo was marked by the full development of Italian literature. Boiardo indeed wrote his lively verse before it began. But it was adorned by the vigorous genius of Ariosto, by the somewhat frigid elegance of Bembo, and by others of less note. Amongst the writers of Italian prose during the early part of the sixteenth century, the foremost are *Niccolo Machiavelli* and *Francesco Guicciardini.* The principal works of Machiavelli are the *History of Florence,* his native city, and a political essay called *The Prince,* in which the qualities and conduct of a man who is fitted to enslave a state are minutely drawn out. Niccolo was a republican, and this shut him out from nearly all patronage, for the Medici expected some substantial return for their support and favour. Francesco Guicciardini, who was also a Florentine, wrote the History of Italy during his own time—from 1494 to 1526.

2. Unsuccessful attempt of Lewis on Milan.—When Leo the Tenth was elected, in 1513, the only two really independent Italian powers were the Pope and the Republic of Venice. The Duchy of Milan, including Genoa, was nominally governed by Massimiliano Sforza, but in reality by the Swiss who upheld him. The Pope had almost boundless influence in Tuscany, and during the reign Florence can hardly be said to have been free. Pope Julius had extended the dominion of his See over the little principalities into which the States of the Church had been split up: and Leo found himself master of a wide extent of territory. Sicily, Sardinia, and Naples were in the hands of the King of Spain. The Pope and King Ferdinand were most anxious to prevent the French from regaining any power in Italy. But the Venetians were aggrieved, because the other members of the Holy League would not give them back the territory which they had lost. In revenge they entered into the schemes of King Lewis, who hoped to regain Milan. The people of the Duchy were weary of the weakness of Massimiliano, and of the greediness of his Swiss supporters. A revolt in favour of France was made at Genoa, and was headed by *Antonio Adorno*. The French crossed the Alps, and were willingly received by the people into Milan. The Duke fled to *Novara*, and was there defended by the Swiss. On June 6, 1513, the French were defeated in a fierce battle under the walls of the town, and were forced to recross the Alps. The Adorni were driven out of Genoa, and *Ottaviano Fregoso* was made Doge by the Spanish Viceroy. The Venetians were attacked by the King of the Romans and the Viceroy, to punish them for having taken the part of France against a member of the League. Their territory was ravaged and the people cruelly ill-treated. King Lewis now became anxious for peace. The Swiss had carried the war into France. His army was routed by the English at *Guinegate.* His allies, the Scots, were defeated at *Flodden.* He therefore made terms with the Pope, the King of the Romans, and the Kings of England and Spain. The schism which he had made in the Church by the Council of Pisa now ended, and the rebellious Cardinals were pardoned. The Swiss alone refused all offers of friendship which he made to them.

3. **Francis the First. Marignano.**— In 1515 Lewis King of France died, and was succeeded by *Francis the First.* The new King immediately asserted his claims to the Duchy of Milan, and began to make preparations for invading it. The Pope saw the movements of Francis with great uneasiness. Giuliano de' Medici and, after him, his nephew Lorenzo, the son of Piero, really ruled Florence for the Pope; and he feared lest, if the French were successful, he and his family should again lose the city. Venice was openly on the side of the French, and sent her army to Cremona to be ready to help them. Ottaviano Fregoso made his peace with the French King, and held Genoa for him. Francis was also joined by *Robert de la Marck,* the leader of a famous free company called the *Black Bands.* The Florentine forces led by Lorenzo, the Spanish under the Viceroy, and the Papal army under Prospero Colonna, advanced northwards. The falseness and indecision of the Pope prevented any united action between them. The Swiss held the passes of Piedmont, and the general of the French, Gian Giacopo Trivulzio, had the greatest difficulty in leading his army across the Alps by *Monte Viso.* Prospero Colonna while on the march to join the Swiss was taken prisoner at Villafranca. The Confederates began to treat with King Francis. The terms of a treaty were settled, and the sum which was fixed upon was just about to be paid by the King,

when a fresh force came down from the mountains. The Cardinal of Sion, who hated the French, urged the Swiss to fight. Some went off, the rest determined to defend the Duchy. Meanwhile Lorenzo and the Viceroy waited each for the other to cross the Po, and thus the Swiss were left alone. On September 13th, the Swiss attacked the French, who were nearly double their number, at *Marignano*. The surprise, and the resolute charge of the Swiss, which was made right against the enemy's guns, made the French waver, but the Black Bands and the men-at-arms retrieved the loss. Still the battle was doubtful that day. When the two armies had fought for some time into the night, and men could scarcely hold their weapons, they separated one from the other, and waited for day to begin the fight again. On the next day the battle was decided by the advance of the Venetian army, which attacked the Swiss in the rear about noon. The Swiss retreated in order and at a slow pace towards Milan, and the conquerors did not dare to follow after them. This fierce battle cost both sides very dear, and the veteran Marshal, Trivulzio, declared that it was a battle, not of men, but of giants; and, that of eighteen battles in which he had been, all of them compared to this were but battles of little children. King Francis was several times wounded during the fight, and, when it was over, he called to him the *Chevalier Bayard*, who had fought by his side, and made him dub him knight upon the field of battle. The Swiss retreated from Milan, and the French entered the city. The Swiss after this never interfered with the affairs of Italy. They made peace with King Francis, and gave him and his successors the right to hire troops of them.

4. **The Schemes of Pope Leo.**—The battle of Marignano made the King of France master of Lombardy, and, if he had known how to push his fortune, he might have overturned the Pope's power both in Tuscany and in the States

of the Church. Leo received the tidings of the defeat of the Swiss with dismay. "We shall put ourselves," he said to the triumphant ambassador of the Venetians, "into the hands of the Most Christian King, and ask for mercy." He met the King at Bologna, and terms of peace were arranged. Among many other conditions to which the Pope had to submit, he was forced to give up Piacenza and Parma. When the immediate danger from France had passed away the Pope devoted himself to the advancement of his family. He took away the territories of Guido, Duke of Urbino, and gave them to Lorenzo, who was, in all things save in name, his vicegerent in Florence. The rightful Duke, with the help of his father-in-law, the Marquess of Mantua, regained his Duchy in 1517. The Pope sent an army against him, and again turned him out of the Duchy, after a war which drained the Papal treasury. Lorenzo de' Medici was the father of *Catherine*, who became Queen of *Henry the Second* of France. Lorenzo died in 1519, and was succeeded in Florence by the Cardinal Giulio, the natural son of that Giuliano de' Medici who was assassinated, in 1478, in the conspiracy of the Pazzi.

5. **Charles of Spain, master of Milan.**—Ferdinand, King of *Spain*, died in 1516, and was succeeded by his grandson Charles. Aragon and Castile had been united through the marriage of Ferdinand and Isabella. Their daughter Joanna married Philip of Austria, the son of Maximilian the Emperor-elect, and of Mary, daughter of Charles the Bold, Duke of Burgundy, from whom she inherited the county of Burgundy and the Low Countries. Their son was Charles, who thus succeeded to the dominions of the houses of Austria, Aragon, Castile, and Burgundy. Charles made a treaty with King Francis, and the Emperor-elect and the Republic of Venice became parties to it. Maximilian died in 1519, and both the young Kings, Charles and Francis,

sought to be elected in his stead. The Electors chose King Charles, who now ruled over Spain, the Low Countries, the two Sicilies, and over wide regions in the New World. He also possessed the right to the Imperial dignity and to the title of King of Jerusalem. Charles, before he was crowned Emperor, called himself *Emperor-Elect*, instead of simply *King of the Romans*. This new title had been first taken by his grandfather Maximilian, with the leave of Pope Julius, when the Venetians prevented his going to Rome for his coronation. Charles also took the title of *King of Germany*, which Maximilian had first used. The Pope knew that so long as the French kept the upper hand in North Italy he was sure to be checked in all his plans. He looked to Charles to support, not only his temporal, but also his spiritual power. In many parts of Western Europe men had become dissatisfied with the power of the Pope, and also with some of the doctrines of the Church; and a widely-spread revolt was made against spiritual despotism. This movement was led in Germany by an Augustine Friar called *Martin Luther*, and was taken up by the *Elector of Saxony* and a strong party in the Empire. Charles was the most fitting ally which the Pope could have. As Emperor-elect, it was his duty and privilege to protect the Holy See. As King of Germany, he would be on the Pope's side, for there was some cause to fear lest the revolt against spiritual authority should also become a revolt against temporal sovereignty. As King of Spain, he was a warm upholder of the teachings of the Church, for he was the grandson of Ferdinand *the Catholic*. In Italy he was the rival of the King of France, who constantly checked the schemes of the Pope. For these reasons the Pope, in 1521, made a treaty with King Charles, and invited him to come and drive the French out of Italy. On the death of Massimiliano, his brother Francesco became the head of the family of Sforza, and the Pope and the King agreed to make him Duke of Milan. The French were much disliked in the city, and the Governor *Odet de Foix*, *Marshal de Lautrec*, was so poorly supplied with money that his Swiss troops left him. He was forced to retreat beyond the Adda. The allied army under the command of Ferdinando, Marquess of Pescara, and the Cardinal de' Medici, entered Milan with scarcely any opposition. Francesco Sforza was proclaimed Duke, and nearly all the cities of the Duchy submitted to him. Parma and Piacenza again returned to the Pope. Leo just lived to hear that he had regained these cities, for which he had greatly longed, and that his enemies the French were humbled, and then he died. The literary and artistic splendour of the reign of Pope Leo often make people forget that he was a vile and sensual man, and an enemy of freedom; that his extravagance and greediness hastened a schism in the Catholic Church, and that his ambition and falseness were a curse to his country. He died in the full enjoyment of success, before the war which he had kindled had become dangerous to the interests of the See. The Spaniards had been brought into Italy by the alliance of Pope Alexander the Sixth with King Ferdinand, against the French. The Holy League, formed by Pope Julius the Second, had opened Central Italy to them. Pope Leo the Tenth made them masters of the Duchy of Milan, for Francesco was only a puppet in their hands, as his brother Massimiliano had been in the hands of the Swiss. The Cardinals chose Hadrian, Cardinal of Tortosa, to succeed Leo. He kept his old name, and was called *Hadrian the Sixth*. He was a native of Utrecht, and was therefore looked upon by the Italians as a *Barbarian*. He had been the tutor of the Emperor-elect, and was strongly inclined to favour his cause. He was a worthier Pope than his predecessor, and tried hard to unite Christendom against the common enemy, the Turks, who had taken Belgrade and the

Island of Rhodes. But Francis was bent on trying to regain the dominions he had lost, and the Pope was almost forced into a direct alliance with the Emperor-elect. Venice had grown tired of her alliance with Francis, which had only brought her into trouble, and she went over to the side of Charles. The Republic engaged to defend the kingdom of Naples against the Turks, and in return all Imperial claims over any part of her territory were sold to her for two hundred thousand ducats. In 1522, the French were defeated near Milan, and left the Duchy. The Imperial army took Genoa, and plundered it. Ottaviano Fregoso was taken prisoner, and Antoniotto Adorno was elected Doge in his stead. The loss of Genoa was a great blow to the hopes of Francis, as it shut him out from sending his troops into Italy by sea.

6. **French Invasion of Milan.**—Francis still hoped to regain Milan, and, in 1523, he made preparations to invade the Duchy. A league was made between the Pope, the Emperor-elect, the King of England, the Archduke Ferdinand of Austria, and the Duke of Milan, and was signed by the Cardinal Giulio de' Medici on behalf of Genoa, Florence, Lucca, and Siena, for the defence of Italy against the French. The French army was already crossing into Italy, and the King was about to follow, when he was delayed by an unexpected discovery. *Charles, Duke of Bourbon*, the Great Constable of France, was much hated by the King's mother, *Louise of Savoy*, and she made a claim on his estates before the Parliament of Paris. The Constable found that he was ruined, and in revenge he made alliance with his King's enemies, the Emperor-elect and the King of England. His plot was found out, and he escaped into the county of Burgundy. This discovery made Francis give up the command of the Italian expedition to *Guillaume de Bonnivet*, the Admiral of France, for he did not dare leave the country lest it should be invaded by the English and Spaniards.

The Admiral was completely out-manœuvred by Prospero Colonna, and could not bring about any decisive action. During this invasion Pope Hadrian died, and was succeeded by the Cardinal Giulio de' Medici, who took the title of *Clement the Seventh*. The new Pope had been the chief adviser of Pope Leo, and was a skilful politician. He had ruled Florence with mildness, though of course as a tyrant, and his accession was received everywhere with joy, for Pope Hadrian had been personally unpopular, both because he was a good man, and because he was a Barbarian. The position of Pope Clement was one of great difficulty. The Spaniards had been made use of by his predecessors to overthrow the French power in North Italy, which was dangerous to the Papacy, and to the families of Borgia, of the Rovere, and of the Medici. But, at the same time, it was by no means for the advantage of the Pope that the kingdom of the Sicilies and the Duchy of Milan should be in the hands of one sovereign. Clement therefore wished for peace, but could not bring it about. The death of Prospero Colonna, which happened at this time, gave the command of the army of Charles to the Constable and the *Marquess of Pescara*. In 1524, as the French were retreating, they were overtaken by the allied army at the river Sesia. The Admiral was wounded, and the rear of the army was defended by the Chevalier Bayard. This famous knight made so gallant a resistance that the French were enabled to continue their retreat in order, but he was mortally wounded by a musket-shot, and was made prisoner. When he felt himself struck, he kissed the cross made by the hilt of his sword and commended his soul to God. The Constable found him as he lay under a tree dying, with his face still fixed against the enemy, and spoke some words of pity. "Pity me not," he answered, "for I die as a man of honour should; it is you who should be pitied, for you fight against your king, your country, and your oath." He died soon after, and his body was sent back with royal honours to his native land of Dauphiny. The French were again forced to quit Italy. The allies carried the war into Provence, but were compelled to retreat from Marseilles.

7. **The Battle of Pavia.**—When the army of the Constable retreated, Francis determined to follow up his advantage by another attack on Italy. He did not pursue the retreating army along the coast, but crossed Mount Cenis, and marched quickly towards Milan in order to get there before the Constable had time to return. Duke Francesco and the Marquess of Pescara were unable to defend the city, and the French entered without any opposition. The Venetians, though they had entered the League, refused to send any help to the allies, either because they thought that it would be dangerous to provoke the French when they seemed likely to be victorious, or because they looked on the power of Charles with jealousy. The French King, instead of following up his success before the allies could recover themselves, laid siege to Pavia, which was defended by the Spanish general *Antonio de Leyva*. The siege was carried on for three months without success. Francis tried to draw away part of the Imperial army by sending *John Stewart Duke of Albany* to attack the kingdom of Naples. The Marquess of Pescara persuaded the other commanders not to heed this movement, and to keep their whole force engaged against the King. Meanwhile the war was carried on feebly by both sides. The French were foiled by the defence of Antonio, and lacked the necessary stores for pressing the siege. The army of the Emperor-elect had been thinned by the expedition into France, and was too weak to force on any decisive action. The cause of Charles seemed almost lost. Papers were even posted in Rome offering a reward for the discovery of the army of *the Cæsar*.

Giovanni de' Medici, son of Giovanni de Pier-Francesco, the grandson of Lorenzo who was brother of Cosmo de' Medici, "the Father of his country," was the leader of a famous Company called the *Black Bands*, which had done good service to the cause of the Emperor-elect. He now changed sides, and brought the French some supplies which they much needed. About the same time the Pope pretended that he was afraid of the Duke of Albany, and sent to inform Charles that he had agreed with the King of France to remain neutral. Meanwhile the Constable was busy gathering troops in Germany to relieve Pavia. At last, in January, 1525, he came back to Italy with a new army, partly furnished by Ferdinand the Archduke, and partly made up of a body of volunteers led by a famous German captain called *George Frundsberg*. With this reinforcement the Constable joined the other generals, and, on February 24th, attacked the French in front of Pavia. The French were utterly defeated. The King of France and his brother-in-law *Henry d'Albret*, King of Navarre, were taken prisoners. It is said that eight thousand were killed by the enemy, or drowned in the *Ticino*. Several of the greatest nobles and captains of France perished, and among them was Admiral Bonnivet. *Richard de la Pole*, grandson of our *George, Duke of Clarence*, was also killed on the French side. Francis was shut up in the Castle of *Pizzighittone* near Milan, and some time after was taken into Spain and imprisoned in the tower of the *Alcazar* at Madrid.

8. **The Conspiracy of the Marquess of Pescara.**—The battle of *Pavia* established the power of Charles in North Italy. The Pope and the Venetians were both alarmed at it, for Charles was too powerful to be a desirable neighbour, and they had reckoned that the war would have ended otherwise. The Venetians tried to persuade Clement to engage in a league with them and with the Duke of Ferrara, in order to take the Swiss into their pay, and then to join the Queen

Mother, who was Regent of France, in an attempt to set Francis at liberty. The Pope did not dare to embark on so hazardous a scheme, and signed a treaty with the generals of Charles. Italy lay at the mercy of the army of the Emperor-elect, and the different states were heavily taxed for its support. The unhappy people of the Duchy of Milan were not only ruined by taxation, but were harassed by the unbearable insults of the victorious army, which was quartered upon them. They were strongly inclined to the French side before this time, and the presence of the Spanish and German troops within their walls strengthened this feeling. Duke Francesco felt that he was only a puppet used to tax the people, for the benefit of masters who treated him and them with contempt. By the advice of *Girolamo Morone*, his Great Chancellor, he determined to make an effort to shake off the yoke. His hopes were privately encouraged by the Pope, and more warmly by the Venetians. The Constable and a large number of the troops had gone into Spain, and other places. The command was left in the hands of the Marquess of Pescara. The Marquess had, or thought he had, cause of complaint against the Emperor-elect, and the Chancellor took advantage of his anger. Morone offered to make a league with the Pope, the French, and the Venetians, and other Italian states, to conquer Naples, which was the native land of the Marquess, and give him the crown, if he would join in driving the Spaniards and Germans out of Italy. The King of France was to acknowledge Francesco as Duke of Milan, and the Marquess as King of Naples, and was to restore liberty to Italy. For a while this extraordinary scheme seemed likely to succeed. The Marquess had, or pretended to have, some scruples of conscience, which were soon overcome. Henry the Eighth of England, who was jealous of the great power of Charles, favoured the design; and the French Government and the Swiss eagerly agreed to second it. But in a short time the Marquess betrayed his confederates, arrested the Chancellor, and besieged the Duke of Milan in his castle. Some people thought that Charles knew all the time of the conspiracy, and that the Marquess acted with his approval, in order that he might have good cause of complaint against the King of France and the Duke of Milan. Others held that Pescara was really ready to revolt at first, and that then, wishing to make his peace, he entered into this conspiracy that he might betray it at a critical moment. By the command of the Emperor-elect the Marquess seized on all the places in the Duchy save the castles of Cremona and Milan, which still held out for the Duke. Before the end of the year 1525, the Marquess died, and the other great traitor, the Constable, again took the command of the army of the Emperor-elect.

9. **The Holy League.**—In the beginning of 1526 Francis obtained his freedom by signing the humiliating *Treaty of Madrid*. By this treaty, amongst other concessions, he renounced all claim to the kingdom of Naples, to the Duchy of Milan, to Genoa, and Asti. As soon as he was back again in France, he declared that all the concessions he had made were to have no force, because they had been made while he was a prisoner. Italy greatly needed his alliance. Naples was heavily oppressed by the military despotism of the Spaniards. The Duke of Milan was still besieged in his castle, and the troops of Charles, who had received no pay since the battle of Pavia, paid themselves by pillage and excess, and levied the most extravagant contributions on the inhabitants of the Duchy. Genoa had suffered from the greediness of the Spaniards. Florence had trembled at their cruelty, and had submitted to their dictation by receiving back the Medici. Venice had been weakened by the conquests of the members of the League of Cambray, and later by the ravages of the Germans. The States of the Church,

Ferrara and Mantua, had been almost ruined by the ambition of Alexander, Julius, and Leo, and the way between Milan and Rome seemed to lie open. The Italians made a great effort to throw off the yoke. The Pope, the Venetians, and the Duke of Milan, made an alliance with the King of France to obtain the freedom of the sons of Francis, who were kept as hostages in Spain, and thus to enable the King to act freely, and to put Francesco again in possession of his Duchy. In case Charles refused these demands he was to be attacked, first in Milan and then in Naples. Henry of England was made *Protector* of the League, which was called *Holy*, because the Pope was at its head. But the King of France had other plans about which he was more anxious than the fate of Milan, and he hoped, by being the mover of a powerful league, to force the Emperor-elect to agree to his wishes concerning them. Francis was not anxious to drive the Spaniards out of Italy, for then the work of the League would have been ended. He rather wished to threaten to drive them out, so that he might make Charles afraid of him. Meanwhile the people suffered greatly. The army of Charles was scantily supplied with food and pay, and the generals were almost forced to content their men at the cost of the Italians. The people of the Duchy of Milan were made to suffer all the more because the Duke was a member of the League. The soldiers lived at free quarters, and robbed, tortured, and murdered their hosts. All the shops in Milan were shut, for, if any one showed his goods for sale, they were sure to be stolen. The army of Venice was led by the *Duke of Urbino*. He failed to relieve Milan, and the Constable forced him to surrender. Cardinal *Pompeo Colonna*, who was a personal enemy of Pope Clement, suddenly marched to Rome. The Papal guards were put to flight, and the Vatican and the Church of St. Peter were plundered. The Pope fled to the strong fortress of St. Angelo, and was glad to make terms with the ambassador of the Emperor-elect. Meanwhile, among other reinforcements which came into Italy to the Imperial cause, George Frundsberg led a splendid army of German infantry into Mantua. He had raised these troops himself, and they followed him only for the plunder which the great military fame of their leader made them count on as certain. Giovanni de' Medici led his Black Bands against him, but was afraid to meet him in the open field. Giovanni harassed the German force, until he died of a wound received in a skirmish. He was only twenty-eight years old at his death, but he was renowned throughout Europe for his courage and skill. If he had lived, the fortune of the war might have been different, for his men loved and trusted him. The army of the Constable was discontented, and mutinous; the men distrusted the character of their leader: they were angry at the scantiness of pay and supplies, and they had lost self-restraint from having indulged in excess at Milan. The Constable was joined by *Charles de Lannoy*, who was Viceroy of Naples, and by George Frundsberg, each at the head of a large force. These new troops were also clamorous for pay, and the Constable had no money for them. He forced all he could out of the Milanese, and, when he could get no more, he led his army southwards, to seek the means of contenting them elsewhere.

10. **Florence on the Approach of the Constable.**—The Pope soon broke the truce which the Cardinal Colonna had forced him to make. He sent *Paolo Vitelli* to ravage the lands of the Colonna family, and invited René, Count of Vaudemont, a member of the old Angevin house, to come and conquer the kingdom. His plans failed for want of money, after he had brought fearful distress on the people of the Neapolitan border. He was disheartened by his failure, and frightened when he heard of the march of the army of the Emperor-elect. After a little hesitation he made terms

with the Viceroy, and disbanded nearly all his troops. The Viceroy promised that the Constable should not advance nearer either to Rome or Florence, for the Pope was very fearful lest the Florentines should revolt from his house if they saw the enemy, and fight for themselves. Still the Constable marched southwards on to Imola. Then the Viceroy remonstrated with him; but he would not hear, for his soldiers were in good humour now that they were advancing, and he either could not or would not stop them. In April, 1527, he crossed the Apennines, and entered the upper valley of the Arno. The younger citizens of Florence loudly demanded arms, that they might take part in the defence of their city, for they looked with distrust upon the army of the allies, which had come to meet the army of the Constable. The two heads of the Medici were *Ippolito* and *Alessandro*. Ippolito was the natural son of *Giuliano*, the brother of the Pope, Alessandro was probably the son of *Lorenzo*, whom the Pope made Duke of Urbino. They were both very young; and the Pope, who managed the Medicean party, was anxious to keep the Florentines quiet until these lads were of age to manage them for themselves. Arms were at first promised to the citizens, but on second thought were denied to them. The spirit of the people rose at being thus held unworthy to defend themselves, and at being trifled with and disappointed. One day, when the Cardinals were away, there was a sudden stir made in the Piazza. One of the guards of the Palace was killed, and the cries of "*Liberta*" "*Popolo!*" were again heard. The Gonfaloniere, *Luigi Guicciardini*, the brother of the historian, is said to have wavered. Two of the Medicean party rushed up the stairs of the Palace to speak with him. As soon as they came into the Council-room, they were turned back with a shout of "We want no more great men, but only to have the People and Liberty!" Unhappily the rising only lasted for one day, for the Duke of Urbino entered Florence at the head of the forces of the League. Francesco Guicciardini, the historian, who was also a statesman, a general, and, sad to say, an enemy to the freedom of his city, made terms between the two parties, and saved much bloodshed. The next day all was quiet.

11. **The Sack of Rome.**—The Constable was so badly in want of provisions that he could not, if he would, have kept his army in Tuscany. He marched quickly on towards Rome. The Pope had made some preparation for the defence of the city, and believed that his generals would be able to hold it. On May 5th, the Constable led his army before Rome. The Lutherans of George Frundsberg were eager for the overthrow of the Pope, and Spaniards and Germans alike greedily coveted the splendid booty which lay before them within the walls. At daybreak on the 6th the Constable led his army to the assault. A thick mist hid his troops as they approached. The scaling ladders were quickly planted, and the assault began. The Swiss guard of the Pope and the troops of the allies met the attack with firmness. The Constable himself climbed one of the ladders. He fell mortally wounded by a musket-shot. His death made his men furious for revenge. The city was stormed between the *Janiculum* and the *Vatican*. The Pope took shelter in the Castle of St. Angelo, and the enemy crossed the Tiber from the *Trastevere*, and made themselves masters of the whole city. The capital of the world lay at the mercy of 40,000 fierce and ungovernable soldiers. Bourbon was dead. Frundsberg had been seized with a fit some time before. The German Lutherans destroyed pictures and statues which were beyond price, for in their eyes they were instruments of idolatry. But the Spaniards surpassed even the Germans in cruelty and avarice. For seven months the City was a scene of robbery, lust, and murder. The arts and letters of the Renaissance were fast perishing by the wars in Italy. The

sack of Rome seemed to crush them at a blow. The Pope remained shut up in the Castle of St. Angelo until June 5th. Then he was forced to surrender because his provisions ran short. He was kept a prisoner until September 9th, and then fled in disguise to *Orvieto*.

12. **Destruction of the French army.**—The sack of Rome, the captivity of the Pope, and above all the triumph of the Emperor-elect, roused the anger of Henry the Eighth and of Francis. They made a fresh alliance against Charles. Henry sent supplies of money, but left the French to carry on the war. The Marshal de Lautrec entered Italy, and took Alessandria. By the skilful management of *Andrea Doria*, the Adorni were turned out of Genoa, and the city declared for the French. The Marshal surprised and sacked Pavia in revenge for his master's defeat under her walls. The Holy League was again published, and included the Pope, the Kings of France and England, the Republics of Venice and Florence, the Dukes of Milan and Ferrara, and the Marquess of Mantua. The Marshal did not push forward against Milan. He turned to Bologna and there met the Florentine reinforcements, which were chiefly made up of the Black Bands, which Giovanni de' Medici used to lead, and which were now taken into pay by the Republic. He next marched into the kingdom of Naples, in the hope of striking a decisive blow at the heart of the Spanish power in Italy. The successes of the French enabled the Pope to escape from the Castle of St. Angelo. The Spaniards saw that they could no longer keep him there, and, while terms were being made for his release, he was kept less strictly. The General of the Emperor-elect, *Philibert of Châlon, Prince of Orange*, with great difficulty gathered together, and led forth from Rome, the remains of the splendid army of the Constable and George Frundsberg. It was wasted by disease, and disorganized by unrestrained violence and rapine.

The French Marshal delayed his march to Naples, and when he at last arrived before the city, he found it occupied by the troops of the Prince of Orange. He blockaded the city, and the French and Genoese fleets beat off the Spaniards, who tried to relieve it. King Francis very foolishly offended Andrea Doria. In revenge Andrea withdrew his ships, and excited his fellow citizens against the French. Thus, in 1528, Genoa again changed sides. Andrea Doria was received by his fellow citizens with great gladness, for they were weary of the French. He assembled a Parliament of the People before his palace. Twelve Commissioners were chosen to remodel the Government. They gave the chief power into the hands of a few noble families, but Andrea while he lived was really master of Genoa. The loss of Genoa was a terrible blow to the French. The blockading army suffered dreadfully from disease. The sun smote them: the bad water poisoned them: and the enemy's cavalry harassed them. The Marshal died, worn out by sickness and trouble. He was succeeded in command by the Marquess of Saluzzo. This new commander was forced, in September, to capitulate at Aversa, and died soon afterwards. Nearly all the French army perished in this disastrous campaign, and the Black Bands of Tuscany were finally broken up. Meanwhile, in the north, Antonio de Leyva surprised and took prisoner the French general, *Francis of Bourbon, Count of St. Pol.*

13. **The Medici driven out of Florence.**—Although Pope Clement was the head of the League against the Emperor-elect, yet he by no means wished it to be too successful. He was anxious that the power of Charles should be somewhat checked, and above all that he should be able to get out of his hands without further humiliation. At the same time it was needful for him to have Spanish help in Tuscany. The Florentines were by no means contented with the rule of the Pope, who governed their city by the Cardinal *di Cortona*,

during the minority of Alessandro and Ippolito. They had been almost ruined by the large demands for money made by Clement; they had lost their freedom under his rule, and now they saw his failure with delight. After the unsuccessful rising which was quelled by the coming of the Duke of Urbino, this discontent began to increase rapidly. The Pope's party in the city were called *Palleschi*, from the Medicean *palle*, while the popular party were called *Piagnoni* or *Frateschi*, because they followed the same line of politics as that which Girolamo Savonarola used to uphold, and were on the French side. When the news of the taking of Rome reached Florence, the people were greatly rejoiced, and the prophecies of Savonarola were in every one's mouth. Then *Niccolo Capponi, Filippo Strozzi*, and other leading citizens, told the young Medici that they must go. Filippo had married *Clarice*, daughter of Lorenzo de' Medici. Filippo, however, had a quarrel with the Cardinal di Cortona, and Clarice hated the young Medici, because they and the Pope were not of the right Medicean line. Filippo rather wavered when he had to send off the young lords. He called his wife Clarice, who had come to see them go off, and begged her to send away the people, who had gathered before the palace. Clarice, however, abused her kinsmen heartily, and bade them begone. So the Medici left Florence for the second time on May 17, 1527. Then Niccolo Capponi was chosen Gonfaloniere, and the Great Council was assembled. The first act of the Florentines, when they had regained their liberty, was to enter into an alliance with France against Charles. They had already angered the Pope, and this alliance brought on them the anger of the Emperor-elect also. The failure of the French, and the expense and loss which the Florentines met with in the war, made them suspicious and discontented. The Gonfaloniere soon lost much of the public favour which he had gained by being foremost in driving out the Medici, for he was suspected of favouring some of the chiefs of their party. He knew that the Medici would certainly come back some day, since the Spaniards had now the upper hand, and he was inclined to make friends with them so as to secure himself when that day came. This made the Republican party distrust him. The members of this party were nicknamed *Popolani*, for the old *popolani grossi* had for the most part become nobles. They were led by *Tommaso Soderini*, *Baldassare Carducci*, and *Alfonso Strozzi*. In order to defeat the Popolani, the Gonfaloniere allied himself with a far more extreme party, and made friends with the *Frateschi*. This gained him his election as Gonfaloniere for another year. He began to imitate Fra Girolamo, and made a wild sort of speech in the Great Council. Florence was wasted by a pestilence; and the Gonfaloniere, at the end of his speech, fell on his knees crying out, "Mercy, O God." He also caused the Saviour to be elected King of Florence, which was just the way in which Fra Girolamo used to act. Still, though he was re-elected, he was much mistrusted because he tried to appease the Pope. The danger of Florence had become very great, but, in spite of the French defeat, the Florentines could not believe that France would desert them.

CHAPTER IX.

ITALY ENSLAVED.

Francis sacrifices his Italian allies by the Peace of Cambray (1)—the coronation of Charles the Fifth (2)—the siege of Florence (3)—its fall (4)—and the return of the Medici: their dynasty (5)—the reign of Pope Paul the Third; his family in Piacenza and Parma; the conspiracy of the Fieschi at Genoa (6)—war between France and Spain (7)—the fall of Siena (8)—Pope Paul the Fourth and King Philip the Second; the Peace of Câteau Cambresis (9)—religious movements in Italy; contrary attempts at reformation; the Council of Trent (10)—the Jesuits; the Waldenses; the Inquisition (11)—wars with the Infidels (12)—Savoy: its Counts (13)—its Dukes; it becomes an Italian State (14).

1. **The Peace of Cambray.**—Pope Clement was fully determined to make himself master of Florence again, and to cripple the power of the Venetians and of the Duke of Ferrara. The French had failed in their struggle against Spain, and the Pope was forced to turn for help to those who were so lately his enemies. In June, 1529, he made an open alliance with Charles at *Barcelona*. By this treaty he promised him the Imperial crown, and the investiture of the kingdom of Naples. Charles, on his part, promised that he would make the Venetians and the Duke of Ferrara give up some territory to the Pope; that he would bring Florence under the power of the Medici again, and would marry his daughter *Margaret* to Alessandro de' Medici, who was now the only lay representative of the family of the Pope, and who was therefore to be his vicegerent in the city. The danger of the Florentines was increased in August by a treaty made

between Charles and Francis, called the *Peace of Cambray*. By this treaty the King of France, in order to gain favourable terms for himself, sacrificed his Italian allies Florence and Venice, the Dukes of Milan and Ferrara, and the Angevin party which still existed in the kingdom of Naples. The Duke of Milan, who was childless and in bad health, made his peace with Charles by a heavy payment, and on his death the Emperor succeeded to his Duchy as a lapsed fief. The Duke of Ferrara submitted his rights to Charles, and met with milder treatment than his enemy the Pope had hoped for him. Venice restored Ravenna and Cervia to the Pope, and gave up to Charles the towns which she had gained in Apulia in the time of King Ferdinand. By these and some further concessions she purchased peace. Genoa had already been persuaded to submit to Charles. The Republics of Lucca and Siena, which had sunk to the position of petty states, were not displeased to be dependent on the Emperor, for they had always been Ghibelin. The Marquess of Montferrat and the Duke of Savoy, who had been nominally neutral during the war, but had on the whole favoured the French, were forced to join the party of Charles, and the *Marquess* of Mantua was rewarded for his services by the title of *Duke*.

2. **Coronation of Charles the Fifth.**—In 1530, Charles was crowned King of Italy and Emperor by Pope Clement. He received both the crowns at once, and the ceremony took place at Bologna instead of at Milan and at Rome. Though this coronation thus lacked somewhat of formal validity, it was no empty pageant. Charles the Fifth reigned over a larger portion of the world than his predecessor Charles the Great. As King of Italy he had greater power than any Emperor since the Barbarian Invasions of the fifth century. All through all the land, from the Alps to the Faro, and to the furthest end of Sicily, there was no one who could withstand his will. This coronation did not bring Italy into

any closer connexion with the Empire. For, after the Emperor's abdication, his Italian dominions remained attached to the crown of Spain, while the Empire passed to his brother Ferdinand, who succeeded him in Germany. No one after Charles the Fifth was crowned Emperor, but each of his successors after his German coronation took the title of Emperor-elect, and usually dropped the latter part of the title. Charles reigned over Italy less as Emperor than as King of Spain, and his coronation marks the end of the long struggle between France and Spain for the possession of that kingdom. It ended in the humiliation of France, and the disgrace of her King—who betrayed his allies—in the exaltation of Spain, and in the slavery of Italy.

3. **The Siege of Florence.**—Florence alone was shut out from the general peace-making. Nothing short of her slavery would satisfy either Pope or Emperor. As long as Niccolo Capponi was in office, the Pope could not take any active part against the city, for the Gonfaloniere was upheld by the Palleschi. In 1520, Niccolo was accused of treason and was deposed, and *Francesco Carducci* was chosen Gonfaloniere in his stead. Francesco belonged to the *Popolani*, who were strongly opposed to any correspondence with the Medici. When Charles came into Italy for his coronation, envoys from the Florentines met him and entreated his protection, but he would not have anything to say to them. Niccolo, who was one of the number, was so overcome by grief and anger that he died of a fever, crying, "Alas! alas! to what have we brought our wretched country!" The Florentines now saw that they must make their choice, and either submit wholly to the Medici, or else stand upon their defence. They chose to struggle for their freedom as long as they had strength to do so, but the news of the cruel treachery of the French King in deserting them by the Treaty of Cambray made them almost despair. Pope Clement,

with the leave of the Emperor-elect, sent the Prince of Orange against his native city at the head of an army of German cavalry and Spanish infantry, men who had shared in the triumphs and cruelties of the war in Lombardy and of the sack of Rome. The Florentines no longer put their trust in mercenaries. Niccolo Machiavelli had taught them to raise bodies of militia for the defence of their city, and the fame of the Black Bands of Tuscany had roused a warlike spirit within them. Michel-Angelo, the sculptor and painter, overlooked and added to the fortifications of the city. Outside the gates were beautiful suburbs, with stately churches and splendid villas, with vines and olives, and fruitful gardens and shady trees. All these were destroyed for a mile round, lest they should give shelter to the enemy. The Gonfaloniere, Francesco, carried on the works for the defence with much spirit, and gained general confidence, but his popularity seems to have waned a little by the end of his term of office. He was succeeded by *Raffaello Girolami*. The Prince of Orange at first hoped to take the city by assault. He was beaten off. He then determined to reduce the city by a blockade, and began to cut off all supplies. In December, 1529, *Stefano Colonna*, who commanded for the Florentines at the fortress of San Miniato, surprised the camp of the enemy by a night attack, and did them much hurt. In the beginning of 1530, *Malatesta Baglioni*, son of the Tyrant of Perugia who had been put to death by Pope Leo, managed to get elected the chief captain of the forces of the Republic, for Stefano Colonna would not take the office. Malatesta was not fit for the post; he tried to stand well with all parties, and ended by deceiving every one. By far the most famous leader on the Florentine side was *Francesco Ferruccio*, who had held an office in the Black Bands under Giovanni de' Medici. He was made commander of the forces without the walls. He seized the little town of *Empoli*, fortified it, and made it into a store-house, from which he supplied the Florentines within the city in spite of the watchfulness of the besieging army. In February, Volterra surrendered to the Pope's army, and Francesco Ferruccio was sent to retake it. While he was engaged in the siege, the Prince of Orange attacked Empoli, and the town was betrayed to him by the very men whom Francesco had left to guard it. The loss of Empoli was a terrible blow to the Florentines, and they soon began to be in want. Still they kept a steadfast heart, and refused to listen to the enticing words of the Pope. Francesco Ferruccio, after he had taken Volterra from the Imperialists, defended it with great skill against *Fabrizio Maramaldo* who besieged it, as well as against the people of the town who were on the side of the Pope. On June 17th, he forced the Imperialists to give up the siege. By this time the distress in Florence had become very great. Then Francesco proposed to turn away the attention of the enemy from Florence. He offered to march towards Rome itself, and give out that he was about to sack the City. He would thus gather together an army by the hope of booty, and would force the Prince of Orange to fall back on Rome to defend the Pope. The Signory thought the scheme too wild, and would not allow him to try it. Then he determined at all hazards to attempt to raise the siege.

4. **The Fall of Florence.** — Francesco Ferruccio was almost worn out with anxiety and weariness. He had been suffering from fever, and was weakened by his wounds and his want of rest. Nevertheless, he set out from Pisa on July 31st, at the head of a small army, in the almost desperate hope of passing over the mountains of Pistoia, and reinforcing the Florentines within the city. He was misled by his guides, who brought his army down from the top of the mountains; and everything which was planned in his camp was carried by traitors to the enemy. The Prince of Orange

with a powerful army met the Florentines, August 3rd, at *Gavinana*, a small village in the hills to the north-west of Pistoia. A fierce struggle took place in the little market-place and at the gate of the village. As the Prince of Orange led his horsemen to the charge, he was shot dead. For a time it seemed as though the Florentines had gained the day, for the Imperialists began to retreat. After a while the German infantry rallied, and the battle began again. Francesco Ferruccio and Gianpagolo Orsini made a gallant stand. Francesco was covered with wounds, and was at last taken prisoner. He was brought faint and dying into the market-place before Fabrizio Maramaldo. There the Imperialist general gratified his spite by striking him with his own hand. The soldiers who stood by finished the murder. He met his death without fear, only saying to those who struck him, "It is a noble thing to kill a dead man." With Francesco Ferruccio died the last hopes of the Florentines. Malatesta had been faithless to the cause of the city throughout the siege, and had worked as far as he could for the enemy. The Gonfaloniere and the Signory were forced by his treachery to accept the fair-sounding offers of the Pope. It was agreed that the Emperor should regulate the government of the city, but that it should still preserve its liberty; that the Florentines should pay a ransom and give hostages; that the Medici should be restored, and that the Pope should show kindness to his fellow citizens. *Baccio Valori*, who entered the city on behalf of the Pope, filled the Palace with armed men, and then called together a Parliament of the people. He asked the few trembling citizens who came together if they would have a Balia. He was answered by faint cries of "*Palle*" and "*Medici*." A Balia was appointed. The republican magistrates laid down their offices, and the freedom of Florence came to an end. The great Guelfic Republic which had lasted for four hundred years, reckoning from the death of the Countess Matilda, was destroyed by the ambition and treachery of one of her own sons, Giuliano de' Medici, Pope Clement the Seventh.

5. **The Return of the Medici.**—The Medicean Balia took ample vengeance on those who had fought for the freedom of their city. Michel-Angelo happily was saved by the Pope, for he wanted him to do some work for him. Many of his fellow patriots suffered torture and death. Then, after a while, Alessandro de' Medici, who had promised to marry the daughter of the Emperor, came with an envoy from the Imperial court. The envoy told the Florentines that they were to receive Alessandro for their Duke. Alessandro moved the seat of government from the old Palazzo Publico to the abode of his own family, which is now known as the *Palazzo Riccardi*. He also broke up the common bell, which in the days of freedom used to call the citizens together to consult or fight for the welfare of their city. The city had been brought very low; it had several times been visited by pestilence, and had suffered much from the war. The fields were desolate and there was great scarcity. Trade languished; there was but little work to do, and but few workmen. All classes were depressed, and looked on with silent and hopeless anger at the signs of their degradation. The Pope kept down all expression of discontent by sending a garrison into the city under the command of *Alessandro Vitelli*, and the violence and debauchery of the soldiers added to the misery of the people. Alessandro de' Medici ruled over Florence for six years. He practised every sort of wickedness and cruelty. In 1537, he was murdered in his bed by his kinsman *Lorenzo*, the son of Pier-Francesco di Lorenzo, and a descendant of Lorenzo, the brother of the elder Cosimo. This murder did not restore the freedom of Florence. Alessandro had had abettors of his tyranny, and they needed support. With Alessandro the elder line of the Medici

ended, but a party headed by Francesco Guicciardini, the historian, chose *Cosimo*, son of the great Captain Giovanni, as *Lord* of Florence, and so the chance of freedom was lost. Before long an attempt was made to shake off the yoke. Pope Clement died in 1534, and was succeeded by *Alessandro Farnese*, who took the title of *Paul the Third*. The new Pope hated the Medici, and wished to make his own family take their place in Italy. He gave Parma and Piacenza, which had been added to the States of the Church by Julius and Leo, to his son *Pier-Luigi*. He persuaded the Emperor to give his daughter Margaret, widow of Duke Alessandro, to his own grandson *Ottaviano*, and thus the dowry of the widowed Duchess had to be paid over to his house. He encouraged the Florentine exiles against their Lord. They raised an army, which was headed by *Filippo* and *Piero Strozzi* and *Baccio Valori*. Their plans were helped forward by a fresh war between the Emperor and the King of France, which broke out on the death of the Duke of Milan. Francis gave them some encouragement, but did not do much for them. They put too much faith in his promises, and miscalculated the power and abilities of Cosimo. Piero Strozzi was defeated but escaped, and, in 1537, the main army of the exiles was utterly routed near Prato. Filippo Strozzi and most of his companions were taken. The conspirators were punished with torture and death. Amongst the number were Baccio Valori, who had entered Florence as the representative of Pope Clement, and a son of Niccolo Machiavelli. Filippo Strozzi perished in prison. After this attempt the Florentines remained quiet under the yoke. Many of the noblest of them had fallen, and the reign of Cosimo crushed in those that were left all that remained of the old republican spirit. The Florentines were no longer free, and they soon learned to follow the vices of their rulers. Cosimo was made Grand Duke of Tuscany by Pope Pius the Fifth in 1570. Florence ceased to have an independent political life; she was no longer a city-state, she had sunk to be the seat of the government of the Grand Duchy. Like his family generally, Cosimo patronized literature and the arts, but both alike withered under the Medici, and this patronage has only served to cast a false splendour over the names of the Tyrants of Florence. Seven Grand Dukes of the Medici family reigned over Tuscany. *Cosimo the Second* alone ruled the state with justice and moderation, and left it in some degree of prosperity when he died. His successor *Ferdinando* undid all the good which Cosimo had done, and left Tuscany impoverished by taxation and crushed with severity. The last Medicean Grand Duke, Giovan-Gastone, a wretched debauchee, died in 1737.

6. **Reign of Pope Paul the Third.**—The advancement of the Farnese family was the chief object of the reign of Pope Paul the Third. He made alliance with the Emperor by the marriage of his grandson *Ottavio*, and he wished also to make an alliance with France. After some time he succeeded in getting one of the natural daughters of King *Henry the Second* for another grandson, *Orazio Farnese*. He wanted to gain some further advantage for his family. The Emperor was the only person who could advance the Farnese house in Italy; and, as he did not seem inclined to give them anything more, the Pope mixed himself up in the schemes of the different exiles from Milan, Florence, and Naples, who were plotting against the Spanish rule, and who hoped for help from France. He thus wavered between Spain and France, while secretly inclined to the French alliance. He made the Emperor angry by giving Parma and Piacenza, with the title of Duke, to his son, *Pier-Luigi*, for Charles wanted the Duchy for his son-in-law, Ottavio. The Pope added to the offence, for he took *Camerino* from Ottavio, and joined it to the States of the Church. He

did this to make up, in some degree, for the more important cities, Parma and Piacenza, which he had taken from the Church for the benefit of his son. Pier-Luigi was the head of all the different parties in Italy which were plotting against the Spanish power. It is almost certain that he helped to bring about an anti-Spanish outbreak at Genoa, called the *Conspiracy of the Fieschi*. When Andrea Doria settled the government of Genoa, he gave the chief power in the state into the hands of an oligarchy. As long as he was able to manage affairs, his will was strictly obeyed. When he became crippled by age and gout, his great nephew *Giannettino* tried to take his place in the State, but he was haughty in manner, and was much hated. The Genoese now began to be grieved that they had allowed their gratitude to Andrea Doria to blind them so far as to make it easy for him and for his nephew to shut them out from the management of their affairs. The discontented party was headed by *Gian-Luigi de' Fieschi*, Count of Lavagna and Lord of Pontremoli, an hereditary foe to the house of Doria. The Duke of Parma promised him his help, and the conspiracy was joined by the party of the Fregosi, and by the French faction. On January 2, 1547, Gian-Luigi gave a great banquet to a number of young Genoese nobles. He placed his servants at the doors with arms in their hands, and then made a speech to his guests, and told them his plans and bade them join him on peril of their lives. All joined him, some with goodwill, and some from fear. They surprised the city that night with cries of "Fiesco" and "Liberta!" Giannettino was slain in the streets, but the aged Andrea escaped. Meanwhile Gian-Luigi seized the galleys of the Dorias, and was about to join his victorious companions on land, when he fell over the side of a galley into the sea. He was clad in heavy armour; he sank, and was seen no more. The conspirators were left without a head, and the next day Andrea Doria came back without opposition, and took full vengeance for the death of his nephew. By mixing himself up in such plots as this, the Duke of Parma made himself much hated by the Emperor. The next year the Duke was assassinated at Piacenza, and it was believed that Fernando da Gonzaga, the Viceroy of Naples, was the cause of his death. The Emperor's troops seized on Piacenza. In return the Pope intrigued with Henry, King of France, and the anti-Spanish party in Italy. He now claimed the Duchy as Church property, rather than allow the Emperor to have it, and seized on Parma. This excited the anger of Ottavio, who declared that, if his grandfather would not give it up to him, he would get it by the help of his father-in-law the Emperor. The Pope died in 1549, in great anger and grief. He was succeeded by the Cardinal *del Monte*, who took the title of *Julius the Third*. The new Pope gave Parma back to Ottavio, who also afterwards received Piacenza from Philip of Spain. *Alessandro*, the son of Ottavio and of Margaret the daughter of the Emperor Charles, became the most famous leader of the armies of King Philip the Second. During the life of his father he was called *Prince of Parma*. He was made governor of the Netherlands by Philip, and after a long siege he took *Antwerp*, the strongest city of the States which had united to gain their freedom. On the death of his father in 1586, Alessandro succeeded to the Duchy. He left the government to others, and still remained in the service of the King. He took an active part in preparing the *Armada*, which was to have taken England in 1588. He was made head of the expedition, but the fleet of *Holland* and *Zeeland* kept him shut up in Nieuport and in Dunkirk while the English destroyed the fleet of Spain. The male descendants of Ottavio reigned over Parma and Piacenza as Dukes of Parma until 1731.

7. **War between Spain and France.**—The treaty of

Cambray was broken by Francis I., who could not give up his hope of regaining the Duchy of Milan. He made extravagant demands upon the Duke of Savoy, in right of his mother Louise, the Duke's sister, and invaded and overran his territory. The Duke turned for help to the Emperor. The Emperor came to the rescue, and carried the war into Provence, but was defeated before Avignon. The death of Francesco Sforza made Francis still more determined to press his claim. The Emperor made his son Philip, Duke of Milan. This step provoked Francis to send his army to overrun Savoy a second time, while his fleet, with the aid of *Barbarossa*, the Algerine corsair, sacked and burned the city of Nizza. Henry the Second, soon after he came to the throne, was engaged in a short war with England. In 1550, when he had made peace with England, he renewed the struggle with Charles. He helped Maurice, the Elector of Saxony, in his revolt against the Emperor, and took up the cause of Ottavio Farnese, who was struggling to regain Parma, and who had quarrelled with his father-in-law the Emperor. This war was decided north of the Alps, but it concerns Italy, for it was the cause of the fall of Siena.

8. **The Fall of Siena.**—When Piero Strozzi heard that his father Filippo had perished in the prison of Cosimo de' Medici, he set himself to avenge his death on Cosimo and on all the Spanish faction. He found an opportunity in the circumstances of Siena. Cosimo greedily desired to gain this city, which was nominally free, but had been forced to receive a Spanish garrison. The Spanish commander, *Don Juan de Luna*, was much hated, both because he and his men oppressed the people, and because the Sienese knew that he was likely to favour the plans of Cosimo for making the city his own. In 1547, the Sienese rose and turned out Don Juan and the party of the nobles, who were on the side of Cosimo. Another garrison under *Don Diego de Mendoza*

entered the city This general also gave great offence to the people by his severity. In 1552, when the war between the Emperor and Henry the Second had begun, the Sienese, with the help of some French mercenaries and a body of exiles, again rose against the Spanish soldiers, and, after some fighting, forced them to leave the city. This time the Sienese received a garrison from the King of France into their city. Piero Strozzi had served the French King with credit for some time, and he was now sent to Siena with the chief command. Cosimo had, as yet, remained almost neutral in the war. He was now aroused, for the coming of Piero stirred up the discontented party in Florence, and endangered his possession of *Piombino*. In 1554, Cosimo suddenly attacked Siena. He hired for his general *Gian-Giacopo de' Medici, Marquess of Marignano*, with an army of Italians, and he received some troops from the Emperor. The Marquess tried to take the city by surprise. He failed, and then formed a blockade. The towns and villages round Siena were attacked one by one, the country was wasted, and many who resisted were put to the sword by order of the Duke. Meanwhile Piero received several reinforcements from King Henry and the French party in Italy. In June he made a daring attack on the Duke's territory, and forced the Marquess to retreat in a skirmish at *Pescia*, near Pistoia. He expected to be reinforced by the French, and by his brother *Leone*, who was to attack the *Maremma* with a sea force. But the French did not come, and, instead of meeting his brother, Piero received the news of his death. He was therefore forced to retreat. This raid turned the Duke's army for a short time away from the walls of Siena, and enabled the people to get a few supplies. Piero received some help from France, and was joined by the French general *Blaise de Montluc*, who took the command of the garrison, while Piero conducted the war outside the city. In August, Piero was defeated in a pitched battle on the *Chiana*. After this defeat Siena was reduced to great straits. Everything which could possibly be eaten was sold at a high price. All the horses and dogs and other animals in the city were eaten up before the people or their French allies would yield. The city surrendered in April, 1555, after a siege of fifteen months. The garrison marched out with the honours of war. A large number of the Sienese went with them, and settled at Montalcino. An Imperial garrison entered Siena, and two years afterwards the Duke received the full sovereignty of the city. This war did terrible damage, not only to the territory of Siena, but also to the country round Florence. The sufferings of the people were very great. From Montalcino to Siena, and from Siena to Florence, it seemed as though no living soul were left; the rich land lay untilled and undrained for lack of inhabitants, and so it became a prey to pestilential fever. It is now at last being reclaimed, and this standing memorial of the cruelty and ambition of Duke Cosimo de' Medici is now likely to be removed by the energy and enterprise of the free Italian people.

9. **Pope Paul the Fourth and King Philip.**—The war between the Emperor and Henry the Second, of which the fall of Siena was a little incident, affected the whole of the West of Europe. As far as it concerned Italy, its results were upon the whole in favour of Charles. The French overran the Duchy of Savoy, but they were not able to gain a footing in the Duchy of Milan, and were driven out of Tuscany. They carried the war into Germany, and there they were completely successful. The Emperor was worn out and disappointed, and, in 1555, he gave up the Low Countries and the County of Burgundy to his son Philip, the husband of our Queen Mary. Philip already ruled over Milan, Sicily, and Naples, and used the title of *King of*

Jerusalem, as the successor of Frederic the Second, who joined it to the title of *King of Sicily*. In 1556, Charles gave up to Philip the crown of Spain, with all the dominions in the New World which were joined to it. The next year Ferdinand, King of Hungary and Bohemia, the brother of Charles, succeeded him in Germany with the title of *Emperor elect*. After a short break the war still went on, but now it was a war between the Kings of France and Spain, and not between the King of France and the Emperor. In Italy the French found an ally in *Gian-Piero Caraffa*, who was chosen Pope in 1555, and who took the title of *Paul the Fourth*. Pope Paul hated the Spaniards, and wished to see the French back again in Naples and Milan. He was helped in his plans by his nephews, by the Duke of Ferrara, and by Piero Strozzi and the Tuscan exiles. He stirred up the war afresh by making a league with Henry against the power of Philip in Naples. This scheme was seconded by *Francis, Duke of Guise*, grandson of René the Second, Duke of Lorraine. The Duke hoped to make himself King of Naples, as his ancestor Charles of Anjou had done. He entered Italy and was received at Rome in 1557. He marched on towards Naples, and besieged *Civitella*, but he was entirely out-manœuvred by the Spanish Viceroy, the Duke of Alva, and was forced to retreat northwards. In the Papal territory the war was carried on by *Marc' Antonio Colonna* on behalf of Spain, with some German Free Companies, and on behalf of the Pope by *Giulio Orsini* and the Swiss mercenaries. There, as in the South, the cause of Spain was victorious. The Pope was obliged to submit, but he received back from the devout Spaniard all the towns which he had lost. It was to strengthen his party in Italy during this war that King Philip restored Piacenza to Ottavio Farnese, and gave the full sovereignty of Siena to Duke Cosimo. The war was really decided in the north of Europe by the defeats of the French at *St. Quentin* and at *Gravelines*. The French King was forced to sign a treaty with Philip called the *Peace of Câteau-Cambresis*, by which, amongst other concessions, he gave up Savoy and Piedmont, with the exception of Turin and four other towns, and withdrew his troops from Montferrat, Tuscany and Corsica.

10. **Religious Movements in Italy.**—The change in religious thought which took place in Germany, and to some extent, though in a different shape, in France, in the beginning of the sixteenth century, found no abiding place in Italy generally, though for a time it exercised considerable influence there. In Italy men lived too near to the Pope to think of making a revolt against him, as was done elsewhere. His presence was, it seemed to them, necessary to the greatness of their land, for it still made Rome the Capital of the World. His position as a temporal prince made his existence as much a given point in Italian politics as the existence of a king in Naples. He was, in nearly every case, an Italian by nation, and this flattered his countrymen and prevented them from having the same feelings about him as Englishmen or Germans had, to whom he was a stranger, and often a political enemy. At the same time the worldly lives of the Popes and of many of the Cardinals, and the scoffing and almost heathenish spirit of the Court of Rome at the beginning of the sixteenth century affected the Italians far more than it affected those who lived at a distance. While therefore nearly all agreed in thinking that no evil could justify men in separating themselves from the Church, many longed for something purer and better than they found in the Church of their own day. Men began to think and to read about religion for themselves. Not a few in Venice, in Padua, and even in Rome itself, adopted the Lutheran doctrine of *justification by faith*. Before long there were some persons of position in almost every town in Italy who were more or less in favour

of a reformation either in matters of faith or in the lives of the Pope and the clergy. Cardinal *Gasparo Contarini*, a noble and a philosopher of Venice, Vittoria Colonna, the widow of Pescara, and many others of high birth and intellect, without leaving the Church, held doctrines which were characteristic of the German Protestants. An attempt was made to check the spread of Reformed opinions, and to remedy some of the evils which existed within the Church, by holding a Council. This plan was looked upon with great favour by the Emperor Charles the Fifth, for the peace of the Empire was much disturbed by religious differences. The Council met at Trent, a bishop's see on the frontiers of Italy and Germany, in 1545. It reformed some abuses, and at the same time made definitions about matters of faith which narrowed the basis of the Catholic Church. Many were definitely shut outside her boundaries who held the new doctrines, but who had not yet separated themselves from her. Thus the breach between religious parties in Italy was really made by Rome. The Council went on, with some breaks, for nearly twenty years, but it was much hindered by the wars between France and Spain, and by the hatred of Italians to both parties.

11. **The Jesuits.**—While some Italians were led by the abuses which existed in the Church to seek into and adopt reformed doctrines, many were influenced by the same causes in an exactly opposite way. Several new religious orders were founded in Italy, for the special purpose of reforming the secular clergy or parish priests, and not as in older times, only to take people out of the world. The greatest help which the Church of Rome received at this time of need came from the Order of the Jesuits. The founder of this Society or Order was *Ignatius Loyola*. He was a Spaniard, and had borne arms against the French. He and a few companions determined to offer themselves to

the Pope to serve him as he should direct. Ignatius took priest's orders at Venice, and began to preach at Vicenza, on his way to Rome. In 1540, with the permission of Paul the Third, he formed the Society of Jesus. The distinguishing features of this new order were devotion to the Pope and unquestioning obedience to authority. Next after Spain, Italy was the country in which the Jesuits had the greatest success. They helped to crush the new opinions which had begun to gain ground, and to uphold the Papal power. They worked with untiring energy and self-devotion. At their bidding the Church was reformed in its Head and its members. The Popes ceased to be heathenish voluptuaries, and became zealous and often austere men. In every city and village of Catholic Europe faithlessness to the interests of the Church was reproved in priests and people. The Jesuits presided over schools and colleges, over the confessional, the pulpit, and the press. They taught Christianity in the remotest parts of the world. There was no place where there was not a Jesuit, and wherever they were they seemed to be natives of the country. They were never lazy, never unfaithful, and never daunted by danger or persecution. They laboured without ceasing to spread the power of the Church of Rome. In this all their policy was summed up, and, because the welfare of that Church seemed to demand it, they have been the enemies of freedom and progress, and have helped to uphold the foreign rulers of Italy. In accordance with the advice of Ignatius Loyola, Paul the Third set up in Rome a system of religious courts, spies, police, judges, and executioners called the *Inquisition*, somewhat after the model of the institution which had been regulated by *St. Dominic*. Persecution and terror began to spread throughout Italy. In each different state the ecclesiastics held a court, and called upon the civil power to help them. The Reformed opinions had spread rapidly among the middle class, especially in Naples. Some of those who were suspected of heresy took shelter in England or Germany, or in the Protestant cities and lands of the Swiss; others suffered the loss of their goods, torture, and death. In Rome, and in most other places, heretics were burned; in Venice they were drowned; in Calabia they were massacred. The new opinions were completely stamped out. They were, however, still held by the *Waldenses* of Piedmont. This sect is said to have taken its name from *Peter Waldo*, a merchant of Lyons, who lived at the end of the twelfth century, but it may have existed before that time. It is more likely that Peter received the nickname of Waldo, when he adopted the opinions of the Waldenses. It is hard to say how the name arose. Perhaps it is akin to *Valais*, *Walloon* and *Wales*, and signifies that the Waldenses were foreigners to the German dwellers in the Alps. The Waldenses of Piedmont believe that their forefathers held a purer faith than those sectaries on the Provençal side of the mountains who were called *Albigenses;* that they read the Bible in their own tongue, and from it learned lessons of purity and truth. They dwelt for the most part in the valleys of the Western Alps. By the middle of the sixteenth century they had much increased in number. Emmanuel Filibert, Duke of Savoy, found these Waldenses politically troublesome. For this reason, and because he was urged to suppress them by France and Spain, he made war upon them. After a short struggle the Duke allowed them to follow their own worship within certain boundaries of territory. In the rest of Italy the old religion became as strong as ever, and was defended and spread by the great spiritual army founded by Ignatius Loyola. The work of reformation was carried on in the North by *Carlo Borromeo*. This remarkable man was the nephew of Pope Paul the Fourth. Instead of making this relationship a means of temporal advancement, he only used it as a means of doing good. He helped the Pope in his business, and raised the character of his ecclesiastical government. After a time he gave up all his offices and dignities, save the Archbishoprick of Milan. He threw himself entirely into the work of his Province. He held constant visitations, and enforced order and discipline. He was untiring in his spiritual work, in ordaining priests, in celebrating the Mass and in consecrations. He was a pattern of purity and devotion, and the people of Milan and the surrounding country were much influenced by his holiness and labours. He has received the honour of canonization. The revival of religion exercised an evil influence on Italian literature and art. The epic of Tasso, who ranks third after Dante and Ariosto, illustrates how fully poetry became the handmaid of religion. Science was discouraged lest it should seem to contradict revelation, and Galileo the astronomer, who lived in Florence during the reign of Cosimo the Second, about 1610, was twice brought before the Inquisition to answer for his discoveries. The Inquisition assumed the censorship of the Press, and a list of forbidden books was put forth by the middle of the sixteenth century. The printers were driven out of Italy. The same Court interfered with teaching by word of mouth, especially at the University of Pisa. Literature disappeared before the Inquisition. Nor was art in a much better state. It was no longer employed either in seeking after and representing the beauties which are to be drawn out from Nature, or in copying the masterpieces of the old world; it returned to religious subjects, and a religious mode of treating them. A new style of painting, that of the School of the Caracci, found its home at Bologna in the latter part of the sixteenth century. It is marked by eclecticism, anatomical accuracy and the force of religious sentiment.

12. **Wars with the Infidels.**—The war between France and Spain not only gave Italy up as a prey to Christian

armies, but also exposed her coasts to the attacks of the Infidels. Francis the First sent to the Sultan Solyman to help him against Charles. The Turkish power reached its greatest height under this Sultan, and this was especially owing to the successes of his navy. His most famous commander in the Mediterranean was *Khaireddin Pasha*, called by Europeans *Barbarossa*, who made *Algiers*, which he took from Spain, the head-quarters of his fleet. He constantly ravaged the coasts of Italy, and carried off into slavery many captives of both sexes. He defeated Andrea Doria, who was then commanding the Genoese fleet for the Emperor, and pillaged the *Riviere*. He sacked Friuli and Reggio, and other towns on the Neapolitan coasts. He defeated the fleets of the Emperor and of Venice off *Prevesa*, and pillaged Corfu and the islands of Venice in the Adriatic. In alliance with the French he took Nizza and burnt it, but was forced to retreat from before the castle by the approach of the Spanish army. During the latter part of the reign of Solyman he was at peace with Venice. Solyman was succeeded by his son Selim, who had his father's ambition without his abilities. He set his heart upon the conquest of the isle of *Cyprus*, which belonged to Venice, and, in 1570, he sent his fleet against it. The island was bravely defended. The Turks took *Nicosia* by storm, and put part of the inhabitants to the sword, and carried off the rest into slavery. *Famagosta* was strongly fortified, and was regularly besieged. The town held out until its walls were almost in ruins, and the defenders were brought to the last extremity of famine. Then, in August 1571, the Venetian commander, *Marc' Antonio Bragadino*, was forced to make terms. The Turkish leader, *Mustapha*, promised that the besieged should be ta' en in safety to Candia. On the faith of this promise the city was surrendered. The infidel broke his promise; he slew part of the garrison, and sent the rest to the galleys. The unfortunate commander was tortured for ten days, and then flayed alive. The Venetians were utterly unable to check the advance of the Turks without foreign aid. The Spanish fleet, which was expected in May, never came until after the island had fallen, and the Venetians were daily fearing to see the Turkish ships enter the Lagoon. The allied fleet, which had been gathered by the exertions of Pope *Pius the Fifth*, met at Messina. It was made up of seventy Spanish galleys, with six belonging to the Knights of Malta, and three sent by the Duke of Savoy; these were under the command of *Don John of Austria*, natural son of Charles the Fifth, who also had the chief command of the whole fleet. Besides these there were the ships of the Pope under *Marc' Antonio Colonna*, and a large Venetian force under *Sebastiano Veniero*. The allies fell in with the Turkish ships outside the *Gulf of Lepanto*, and gave them battle on October 7, 1571. The loss on both sides was heavy. The Christian fleet was entirely victorious. This victory possibly delivered a great part of Christendom, it certainly delivered Italy, and especially Venice, from the infidels. The allies did not follow up their success, and, in 1573, the Venetians were forced to make peace. They gave up their claim on Cyprus, and paid a large tribute to the Sultan, so that it seemed as though the Turks and not the Christians had been the conquerors of Lepanto.

13. **The Counts of Savoy.**—The only commonwealths which were left in Italy at the peace of Câteau Cambresis were *Venice, Genoa, Lucca,* and the little *San Marino*. These were under the influence of a few great families, and Venice alone was of any importance. The King of Spain was master of the Kingdoms of Naples and Sicily, and of the island of Sardinia. Genoa was now secured in her possession of Corsica; but both she and Lucca were in all but name the subjects of the same King. The Duke of Ferrara

had in vain tried to shake off his yoke. The Spaniard had made the Medici Grand Dukes of Tuscany, and established the Farnesi in Piacenza and Parma Pope Paul the Fourth had learned how useless it was to try to thwart Spain, and his immediate successors had no wish to do so. The King of Spain was by far the greatest power in Italy, and after him came the Pope. Meanwhile a power was growing up in the north-west corner of the land which was destined after three centuries to give freedom and union to the whole, and which had already begun to be the most truly Italian state in the peninsula. This was Savoy. When *Rudolf the Third*, King of *Burgundy* or *Arles*, died, in 1032, his kingdom became joined to the Empire. The nobles of Burgundy thus became subjects of the Emperor Conrad. The most famous of these was *Humbert*, called the Count of Burgundy. His son married *Adelaide*, daughter of the Count of Turin. By this marriage the frontiers of Burgundy and Lombardy came to be subject to one family, that of the *Counts of Maurienne*, who became *Counts of Savoy*. This family by degrees lost its Burgundian or Transalpine possessions, but kept gaining new ones on the Italian side of the mountains. In the thirteenth century the House of Savoy played a conspicuous part in the history of the courts of Europe. A daughter of one of its Counts married Raymond Béranger, last Count of Provence, and became the mother of *Margaret*, Queen of Lewis the Ninth of France, of *Eleanor*, Queen of Henry the Third of England, of *Sanchia*, Queen of Richard King of the Romans, and of *Beatrix*, Queen of Charles of Sicily. By the marriage of Eleanor with King Henry her family came in for a large share of the wealth and honours of England, and her brother Boniface was made Archbishop of Canterbury. Though this family did well abroad, yet for a long time it was not so successful at home. At the end of the thirteenth century two younger branches each obtained a share of its dominions.

Thus one line ruled in Savoy, another in Piedmont, and a third over the northern shores of Lake Leman. The House of Savoy was very often at war with its neighbours on the north-west and north-east, with the *Dauphins* of Vienne, and with the House of *Habsburg*. When the dominions of the Dauphins were purchased by Philip the Sixth of France, the Counts of Savoy were forced to make peace in 1355, and thus their hopes of extending their dominions on that side came to an end. On the north-east they tried to extend their boundary at the expense of the lords of *Zähringen* and *Kyburg*, and were successful in Vaud and in the land which afterwards became the Lower Vallais. When *Rudolf of Habsburg* succeeded to the dominions of these lords, and even after his election to the Empire, the Counts of Savoy were able to stand their ground with the help of Bern. At the death of Rudolf their power was much strengthened by the war between his son Albert and Adolf of Nassau. By the middle of the fourteenth century, however, the German people began to check the conquests and wars of the Dukes and Counts who were treating them as their property. The men of Vallais rose against their Bishop and turned him out, in spite of *Amadeus*, the Red Count of Savoy, and, after peace was made, the men of the higher valleys, in 1416, took the Val d'Ossola from his House. Thus Savoy was prevented by the Old League from making conquests on the north-east. While the Counts of Savoy were thus hemmed in by the French King and by the German League on the north-west and north-east, they were gradually getting back the territory on the south which they had lost by division, and adding more to it. They were losing in what had once been Burgundy, but were gaining in Italy. The three powers which tried to check Savoy on the south and east at the beginning of the fourteenth century were the Marquesses of *Montferrat* and of *Saluzzo* and the Princes of *Achaia*, who were a branch of the house of Savoy. These princes reigned at Turin and Pinerolo; they inherited their eastern titles of *Princes of Achaia and Morea* from Philip of Savoy, who joined in the Latin conquest of Constantinople. Besides these powers the Count of Anjou, as the heir of Raymond Béranger, ruled over Nizza, and the Visconti had gained considerable power over Vercelli and Novara. In the war between the Angevin houses of Naples and Provence, Nizza separated herself from Provence. She joined, first Charles of Durazzo, and then his son Ladislas, and on the death of Ladislas gave herself, in 1388, to the Count of Savoy. *Amadeus the Eighth*, Count of Savoy, and his kinsman the Prince of Achaia, conquered Saluzzo; and by the death of the Prince, which happened soon after, Amadeus succeeded to his territory. By an alliance with Filippo Maria Visconti, Amadeus gained Vercelli, and soon after forced the Marquess of Montferrat to give up Chivasso. Thus by the middle of the fifteenth century the Counts of Savoy gained an Italian state, while their advance was checked beyond the Alps.

14. **The Dukes of Savoy.**—Amadeus the Eighth, who succeeded in adding so much Italian territory to Savoy, received the title of *Duke* from the Emperor Sigismund. He had hoped to have gained a larger piece of the Duchy of Milan when Gian-Galeazzo died, but Filippo Maria was too strong for him to fight against, and he had to be contented with the small increase which the Duke gave him. His hopes were again raised at the death of the Duke, and he sent some help to the people of Milan when they tried to set up self-government. His schemes were checked by Francesco Sforza, and, though he seized on Pavia and Novara, he had to give them up again. Amadeus after a while gave up the Duchy to his son. In 1440, he was chosen Pope by electors appointed by the Council of Basel. Then again after a while he gave up the Papacy. His son *Lewis* married *Anne* of

Lusignan, the daughter of the King of Cyprus; their second son, *Lewis*, married *Charlotte*, daughter and heiress of King John of Cyprus. Lewis and Charlotte were crowned King and Queen of Cyprus, but were driven out of the island by an illegitimate son of King John. Queen Charlotte on her death left her rights to the reigning Duke of Savoy, and from that time the Dukes of Savoy claimed the title of King of Cyprus. They fought with the Venetians for this empty honour: even after the island had been taken by the Turks. After the abdication of Amadeus the power of his house decreased, for his successors lacked his abilities. In the war between Charles the Bold and the Confederates, the House of Savoy lost some lands north of the lake of Geneva. The Marquess of Montferrat attached himself to Milan as a defence against Savoy; and the widowed Marchioness of Saluzzo submitted herself to Charles the Eighth of France. The weakness of Savoy was increased by the changeful policy of Duke *Charles the Third*. Instead of striving to keep his Italian territories safe amidst the wars and combinations which followed the invasion of Charles of France, he mixed himself up in these changes. He hoped to gain more, and lost what he had before. He refused to learn the lesson which the Confederates of the League had given to his ancestor, and tried to extend his territory to the north-east. The free Imperial city of Geneva had long been closely connected with the Dukes of Savoy. Since the time of Amadeus the Eighth, its Prince-Bishops had been either members of their House or its firm allies. One of these Bishops gave up all the temporal power of his see to Duke Charles. The Duke without delay entered the city and began to exercise in his own name the authority which, though it had been really his before, had been exercised in the name of the Bishop. This change excited great wrath in the city. The republican party were helped by the men of Bern and Freiburg. The cause of the Duke was upheld by the nobles of Vaud. The quarrel was embittered by difference of faith. The citizens of Geneva adopted the new doctrines, while the inhabitants of Vaud rejected them. In this war *Bonnivard*, one of the leaders of the Republic, was taken prisoner, and kept for six years in the Castle of Chillon. His sufferings have been made famous by Lord *Byron* in the poem called *The Prisoner of Chillon*. King Francis the First abetted the spread of the Reformed Faith to annoy the Emperor, and quietly helped the republican allies. The war was decided in 1536. Savoy finally lost the rest of her lands north of the lake of Geneva. The Catholic nobles of Vaud were crushed. The independence of Geneva was secured. Thus the Duke's power was cut short on the north. Immediately after this the French invaded Savoy, and took away a great part of the Duke's dominions. Savoy and Piedmont now became one of the theatres of the war between France and Spain, and when the Duke Charles died his son *Emmanuel Filibert* was left a Duke without a Duchy. He took service under his cousin, King Philip of Spain, and held the chief command in his army at the battle of St. Quentin, in which the French were completely defeated. The defeat of the French in the Low Countries led to the Peace of Câteau Cambresis. The interests of the Duke were neglected by this treaty, for the French kept Saluzzo. They had to give up the other possessions of the Duke, with the important exceptions of Turin and four other fortresses, which were to be occupied for three more years. Meanwhile Spain was to keep Asti and Vercelli, but Philip gave the latter to his cousin at once. This treaty made the Duke again a real sovereign, though it did not give him back all that was his. At the same time a marriage was arranged between the Duke and Margaret, sister of King Henry the Second. This marriage was, after long delay, the cause of the restoration of all his Italian territory, except Saluzzo, which was kept by France until it was reconquered in 1588. From the reign of Emmanuel Filibert, the Dukes of Savoy and their descendants became Italians instead of successors to the old Burgundians. From that time Italian became the language of the Court and of the Government. He made Turin the capital of his Duchy instead of Chambéry. Piedmont, and not Savoy, was the chief state in his dominions. Thus, after so many changes, the Dukes of Savoy finally became Italian, though as yet they possessed Savoy, Nizza, Bresse, and other territories to the north-west of the Alps.

CHAPTER X.

ITALY DIVIDED.

Savoy gains Saluzzo, and loses on the West of the Alps; the French shut out of Italy (1)—*restlessness of Duke Charles Emmanuel; his wars with Spain* (2)—*Ferrara and Urbino added to the States of the Church; the Papal government* (3)—*Venice and Pope Paul the Fifth* (4)—*the decline of Venice* (5)—*decline of the power of Spain; insurrection in Naples and Sicily* (6)—*the war of the Spanish Succession; the Treaty of Utrecht; the Duke of Savoy becomes King of Sicily* (7)—*the Succession to Parma; the King of Sicily becomes King of Sardinia* (8)—*the war of the Polish Succession; the treaty of Vienna; the power of Spain again established in South Italy* (9)—*the war of the Austrian Succession; the revolt of Genoa* (10)—*the Peace of Aix-la-Chapelle; the independent sovereignties of Italy; the suppression of the Jesuit order* (11)—*the French Republican invasion* (12)—*Buonaparte King of Italy; his fall* (13)—*the Congress of Vienna* (14).

1. **Savoy and France.**—The invasion of Italy by Charles the Eighth of France led to the slavery of Italy under the Emperor Charles the Fifth, and his Austrian successors on

the throne of Spain. From the fall of Siena on to the nineteenth century, Italy can scarcely be said to have existed at all except as a geographical expression. Italians still ruled over certain parts of the land, but they had the vices without the virtues of their nation, and reigned more as the dependants of foreign sovereigns than as independent princes. During the seventeenth, the eighteenth, and the early part of the nineteenth centuries, Italy was made the scene of wars in which her people had no interest, and was divided by treaties which brought her no good. This chapter will be chiefly taken up with these divisions. The wars of Europe which brought them about will only be noticed so far as they affected Italy, and especially as they affected the Dukes of Savoy. With the history of their house are connected the deliverance of Italy from the foreigner and its union into one State. On the death of Emmanuel Filibert (1580), his son, Charles Emmanuel, succeeded to the Duchy. He was full of schemes for extending his dominions, and set his heart first of all on the recovery of Saluzzo. He married *Catherine*, sister of King Philip the Second, and was thus sure of the support of Spain. His ambition and his Spanish alliance made the rest of the Italian Powers uneasy, more especially as they were for the most part tired of the bondage in which Philip kept them, and looked to France as the best means of keeping his power within bounds. This was especially the case with Ferdinand, Grand Duke of Tuscany, who was drawn towards France by the influence of his cousin, Catherine de' Medici, the Queen Mother. France, however, was torn by the *Religious Wars* between the *League* of the Catholics headed by the Duke of Guise, and the Huguenots, headed by the King of Navarre. The Duke of Guise nominally commanded the army of King Henry the Third. He really acted as though he was King himself, and after a while the King had him assassinated. While France was in this distracted state, in 1588, the Duke of Savoy made a sudden inroad on Saluzzo, and easily conquered it. The murder of the Duke of Guise gave rise to a war between the Catholic League and the King, who was now upheld by the Huguenots. The Duke of Savoy joined the League, he invaded Provence, and at the same time laid siege to Geneva. His hopes were flattered by the Leaguers, and, when the King was assassinated in 1589, there were some who upheld his claim to the throne of France, which he made in right of his mother, Margaret, daughter of Francis the First. Henry of Navarre, however, secured the throne. A long war followed. The French drove the Duke out of Provence. The famous Huguenot leader Lesdiguières defeated him and the Spaniards. The Waldenses revolted, and, in 1601, the Duke was forced to make the *Treaty of Lyons*. He was allowed to keep Saluzzo, but in exchange had to give up *Bresse*, *Bugey*, and the *Pays de Gex*. The cession of Saluzzo caused great annoyance to the Grand Duke of Tuscany and the rest of the French party, because it shut the French entirely out of the Peninsula, and gave, as it were, the keys of Italy on the French side into the hands of the Duke of Savoy. The exchange was a loss to the Duke, and put an end to his hopes of conquest in Provence. It was another and a most important step in the process by which the Duchy was turned into a purely Italian State.

2. **Savoy and Spain.**—Charles Emmanuel thought that he had been badly treated by Spain, because he had been left to make what terms he could with France, and his interests had been neglected by the *Treaty of Vervins*, which had been made between the two kingdoms. His discontent was soon increased. The Duke had married his daughter to Francesco, Duke of Mantua and Montferrat. Francesco died, leaving a daughter. His brother Ferdinand succeeded him. The Duke of Savoy, as guardian of the heiress,

invaded Montferrat. He was ordered by Philip the Third to evacuate the Duchy, and he went to war with Spain. After this quarrel was ended another question arose, which gave the Duke an opportunity of trying to push forward his schemes for gaining territory at the expense of Spain. A religious war broke out in the Valtellina, which had been occupied by the Leagues of the Grisons in 1512. Philip the Third, and his successor Philip the Fourth, were anxious to get hold of the Valtellina, in order to establish a communication between Austria and their Italian dominions, and they therefore sent help to the inhabitants, who were Catholics. On the other hand, in order to thwart the schemes of Spain, Lewis the Thirteenth of France, the Venetians, and the Duke of Savoy made an alliance with the Grisons. In the course of the war the Duke made an attack on Genoa, but he was forced to retreat, because the German and Spanish allies invaded his Italian territory. Although the Genoese joined with the Spaniards against the Duke, there were many amongst them who were anxious for change. The narrow oligarchy which had been set up by Andrea Doria, gave great offence to a large class of citizens who had risen to riches and social position, and yet were shut out from all share in the government. One of these men, *Giulio Cesare Vachero*, a rich merchant, made a plot with several other men of the same rank to seize on the public Palace, slay the nobles of the older families, and set up a new kind of government under the protection of the Duke of Savoy. The plot was found out, and the conspirators were put to death. When the direct male line of the house of Gonzaga came to an end in 1627, the Duke again seized Montferrat. This time he was opposed by France. Mantua and Montferrat passed to Charles, Duke of Nevers, who married the daughter of Francesco da Gonzaga. Savoy gained some places in Montferrat. On the other hand, the French power was again established south of the Alps in Pinerolo.

3. **The States of the Church.**—After King Henry the Fourth had gained the crown of France, he was willing to keep on good terms with the See of Rome, if he could do so without hurting himself. He accordingly helped Pope *Clement the Eighth* in his designs upon the Duchy of *Ferrara*. When *Alfonso of Este*, Duke of Ferrara, died without children in 1597, he left his dominions, consisting of Ferrara, Modena, and Reggio, to his kinsman Cesare. Pope Clement immediately claimed Ferrara as a fief of the Holy See, and the King of France offered to help him enforce the claim. The King of Spain took the part of the new Duke, but Philip the Second was now old and in bad health, and would not interfere actively. The Pope took possession of Ferrara with a high hand, and the Duke, without striking a single blow, retired to Modena, which was a fief of the Empire. The family of Este continued to reign in Modena until 1794. During the reign of Urban VIII. (1623-44), the Holy See was still further enriched by the addition of the Duchy of Urbino, which became a lapsed fief upon the failure of the line of *Giovanni della Rovere*, who had married the heiress of the *Montefeltri*. The States of the Church now extended over a rich and beautiful territory, which at the end of the sixteenth century produced much more than the inhabitants could consume. The way in which these states were governed varied somewhat with the characters of the different Popes, but during the sixteenth and seventeenth centuries their condition on the whole grew continually worse. When Julius the Second conquered the cities of Romagna, each received some sort of charter of liberty; but, as almost every Pope who reigned for some years had secular designs, which he wanted to carry out, these rights were disregarded. The Popes levied taxes on alum, salt, flour, and even on meat. Gregory XIII. (1572-85) pushed all his rights to the utmost, and ruined Ancona by his heavy custom dues. Old claims were revived;

agitation and violence filled the Romagna. The central government was weak, and all things fell into disorder. His successor Sixtus V. sternly repressed the disturbers of the peace. Unhappily he increased the imports and burthened his revenues with debt. The Popes always wanted money, and, for the most part, treated their dominions as a selfish landlord would treat his private estate. The tendency of their rule has been to check reform, to blight the fruitfulness of the land, and to crush free thought and liberal education. The unhealthiness of the *Campagna* is partly the result of the destitution to which their system of taxation and their general bad management brought the labouring class. Some of the earlier Popes made efforts to drain the waste land, and bring it under cultivation. The first serious attempt of this kind was not made until the reign of *Pius the Sixth* (1785-1800), when the evil had grown very great. His example was followed by his successors, *Pius the Seventh* and *Leo the Twelfth*, but their plans failed for want of money.

4. **Venice and Pope Paul V.**—The Venetians upheld Henry the Fourth in his struggle with the League, and found his alliance useful in a quarrel which they had with Pope *Paul the Fifth*. The Venetians never allowed the Pope to meddle much in their ecclesiastical government. No Archbishop dwelt within their walls to vie with the Doge in splendour or authority. Their chief ecclesiastic was no mere Archbishop, he was a *Patriarch*, like the Patriarch of Rome, though he acknowledged the supremacy of the Pope. He dwelt first at Aquileia, and afterwards at Grado; and thus, while his position was a source of pride to the Venetians, he was shut out from taking part in their politics. During the time in which the Popes were foremost in the political intrigues of Italy, the lofty spiritual pretensions of the Papacy were kept in the background. The Popes used excommunications and interdicts against their enemies, but it was against

those who endangered their temporal power, rather than against offenders in spiritual matters. The schismatical Council of Pisa was the last quarrel about ecclesiastical matters which had taken place in Italy, and even this had its rise in purely political questions. During the latter part of the sixteenth century the Jesuits insisted on the supremacy of the Pope, and the consequent exemption of the clergy from other authority. These pretensions were put forward by *Cardinal Bellarmino*, and other ecclesiastical writers, at the beginning of the seventeenth century. They were received with no favour by the Venetians. In the early part of the sixteenth century Venice was famed for her printing-presses, and especially for the well-known types of *Aldo Manuzio*. The restrictions which the Popes laid on the publication of books injured, and at last drove away the Venetian printers. In 1605, *Cardinal Borghese* was chosen Pope, and took the title of *Paul the Fifth*. He held the most exalted ideas of the greatness of his office, and of the claims of the Church. He soon had some disputes with the Republic concerning the boundaries of his States, and, being angry at the independent tone of the Venetians, he began to interfere in their ecclesiastical matters. He claimed to manage the *tithes*, which had always been regulated by the State, and to be the supreme judge in all matters which concerned ecclesiastical persons or causes. These claims were resisted by the Senate. This body was upheld in its decision by *Fra Paolo Sarpi*, an eminent theologian and lawyer of Venice. The Pope laid the Republic under an interdict. The Senate took vigorous measures to make the sentence ineffectual, and threatened to hang any priest who acted upon it. The Jesuits tried to temporize. They offered to perform the ordinary services, but refused to celebrate the Mass. Neither the Pope nor the Senate would have any such half obedience, and for the first, but by no means the last time, the Jesuits were forced to leave a State of which they were unfaithful subjects. The Republic hoped that Henry the Fourth of France, and James the First of England, would uphold her. Henry, however, refused to act against the Pope lest he should offend his Catholic subjects. James, though he would not go to war for such a cause, used his influence in favour of Venice. Henry made peace between the two parties. The Venetians gave way as regards the power of the Pope over ecclesiastics, though they managed to veil their submission. The Pope took off the interdict. The Venetians, nevertheless, steadily refused to let the Jesuits come back again, and so far "St. Mark triumphed over St. Peter."

5. **The Decline of Venice.**—Venice took no part in general Italian politics after the war in which she helped Duke Charles Emmanuel against Spain. In the early part of the seventeenth century she freed the Adriatic from the fierce pirates who infested it. They were called *Uscocchi*, from a Slavic word meaning *runaways*. They seem originally to have been Bulgarians by race, but their numbers were kept up by the offscourings of all nations. In 1645 the Republic began a war with the Turks, which lasted till 1669, when, after a gallant defence, *Candia* was taken and *Crete* was lost. In 1684, roused by the success of *John Sobieski*, Venice again ventured on war. She made alliance with the Emperor Leopold and the Poles, and her general, *Francesco Morosini*, conquered the whole of Peloponnêsos. But, in 1715, when he was dead, she lost her new conquest. Thus she was bereft of almost all her share in the Eastern Empire, save the *Ionian Islands*. Her war with the Infidels, which had gone on more or less for five hundred years, ended with the *Peace of Passarowitz* in 1718. Venice took no share in the great wars of the eighteenth century; it was a period of decline and social disorder in the Republic. The success of the Ottoman Turks cut the Venetians off from the trade of the

Levant, and hindered their trade through Egypt and the Red Sea. The discovery of the passage round the *Cape of Good Hope*, and the maritime greatness of England and Spain, checked the import overland of the wealth of the East. The strict oligarchy of Venice, which had supplied her with leaders and had made her famous in old times, failed to meet the needs of modern days. Her public debt rapidly increased, luxury was unchecked, and pleasure was made the chief business of life. The privileged class of nobles lost all nobility, save that of birth. Its members became sunk in helpless indolence and in vice; some managed public gaming-tables, and some begged in the streets for alms, when their own vices, or those of their fathers, had left them penniless. Nobles and people alike were at the mercy of the Council of Ten, which was valued and preserved as a check on the numerous rulers of the State. The secrecy of this Council enabled it to crush conspiracies, when those who were engaged in them thought that all was secure. In this way it defeated an obscure conspiracy which was made by the Viceroy of Naples, the Governor of Milan, and the Spanish Ambassador at Venice in 1618, which seems to have had for its object the sack of Venice, the overthrow of the power of Spain, and the accession of the Viceroy to the throne of Naples. The plot was revealed to the Council, and all on whom the slightest suspicion rested and who were in the city, save the ambassador, were quietly put to death without public trial.

6. **Decline of Spain. Insurrections.**—In the early part of the seventeenth century, *Cardinal Richelieu*, the minister of Lewis the Thirteenth of France, set himself to humble the Austrian successors of Charles the Fifth, both in Spain and Germany. The French cause was taken up by the Regent of Savoy, *Christina*, the daughter of Henry the Fourth. The Princes of the ducal family upheld the cause of Spain,

and a civil war broke out which had no lasting results. The greatness of France was marked by the *Peace of Westphalia*, which was made between the Emperor and the States of Germany, France, and Sweden, in 1648. The war with Spain went on until the *Treaty of the Pyrenees* in 1659. By this treaty France still kept Pinerolo. Though the Italian subjects of Spain were not able to take much advantage of her weakness, two insurrections were made in the South, which were connected with these wars. The Habsburg kings of Spain looked upon their Italian dominions simply as an inexhaustible treasury. Ferdinand and Charles the Fifth had both promised that no new taxes should be levied in the Kingdom of Naples without the consent of the Neapolitan Parliament, which consisted of nobles and people. The Viceroy of Philip IV. did not summon the Parliament, yet he taxed the most common necessaries of life, and thus greatly oppressed the poor. At last, in 1647, a tax on fruit, which seems to have been almost the only sort of food yet untaxed, roused the poor of Naples. They were headed by a young fisherman of Amalfi, named *Tommaso* or *'Mas Aniello*. They burned the Custom-house, and forced the Viceroy, the Duke of Arcos, to take shelter in the Castle of *St. Elmo*. At the same time an insurrection was made at *Palermo* against the Viceroy of Sicily, which added to the danger of Naples. The Duke of Arcos made terms with the people, but deceived them with false promises. At the same time he gained over the upper classes by telling them that the populace would be revenged on them, as well as on the Spaniards. He succeeded, after one failure, in getting 'Mas Aniello assassinated, and then the outbreak subsided for a while. In August the people rose again. *Don John of Austria*, natural son of King Philip the Fourth, came to restore order. He was forced to draw off his men after two days of street fighting. But the Neapolitans could not form a government for themselves. They seemed helpless without 'Mas Aniello, in whom they had believed with an almost childish faith, for they looked on him as a saint and a miracle-worker, just as our forefathers looked on Earl Simon of Leicester. They next put all their trust in a certain *Gennaro Annese*. By his advice, they sent for help to the *Duke of Guise*, who came readily, hoping to regain the possessions of the House of Anjou, from which he was descended. But the Neapolitans wanted a protector, and not another foreign master. Gennaro found himself set aside by the Duke, and in his anger he betrayed the city to Don John. The Spaniards crushed the spirit of the people by putting many to death, and by laying heavier burthens on the rest. Amongst those who were put to death was the traitor Gennaro. The outbreak in Sicily was quelled far more easily, for the Viceroy made a proclamation of pardon, and then fired on the people in the streets of Palermo. Towards the end of this century Lewis the Fourteenth further weakened the power of Spain. The people of *Messina* took advantage of the Dutch war in which Spain took part against Lewis. They were much oppressed by the Governor, who disregarded their rights, and, it is said, even planned a massacre of their senators. They rose against the Spaniards, and drove them from their city; and, in 1674, they sent to Lewis for help, and proclaimed him King of Sicily. Lewis sent a fleet to secure the island, and, in 1676, the French gained three victories by sea over the Dutch allies of Spain, off *Stromboli*, *Catania*, and *Palermo*. In 1678, Lewis made peace with Spain by the Treaty of *Nimwegen*, and withdrew his forces from Messina. The Spaniards took away all the ancient privileges of the city, and confiscated much property. The treaty of Nimwegen added much to the glory of Lewis, and made him none the less anxious to disturb the Spaniards in Italy. He made alliance with Duke Victor Amadeus of Savoy, and commanded the alliance of

Genoa. The city dared to refuse, and, in 1684, was cruelly bombarded by the French fleet until it submitted.

7. **The Treaty of Utrecht, 1713.**—The eighteenth century was marked by European wars about rights of succession. These wars were partly fought in Italy, and this brought much distress on the people. They were followed by treaties by which different powers divided Italy between themselves and their allies, without in any way asking the wishes of the Italian people. In 1700, Charles the Second of Spain died without children, and thus the line of the Habsburg Kings of Spain came to an end. Lewis the Fourteenth claimed the throne for his grandson *Philip, Duke of Anjou*, whom the last king named as his heir, and who derived his right from his grandmother *Maria Theresa*, Queen of France, daughter of Philip the Fourth of Spain. His claim was opposed by Charles, Archduke of Austria, the son of Leopold, the Emperor-elect, who was grandson of Philip the Third. The army of France occupied Lombardy. The French cause was upheld by *Cosimo the Third* of Tuscany, and *Ferdinando da Gonzaga* of Mantua, and for a time by Victor Amadeus of Savoy, the father-in-law of Philip. In 1704, Austria gained over Savoy. The French under Vendôme defeated the Austrians and conquered the whole Duchy except Turin. Prince Eugene saved this city by a brilliant victory. In 1706, the French were driven out of Lombardy and Naples, and Charles the Third was proclaimed. The war in Italy was of small consequence compared to that which was carried on north of the Alps, in which France was opposed by *The Grand Alliance* of the Emperor, England, and Holland, and in which our Marlborough won his splendid victories. In 1713 the war was ended by the *Peace of Utrecht*. The Austrian Charles, who had now become the Emperor Charles the Sixth, received Milan, Naples, and Sardinia; and to punish Ferdinando for his alliance with France he took away

Mantua from him. The Duke of Savoy, as a reward for his timely help, received Sicily, with the title of King, and the same year was crowned at Palermo. Thus the Bourbon king of Spain lost the dominions in Italy which the Habsburg kings of Spain had gained. The Italians passed from under the power of Spain to be under the power of Austria. They did not gain any freedom by the change, though the rule of the Austrians, bad as it was, was yet better than the rule of the Spaniards. The Duke of Savoy had gained Pinerolo in 1696. By this war he gained Montferrat, Alessandria, and some other places. By the Treaty of Utrecht his Duchy was recognized as an independent power, which means that it was now free from all Imperial claims.

8. **The Kingdom of Sardinia.**—King Philip of Spain did not give up all hopes of gaining Italian territory. On the death of his queen, who was the daughter of the Duke of Savoy, he married *Elizabeth Farnese*, heiress of the Duke of Parma. This marriage not only made the Spanish King the immediate heir to Parma and Piacenza, but gave him a good chance of succeeding to the Grand Duchy of Tuscany. *Gian-Gastone de' Medici*, who was the immediate heir to the Grand Duchy, had no children. The Queen of Spain claimed to succeed him, because she was descended from a daughter of Duke Cosimo the Second. The claim of Spain was disputed by Austria. The Emperor Charles the Sixth claimed to succeed to the Grand Duchy through *Anne*, the wife of the *Elector Palatine*, the sister of Gian-Gastone. The marriage of Philip of Spain was therefore highly displeasing to the Emperor. Philip was stirred up by his Queen to secure an inheritance in Italy for their son *Don Carlos*. In defiance of the Treaty of Utrecht, he made a sudden attack upon Sardinia, and took it away from the Austrians. He also purposed to occupy the new kingdom of Sicily with his troops. But England, France, the United Provinces, and Charles of

Austria, made a league called the *Quadruple Alliance*, to enforce the Treaty of Utrecht, and the Spanish fleet was put to flight by the English under *Admiral Byng*. Victor Amadeus was on the side of Spain in this breach of the peace of Europe, for he hoped to gain Lombardy. To secure Austria the allied Powers made him give up his new kingdom of Sicily to Charles the Sixth in exchange for the kingdom of Sardinia. The Austrian already had possession of Naples, and now, by the addition of the island kingdom, he became King of the *Two Sicilies*. The wild and rocky island of Sardinia was but a poor return for the surrender of Sicily. By this means the Austrian power was strengthened in Southern Italy. The reversion of Parma and Piacenza was promised to Don Carlos to be held as fiefs of the Empire. Savoy was forced to look to the North for its development. The reign of Victor Amadeus is an important epoch in the history of Italy, for it was a step in the greatness of Savoy. The Counts of a land of which a small part only was Italian, had, under Amadeus the Eighth, become Dukes of a Duchy which they did not succeed in extending on the north and west. Under Emmanuel Filibert, the Duchy of Savoy became truly Italian. Victor Amadeus changed the Duke of Savoy into an independent and Italian King. He reigned as a despot, but his despotism was liberal and enlightened. He paid great attention to the education of his people. The Jesuits had taken all the management of the University of Turin, and of the schools of Piedmont, into their own hands. The King saw that this gave them an undue power in the State, and accordingly took from them all share in public education. This decisive step strengthened the national feeling in his kingdom. Amid the general ruin Piedmont stood alone as a strong and independent Italian state. In 1730 the King gave up the crown to his son Charles Emmanuel the Third. The year after his abdication, he and his second wife, whom he had lately married, grew weary of the stillness and obscurity of their lives in the old fortress of Chambéry. They determined to try to get back their former dignity, and set out for Turin. The new King had only just time to reach the capital before his father, who had come as far as *Rivoli*. Although this scheme was defeated, the old ex-King made others, and endangered the peace of the kingdom, until his son put him in prison in the Castle of Rivoli, where he remained shut up till his death, which happened in 1732.

9. **The Treaty of Vienna, 1738.**—The Queen of Spain was still anxious for a better provision in Italy for her son, Don Carlos. The *War of the Polish Succession* gave Spain an opportunity of regaining her position in the peninsula. Philip made alliance with France and with Charles Emmanuel (1733). They agreed to drive the Austrians out of Italy; to place Don Carlos on the throne of the Two Sicilies, and to secure his succession to the Duchies; and to give Milan to Charles Emmanuel. The King of Sardinia, with French help, made himself master of all the Duchy of Milan save Mantua. In the mean time Don Carlos was acknowledged in Naples, and soon drove the Austrians out of Sicily. At the close of the war, France and Spain sacrificed the interests of their ally. By the Treaty of Vienna, 1738, Lorraine was given to Stanislas, who could not gain Poland. He ceded it to France. In exchange, Francis of Lorraine, who married *Maria Theresa*, the daughter of the Emperor Charles the Sixth, received the Grand Duchy of Tuscany, which had just fallen vacant by the death of Gian-Gastone. Don Carlos was acknowledged as King of the Two Sicilies, and gave up his claim to Tuscany and Parma. Parma and Piacenza were given up to the Austrians, who were also allowed to keep Milan and Mantua. Thus the power of Spain was re-established in Southern Italy. Charles Emmanuel was cheated of his hopes. His frontier, however, was extended, for he

received Novara and Tortona, which were cut off from the Duchy of Milan.

10. **The War of the Austrian Succession.**—The arrangements made by the Treaty of Vienna were soon partially overset by the *War of the Austrian Succession.* On the death of the Emperor Charles the Sixth, in 1740, Frederic of Prussia claimed Silesia. Then the Bourbons reigning in France, Spain, and Naples, joined with Bavaria and Saxony, to despoil Maria Theresa, the daughter of Charles, of the succession to all the hereditary estates of her father. Italy was again made a scene of war. Both parties courted the alliance of the King of Sardinia, for he was able to bring Lombardy to whichever side he upheld. Soon after the war began, the King of Sardinia made alliance with Maria Theresa. Spanish troops were landed in Italy under Don Philip, brother of Don Carlos. Naples was forced to neutrality by an English fleet. The alliance between the King of Sardinia and the Queen of Hungary, and the neutrality of Naples, checked the French and Spanish. Genoa, however, was alarmed at it, for it was known that Charles Emmanuel coveted the city for a seaport. The Genoese, to foil his plans, allowed the French and Spaniards to pass through their territory, and gave them reinforcements. The King was utterly defeated in 1745, and the invading armies conquered Milan and Parma. In the same year the husband of Maria Theresa, Francis of Lorraine, Grand Duke of Tuscany, was elected Emperor, and peace was made with Saxony. The Empress-Queen was now able to spare more of her forces to carry on the war in Italy. In 1746, the King of Sardinia and the Austrians defeated the French and the Spaniards in a great battle at *Piacenza.* The victorious Austrians marched to Genoa and demanded to be let into the city. The Republic had been brought very low, for it had been engaged in a long struggle to keep the two Rivieras and

the island of Corsica. It also suffered from internal discord; for the ruling oligarchs were very unpopular, and did not dare to give arms to the people that they might defend the city. Terms were therefore agreed upon, and the gates were opened. As soon as the Austrians were inside the city, they set aside the agreement which had been made. The leader of the Austrians was the *Marquess Botta Adorno*, who was half a Genoese by birth, but he seemed all the more determined to prove that he had no loyalty towards Genoa. The city was treated as though it had been conquered; the goods of the citizens were confiscated, and they themselves were insulted. No resistance seemed possible, for the Genoese soldiers had been disarmed, and the great men were so dependent on the support of the Austrians against the people, that they did not dare make any remonstrance. The people were in evil case. On a sudden their own arms wrought their deliverance. On Dec. 5th, 1746, it chanced that, as the Austrian soldiers were taking a cannon through the streets, an underground vault gave way beneath the weight, and the heavy gun sunk, and stuck fast in the ruins. On this, the soldiers tried to make the by-standers pull it out, and urged them to work with blows, as though they were lazy cattle. The Austrians had been wont to see their insults borne in silence. Now at last they had gone too far. A young man who stood by, in the bitterness of his soul, threw a stone at the soldiers. Then, all at once, from roofs and windows stones came flying down upon them. The soldiers fled, but the streets were narrow, and the houses were of great size and strength, and they could not burst them open. For five days they fought with the citizens in the streets, and then they fled out of the city as best they could. The people seized on the artillery which the Austrians left behind them, and pointed the guns at the camp which had been made outside the walls. When the Austrians saw this, they retreated across the Apennines, and left Genoa in peace.

11. **Time of Peace**, 1748–1792.—The war of the Austrian Succession was ended, in 1748, by the *Peace of Aix-la-Chapelle* (*Aachen*). From this treaty on to the French invasion there was peace in Italy. Almost all the land, except Lombardy, was under sovereigns who were independent of foreign Powers, and who were absolute rulers. By this treaty Parma, Piacenza, and Guastalla were given to *Don Philip*, the son of the King of Spain, and the brother of the King of the Two Sicilies. Besides Genoa there yet remained free Venice, with diminished glory; Lucca, in timid silence, and San Marino, in native obscurity. Genoa, and the Duchy of Modena with its dependencies, which still belonged to the family of Este, were placed under the protection of France. Genoa was confirmed in her possession of the two Rivieras. After a time she ceded Corsica to her new protector. The island had become stronger than the city which ruled over it, and the greater part was freed by an insurrection led by General *Paoli* in 1755. During the life of the Emperor Francis the First, the Grand Duchy of Tuscany was almost a province of Austria. On his death, in 1765, it again became an independent state under his third son, *Peter Leopold*. Although this sovereign reigned as a despot, yet he did much to forward the welfare of his subjects. He made many reforms in the management of the finances, and in the administration of criminal law. He checked, as far as he could, the overweening power of the clergy, he greatly reduced the number of monks, and abolished the Inquisition in his dominions. One noble monument of his reign is the improved state of the *Val di Chiana*. This valley is a tract of land lying between two mountain ranges, and bounded by the Arno and the Paglia. The greater part of the water of the valley slowly found its way into the Tiber, and nearly

fifty miles were thus made a prey to swamp and malaria. Leopold changed the whole flow of the water, he drained it into the Arno, and thus made the valley wondrously fruitful. He also began to drain the Maremma, where the wars of Florence and Siena, and the ambition of the Medici, had completed the desolation of a once flourishing tract of country. In 1790, Leopold succeeded to the Empire. He appointed his second son, Ferdinand, to succeed him in Tuscany. After the Peace of Aix-la-Chapelle, Charles Emmanuel engaged in no more wars. Like the rest of the rulers of Italy, he was a despot. His will was law, not only in politics, but in religion, and in everything else. He followed his father's example in keeping down the temporal power and wealth of the Church, and especially in opposing the Jesuits. He did this not because they and the Churchmen generally were, for the most part, enemies of Italy, but because they were a power which threatened to interfere with his own sovereign will. In the same spirit he swept away the privileges and constitutional rights of different parts of his kingdom. He dealt in this way with the Island of Sardinia; for, while he tried to bring the wild mountain people into some sort of order, his only wish was to make them feel his power. His Minister in the island greatly oppressed the people, and abolished the remains of their representative Chamber. At the same time the King encouraged agriculture in the island, and, like his father, patronized education. Though he did something for the cause of learning, yet he was too stingy to give it any real help, and too illiberal in his own feelings to allow it to flourish. *Piero Giannone*, who wrote a history of the kingdom of Naples, lived at this time. He offended King Charles of Sicily, who was a thorough Papist, by showing the proper position which the Pope ought to hold; and, to please King Charles, the King of Sardinia allowed the historian to be caught and shut up in one of his prisons. *Muratori* produced his vast historical collection and his *Annals of Italy* earlier in the century. After the death of Charles Emmanuel, 1773, his son *Victor Amadeus the Third*, allied himself to the French Bourbons, and imitated them in everything. Towards the end of his reign the Piedmontese Count *Alfieri* began to write poems and prose works, which are full of hatred to tyrants, and which even in this period of dull absolutism made men hope for the freedom of their country. At this time also *Beccaria*, a Milanese marquess, wrote on philosophy as it concerns man, on crimes and punishments. He exhibited in Italy the foundation of that humanitarian philanthropy which was made popular in Europe by *Voltaire*. About the same time *Alessandro Volta*, a native of Como, discovered the theory of *galvanism* by contact, and, in 1800, invented the *voltaic pile*.

The war of the Austrian Succession left nearly all Italy in the hands of the Bourbons. This was much against the will of the Popes, for it weakened their power considerably. From the time of the Peace of Aix-la-Chapelle they were engaged in constant disputes with the courts of France, Spain, and Naples, about the powers of the Church. The Jesuits upheld the most violent pretensions of the Pope, and by their advice Pope *Clement the Thirteenth* refused to give way in the smallest degree to the demands of the temporal powers. All Italy, as well as the Bourbon families, was against this order, which by its obstinate pride threatened to set the temporal powers at war with the Holy See. Pope Clement died in 1769, and was succeeded by *Lorenzo Ganganelli*, who took the title of *Clement the Fourteenth*. He was a liberal by education and disposition, and had been raised to the Papacy chiefly by the French and Spanish influence in the conclave. In spite of very strong opposition he issued a "Brief," in 1773, which abolished the Society altogether.

12. **The French Invasion.**—At the end of the eighteenth century, it seemed as though the despotism which was crushing Italy in the Sardinian kingdom and in the dominions of the Bourbon families was about to come to an end. In 1792 the French abolished their monarchy, and formed a Republic. They immediately began to try to make other nations accept the same form of government, and invaded Savoy and Nizza, and made them parts of their own Republic. Victor Amadeus the Third joined the European alliance against France in 1793. He was only able to keep up a defensive war on the Alps. The next year the French took the passes. In 1795, a new government was formed in France, and peace was made with all the foreign States except England, Austria, and Sardinia. The next year the French army crossed the Alps under *Napoleon Buonaparte*. This famous General was of Italian blood and name, and was a native of Corsica. King Victor Amadeus the Third was forced to surrender his claim to Savoy and Nizza, and to give up Alessandria and Tortona on the Italian side of the Alps. He died shortly after. Buonaparte next met the Austrians. He defeated them at Lodi and entered Milan. He dictated terms to Pope Pius the Sixth and Ferdinand of Tuscany, to the Dukes of Parma and Modena. The victories of *Arcola* and *Rivoli* completed the conquest of Lombardy. He entered the States of the Church. He made the Pope give up part of his territory, and pay tribute. He compelled him also to yield up some of the most precious works of art in the Vatican, and sent them to Paris. The French, as they advanced, brought with them the doctrines of their own revolution. These doctrines were gladly embraced by the democrats of Milan, Brescia, Bologna, Modena, and Parma. The Austrian garrison in Mantua yielded after a long siege. Aristocratic Genoa was frightened by severity into submission. The peasants of Romagna rose on the Pope's side, but quickly submitted to the French. The

Italians soon found that the French were not fighting simply to set them free. The French cared nothing for the old republics of Italy; their aim was not to establish Italian, but French republics in the peninsula. The Italians were heavily taxed to pay for the glories of the French arms. Attempts against the new government were put down with severity. The doom of Venice was already decided. The peasants, excited by the priests and joined by Venetian troops, rose against the French at Verona and massacred the wounded in the hospitals. This outrage gave Buonaparte an excuse for pushing forward. The Austrian Emperor was forced to make peace, and with his sanction Buonaparte advanced to Venice. The Doge *Luigi Manini* was so frightened that he did not attempt to defend the city. At the first sound of the French firing, the Great Council in dismay voted the dissolution of the government. The French landed without opposition, and were hailed by the cheers of the people. The signs of the greatness and independence of the Republic were destroyed. The *Bucentaur*, or galley from which the Doge yearly wedded the Adriatic by dropping a ring into the water, was broken up. The *Golden Book* which contained the names of the nobles who ruled the city was burned. Many splendid works of art were carried off to Paris, and amongst them the bronze horses of St. Mark's, which Enrico Dandolo had brought from Constantinople, and which Luciano Doria had sworn to bridle. The same year, 1797, the *Treaty of Campo Formio* was made between France and Austria. Lombardy, Parma, and Modena, the Papal States of Bologna, Ferrara, and the Romagna, and the Venetian territory as far as the Adige, were declared independent under the name of the *Cisalpine Republic*. To make up for these and other losses, the French gave Venice and her dependencies in the Adriatic to the Austrians, who took possession of the city at the beginning of the next year. Besides the *Cisalpine Republic*, the French

General set up the *Ligurian, Cispadane,* and *Tiberine Republics,* with Genoa, Bologna, and Rome, as their capitals. At the close of 1798 Naples surrendered, and was made the seat of the *Parthenopæan Republic.* The same year *Charles Emmanuel the Fourth* was forced to give up his throne, and the French took possession of Piedmont. The Vatican was occupied. Pope Pius VI. was led captive to France, where he died in 1799. The victories of France were now checked for a time. Austria, Russia, and England formed an alliance against her. The Russian Suwarrow turned the French out of Northern Italy. An army of Calabrians under Cardinal Ruffo, with the help of the English fleet, regained Naples and Rome. At Naples, Nelson was guilty of delivering the Republicans to the vengeance of the Court. Pius VII. was chosen Pope at Venice. All this soon ended, for Buonaparte came back from the war in Egypt. He was made First Consul, and, after the decisive battle of *Marengo,* regained all that had been lost. He compelled Pius to agree to Concordats both for Italy and France. He then allowed him to remain at Rome. King Ferdinand also was allowed to reign at Naples.

13. **Buonaparte, King of Italy.**—In 1804, Buonaparte chose to call himself *Emperor of the French,* and sent for the Pope to anoint him. The next year this successful Corsican changed the Cisalpine Republic into a monarchy, and was crowned *King of Italy* in the church of St. Ambrose. He joined the Ligurian Republic to the new kingdom; and made his stepson, *Eugène Beauharnais,* the grandson of a West Indian planter, the Viceroy of Italy. At the close of the year, the Austrians, by their defeat at *Austerlitz,* were forced to give up the whole of the Venetian territory to Buonaparte. This he joined on to his Italian kingdom. Early in 1806, Buonaparte again turned the Bourbons out of Naples, and made his brother *Joseph* King. When he made Joseph, King of Spain, in

1808, he appointed *Joachim Murat*, one of his generals, to succeed him in Naples. These changes met with strong opposition. The bad government of the Bourbons had filled their kingdom with *Brigands*. The people of the lower class were left without education, and were ruled by force. They became tools in the hands of the priests. They were at once childishly superstitious, and wholly without any moral restraint. They were idle, dishonest, and cruel. The robber chiefs, who were the heroes of the populace, were stained with every sort of wickedness. They were without mercy or honour. The Bourbons had made no serious effort to put down this evil. Now, in the days of their adversity, they encouraged it for their own ends. The priests, who were all on the Bourbon side, stirred up these brigands against the French. The Basilicata, Calabria, and the Abruzzi swarmed with men who lived by plunder, and who willingly took up a cause which gratified the priests, which raised them even higher than they were before in the opinion of the populace, and which held out the hope of indulging their passions by murder and robbery. *Caroline*, Queen of Ferdinand, who had been driven out of Naples, but who was still King of Sicily, organized the insurrection in Calabria, and received some help from the English fleet. Soon after Joseph was made King, the English General, *Sir John Stuart*, defeated a large number of French troops at *Maida*, but his force was too small to enable him to carry on any long struggle. The French met the brigands with almost equal cruelty, and a savage guerilla war was carried on, which ended, in 1811, in the entire defeat, and almost in the extirpation, of the robber peasants of Calabria. In 1807, Buonaparte changed the constitution of the kingdom of Italy, and did away with everything which remained of the short-lived liberty which the Italians gained by the invasion of the Revolutionary army. He also made Tuscany, where he had set up a Bourbon as king, a part of the French Empire, and turned away Charles Lewis, whom he had set up. In 1809, Pope Pius dared to complain of the injuries which had been done to the Holy See, and refused to acknowledge Joachim Murat as King. In reply, Rome was occupied by the French, the Papal States were declared part of the French Empire, and the Pope was taken prisoner, and carried off to France. The same year Buonaparte changed the government of Tuscany. He turned it into a Grand Duchy, and set over it his sister *Eliza*, the wife of a Colonel *Bacciocchi*. Eliza was also made Duchess of Lucca and Princess of Piombino. Her government was on the whole popular, and lasted until 1814. The reason of these divisions, and of many others not worth mentioning which Buonaparte made, was his wish to make Italy into a number of states to be held by his generals. By this means he thought that he could secure their obedience, and reward their success. At the same time he would raise up a territorial nobility, to make his court respectable, and supply the place of the nobility which had been almost destroyed by the Revolution, and the remains of which were not likely to become his courtiers. The period of the French rule in Italy was marked, on the whole, by a strict observance of law, and by order in the administration. It was during this time that an intellectual movement began, which reached its full development about thirty years later, but which probably would have never arisen under the dull despotism of the Bourbons. It was now also that the idea seemed first to arise that Italy might become one. For now, for the first time, natives of different parts of Italy fought side by side in the armies of Buonaparte, in Russia and other places. But still the presence of the French troops, the heavy taxes levied for their support, and the marches and engagements of armies, brought Italy into great distress. No one could stand against the conqueror. He divided and redivided, he created and destroyed, he set up one and put down another just as he would. Sicily and Sardinia alone were safe from him, for the English fleet was master in the Mediterranean.

14. **The Congress of Vienna**, 1815.—The power of Buonaparte was at last overthrown by an alliance of the Powers of Europe. In the war of 1814, Joachim, King of Naples, deserted his patron. He joined the Allies and seized on Rome and Ancona. A Piedmontese legion was raised under the flag of King Victor Emmanuel. The Allies carried the war into France, and, on March 31st, entered Paris in triumph. Buonaparte was forced to give up all claims on Italy and on the rest of his conquests, and was sent off to reign over the little isle of *Elba*. In 1815, the Allies met in congress at Vienna, to settle the fate of the countries which Buonaparte had lost. The gaieties and negotiations of Vienna were interrupted by the news of the escape of Buonaparte. Europe escaped from this fresh danger by the battle of *Waterloo*, and the new arrangements came into effect. The people of Italy hailed with delight the success of the Allies, and joined in driving the French out of their land. They looked forward with hope to the Congress at Vienna, for they thought that the Allied Powers would give them liberty. They were deceived. In almost every case they were handed over to the masters who had ruled them before the French Revolution. Italy was made the means of gratifying the selfish ambition of the sovereigns of Europe. By the Treaty of Paris, Victor Emmanuel received much the same dominion as had belonged to his house before 1792. The restoration of the King of Sardinia was held to be the best safeguard against another French invasion, but it was useless so long as a French army could be landed at Genoa. The Genoese had been encouraged by an envoy from England to drive out the French, and restore their old Republic. They were basely deceived, and the city was handed over to the King

of Sardinia, and became part of his kingdom. Genoa has gained greatly by this change, though this does not lessen the crime of betraying her independence. The only excuse which can be put forward for this act is that, the change has turned out to have been necessary for the welfare of Italy. No such excuse can be pleaded for giving Venice over to Austria, to make up for the large share of Poland which Russia took. *Milan* also was given back to the Austrian Emperor, Francis the Second, and thus the Austrian kingdom of Lombardo-Venetia was set up. *Parma* and *Piacenza* were given to *Maria Louisa*, the wife of Buonaparte, the daughter of the Austrian Emperor. *Lucca* was given to the Bourbons of Parma. On the death of Maria Louisa, this family was to regain its former possessions, and was to give up Lucca. Lucca was then to pass to the family of the Austrian Ferdinand the Third, who was made Grand Duke of Tuscany again. Francis the Fourth, the son of Beatrice, heiress of the ancient house of Este and of the Austrian Archduke Ferdinand, was made Duke of *Modena*. When Lucca should be joined to Tuscany, he was also to receive *Lunigiana* from the Grand Duke. Pope Pius the Seventh regained all the *Papal States*, including Bologna, Ferrara, Forli, and Ravenna, which had been taken away from the See in 1796. These were called the Northern *Legations*. Austria claimed the right to place garrisons in Ferrara and Commacchio. The Pope protested against this, but a small body of troops was placed in each of these towns. As soon as Pope Pius re-entered Rome, he restored the Order of the Jesuits. This was agreeable to the wishes of the very same powers which had been foremost in causing the suppression of the Order, for the Jesuits had shown themselves good allies to the Bourbons in their distress. The kings of the South of Europe who had suffered from the French Revolution now with one accord made alliance with the Pope and the Jesuits. They saw in them the representatives and upholders of the old state of tyranny. The kingdom of Naples was restored to King Ferdinand the Fourth of Sicily, and he took the title of King of the Two Sicilies. By these arrangements the Austrians became dominant in Italy, just as had been the case after the War of the Spanish Succession. One thing which the wars of Buonaparte had destroyed was not set up again at Vienna. This was the Holy Roman Empire, of which for so long a time the kingdom of Italy had formed a part, first in reality and then in name alone. The Empire, which was in theory elective, had become practically hereditary in the reigning family of Austria. It was founded by Augustus, it was renewed by Charles the Great, it was restored by Otto, and it came to an end by the abdication of Francis the Second. The peace of Italy was for a moment disturbed. Murat declared for Buonaparte when he returned to France. He was defeated and fled to Corsica. In the autumn he landed with about thirty followers on the coast of Lower Calabria, and was immediately taken and shot.

CHAPTER XI.

ITALY FREE AND UNITED.

Italy kept in slavery by her rulers, who are upheld by Austria; the Carbonari and the insurrections in the North and South (1)—the insurrections in Romagna, Modena, and Parma (2)—Charles Albert, Giuseppe Mazzini and Young Italy; the Bandiera attempt (3)—the Moderate party; Cesare Balbo and the Abbate Gioberti; Giuseppe Giusti, the Marquess Gino Capponi, and Baron Bettino Ricasoli; Alessandro Manzoni (4)—Pope Pius the Ninth; his liberalism, punished by Austria (5)—the War of Independence; the defeat of Charles Albert, and the end of the Pope's liberalism (6)—the war carried on by the Republicans; the sieges of Rome and Venice (7)—King Victor Emmanuel and Count Cavour (8) —L. N. Buonaparte and Villafranca; the cession of Savoy; the freedom of Lombardy and of Central Italy (9)—Giuseppe Garibaldi works the freedom of Sicily and Southern Italy (10)—the Kingdom of Italy; the difficulties of the Government (11)—Urbano Rattazzi and Giuseppe Garibaldi; the Aspromonte affair; the September Convention; the change of capital (12)—the freedom of Venetia (13)—the Mentana affair (14)—Rome, the capital (15)—Italy since 1870 (16).

1. **The Insurrections of 1820-1.**—After the Treaty of Vienna Italy was at peace, but she was still enslaved and divided. The only Italian Republic was the little *San Marino*. The only native Italian ruler, besides the Pope, was the King of Sardinia, and Victor Emmanuel was an indolent despot. Three centuries of foreign tyranny had lowered the character of the Italian people, although during the French rule a change for the better had begun. The Italians of the Southern Kingdom were sunk lower than

those of the north, for they had borne the yoke far longer. All through the peninsula a low standard of morals had become general, save among people of education. The Italians learned some social vices from the Spaniards. The want of courageous perseverance and, above all, of good faith, which, for a time, hindered the work of their statesmen, was the general result of tyranny. The people had long been shut out from political life, and they sought distraction in frivolous amusement. This was supplied by the *Lottery*, which brought money into the exchequer of the governments which set it up. Gambling made the people idle and reckless. Italy was ruled by despots, who had to keep their power by violence and by means of spies; the people naturally met violence by treachery, and foiled the police by secret societies. The Austrians helped the weaker sovereigns to keep the people in slavery, and encouraged them to refuse all demands for constitutional government. All the Italian sovereigns were in strict alliance with the Austrian Emperor, who, in return, guaranteed to keep them on their thrones. It was hopeless for the Italians by themselves to try to get rid of rulers who were upheld by so great a power: it was still more hopeless to make the attempt without unity of design and action. Nevertheless, such attempts were made, and failed again and again. At length the deliverance of Italy was brought about by the wisdom of statesmen who were content to bide their time, as well as by the energy of patriot soldiers who were ready to act when the time came. Before the treaty of Vienna, plots were made by the members of a secret society, who were called the *Carbonari*. These men were violent democrats, and they now hoped to get rid of the rulers of Italy, and to set up a democratic government. The Neapolitans were much influenced by this society, and, in 1820, they called on King Ferdinand to grant them a constitution. They made a revolt so suddenly that the King was forced to grant them all that they asked for. But a few months later the Emperors of Russia and Austria, and the Kings of Prussia, Sardinia, and Naples, had a conference at *Laybach* in Austria, and agreed to put down the insurrection. King Ferdinand, with the help of the Austrians, soon crushed the movement. A plot of the Carbonari was also discovered at Milan. It had for its aim the expulsion of the Austrians, and perhaps the murder of the Viceroy and some of his ministers. An insurrection of a better kind was made in Piedmont. Although Victor Emmanuel had married an Austrian, yet he could not forget that the Austrians had not made a single effort to keep his father on the throne. This feeling was encouraged by the Liberal party in the kingdom, headed by the minister *Prospero Balbo*. These men wished to see their State liberally governed. They held that if the government of the kingdom were to become liberal, Piedmont might then take the headship of Italy, and a centre would be made to which Italians might look with hope. The people tried to force their King to take up a liberal policy. In March, 1821, first Alessandria and then Turin made an insurrection: the people of both places crying out for a constitutional government, such as Ferdinand of Naples had for the moment granted, and for war with Austria. Unhappily the King had been at Laybach, and had there promised that he would not make any concessions. He kept his word to the great sovereigns, and chose to give up his crown rather than have his power cut short. He was succeeded by his brother *Charles Felix*, who was at the time at Modena. In his absence *Charles Albert, Prince of Carignano*, was made regent. This prince was descended from Charles Emmanuel, and, as Charles Felix had no children, he was the next heir to the throne. He was much pressed by the more violent Liberals and by the Carbonari; and either willingly, or from fear, or perhaps to secure his own succession, he granted the people the liberties for which they asked. When Charles Felix heard this he was very angry, and threatened to bring the Austrians down upon his people unless they yielded. Charles Albert had to retire into private life, and the King came to Turin, and for a time put an end to the hopes of the Liberals.

2. **Central Italy**, 1830-1.—Francis, Duke of Modena, had married a daughter of Victor Emmanuel and his Austrian Queen. The Jesuits and the Austrian party tried hard to make Charles Felix name Francis as his successor. They wished to shut out Charles Albert, who was, they thought, inclined to liberalism. The King, however, would not consent to do this. Charles Felix seems to have had a liking for his cousin, and Charles Albert himself was suspected by the Liberal party. Francis of Modena took advantage of this suspicion, and intrigued with the Liberals. He made *Ciro Menotti*, one of the leaders of the party, believe that, if they would declare him King of Italy, he would head their party, and be himself a Liberal. Thus he beguiled the Liberals with his fair speeches. The French Revolution of 1830 raised the hopes of the Italians. The Austrians made fresh efforts to work upon the mind of the King, but he refused to listen, and called Charles Albert to his court. In the beginning of 1831 Ciro Menotti and his party found that Duke Francis had deceived them. The insurrection broke out all the quicker. The Duke of Modena and the Duchess of Parma were forced to flee, but, before he went, the Duke caught Ciro and his friends. The revolt broke out also in the Romagna against the government of the Pope. The new Pope, Gregory the Sixteenth, had no power to withstand the movement; he had no troops and no money. He sent to beg the help of Austria. This was readily granted. The Duke of Modena and the Duchess of Parma were brought

back by the Austrians. The revolt in the Romagna was put down, and the Pope was strengthened by the presence of Austrian troops. The Duke of Modena put Ciro and his companions to death, and filled his prisons with political offenders. This insurrection of Central Italy was caused by the hope of support from France. In this the Italians found themselves mistaken, for *Louis Philippe*, the King whom the French set up, could not help them in any way. At the same time the French were jealous of the presence of the Austrians in the Papal States, and, in 1832, they took possession of *Ancona*, and kept a garrison there until the Austrians withdrew their troops in 1838. As soon as the Austrians had crushed the revolt, Charles Felix died. He left his kingdom almost without an army, for he relied on the Austrians in case of need, and, he said, needed no other troops.

3. **Young Italy.**—When the revolt of 1831 was put down, Italy was more than ever at the feet of the Austrians. All her rulers held their power simply by Austrian leave. Charles Albert was, from his former history, the most likely to take the headship in any attempt to throw off the yoke. He seems to have been willing to grant to his subjects, as King, the same charter which he had granted as regent. But this would have brought on a war with Austria, for which he had not sufficient strength. France, whither the hopes of the Italians turned, could not give him any help. Nevertheless, a party in Italy determined to give the King a chance of taking a decided step. A society chiefly composed of young men, many of them political refugees, was organized by a native of Genoa, *Giuseppe* or *Joseph Mazzini*. This society was called *Young Italy*, and its members aimed at making their country united and republican. It was strongly democratic, because Giuseppe Mazzini, and others like him, thought that the working people were the noblest class, and that all others were selfish

and corrupt, and also because there did not seem any chance of Italy being saved by any of her rulers. Mazzini was a man of far greater ability than most of his party. He was an eloquent speaker, and his hopes and thoughts were lofty though somewhat undefined. He had a restless spirit, and a passion for intrigue. The turn of his mind was unpractical, and he had no patience. He was the first Italian statesman who declared that Italy might and would some day exist, not merely as the common name of different confederate powers, but as one free state. Mazzini and his party hoped to gain their end by secret plans and actions, and they were sometimes guilty of rash and unjustifiable deeds. They have often been accused of assassination, but without good ground. Assassinations were unhappily frequent in Italy at this time. Many of these crimes had doubtless political motives. Many may have been committed by members of Young Italy, yet there is no ground for thinking that assassination was the policy of the party. Mazzini and his followers hoped to drive out the Austrians with a volunteer army composed of patriots from all parts of Italy. When Charles Albert came to the throne, Mazzini called upon him to take the command of the patriots, to defy Austria, and throw himself on "God and the People." The King was neither able nor willing to take such a step. Mazzini then tried to seduce the King's soldiers from their allegiance, and thus did what he could to weaken the only really Italian army that existed. These attempts were met by severe and cruel measures, and a large number were put to death by court-martial. Mazzini made Geneva his head-quarters, and there gathered together a small army of political refugees of different countries. In January 1833, he made a raid upon Savoy. The expedition utterly failed, and he took shelter in London. This wild invasion quite changed the feelings of the King. He was now exposed to danger from the same quarter which threatened Austria. He allied himself more closely with that power and with the Jesuits' and ruled his people with great severity. On the other hand, this raid of Polish and other refugees excited the anger of the Piedmontese against the extreme party, and the belief that the King's life was in danger helped to awaken a spirit of loyalty. During the next fourteen years several attempts were made against the rulers of Italy by members of the republican party. In most cases they were foiled by spies and traitors. Towards the end of this period the conspirators tried to find allies in the Austrian navy, in which there was much disaffection. The two sons of Admiral *Bandiera*, an Italian by nation, in the Austrian service, tampered with the officers of the fleet. The plot was found out, and the conspirators fled. The two brothers still persevered in their plans, and arranged an outbreak at *Cosenza*. The revolt, which was made in 1844, was easily quelled. The two brothers were betrayed to the police, and were put to death.

4. **The Moderate party.**—A large number of Italians were waiting and working for the deliverance of their country in another way. The *Moderate* men did not expect to gain the freedom of Italy by violence without policy. They were strongly opposed to the schemes of Mazzini: and the greater part of them looked to Charles Albert as the King under whom Italy should become free and united. They were brave enough to speak and to write in the cause of freedom, and to act when the time came; but they were content to wait till then. This party was strongest in Piedmont and Tuscany, for in both, though there was much evil, yet there was less oppression than in the rest of the land, and men were not goaded on to action. The opinions of this party were spread by a book called *Delle Speranze d'Italia* (On the Hopes of Italy), published about 1843 by *Cesare Balbo*, a son of the minister of Victor Emmanuel, which pointed out the King of Sardinia as the future liberator. About the same

time another book, *Il Primato*, was written by the *Abbate Gioberti*, which, while it pointed out the King as one great means of the future happiness of Italy, at the same time it spoke as though it were possible to join the different states of Italy together in a confederation of which the Pope should be the head. A third leader of the moderate party was *Massimo d'Azeglio*, a Piedmontese nobleman of high character and ability, who strongly condemned the democratic movements. The Grand Duchy of Tuscany, from 1815, had suffered less from oppression than any other part of Italy. Neither Ferdinand the Third nor his son Leopold the Second were cruel men, though they both of them ruled as despots. Their minister *Vittorio Fossombroni* was an enemy to all reform. His policy was indeed to withstand all papal encroachments, and uphold religious toleration, yet none the less he treated the Tuscans like children. The press was under State control; all progress was checked; there was little education, and the government took care to see everything, and meddle in everything. This treatment caused all men of education and culture to join the Liberal party. The foremost amongst them during his short life was *Giuseppe Giusti*, who wrote satires in poetry. These writings, which were for some time put forth without his name, were received with the greatest eagerness. They are full of noble wrath against the rulers of his land, against the Pope and the Italian Princes who bowed down to Austria. They call on the Italians to remember that they are one, that "they were all born in the Boot"—a name which signified the shape of Italy—and that they have a glorious heritage of noble deeds. To the same party also belonged his friend the *Marquess Gino Capponi*, the descendant of the famous *Piero*, and the more widely known *Baron Bettino Ricasoli*. In Milan *Alessandro Manzoni* raised his voice against the rule of the foreigners in his charming novel, *I Promessi Sposi*, in his poems, and in his tragedies; but while he wrote against this rule, as Might overcoming Right, he shrank from the evils which must needs be, before Right could also have Might on her side. He looked to a land where the slave and the freeman should be as one; in this world evil, he thought, could only be overcome by evil.

5. **A Constitutional Pope.**—During the reign of Gregory the Sixteenth the breach between the Liberals and the Papalists grew wider each year. The Pope was kept on his throne by the Austrians, and he followed the policy which pleased Metternich, the Austrian Minister. He would not suffer any reform to be so much as named before him. On his death, in 1846, Cardinal *Mastai Feretti* was chosen Pope, and took the title of *Pius the Ninth*. The new Pope immediately began a different policy. The power of the *Gregoriani*, as the Papalists of the last reign were called, came to an end. An amnesty to political offenders was put forth: liberty of speech and of complaint was granted; convents were inspected; even railroads were promised. Two opposite parties looked on these reforms with anger. The Gregoriani were indignant and helpless; for the Roman people were delighted with their liberal Pope, and triumphed over the party which had so long oppressed them. The extreme Republicans were angry and suspicious, because these reforms made the Pope popular, and increased his authority. In the autumn some disturbances were made in the streets of the city. During the early part of the next year these tumults became more frequent and serious. The Cardinals were insulted and threatened. The Papal Guard and Police were not strong enough to keep the peace. The Liberal party demanded that a *National Guard* should be formed. The Austrian government sent a strong remonstrance against this plan. Nevertheless, on July 6, 1847, the Pope gave his consent to the formation of a National Guard, not only in Rome but throughout all his States. In order to punish the Pope for

his disobedience, and to keep in check the people of his States, who had now become powerful because they were armed, the Austrian government sent troops into the Pope's territory. A large detachment of *Croats* marched into Ferrara, and took possession of the city in spite of the Papal legate. There had been for some time causes of dispute between Austria and Sardinia, chiefly about levying duties. The conduct of the Pope now definitely changed the policy of Charles Albert. He turned for support from Austria to his own people, and declared that, if the Austrians went further, he would fight to the death for Italy and the Pope.

6. **The First War of Independence,** 1848.—The strength of the Republicans throughout Europe, and the example of the Pope, stirred up the people of Italy to make a struggle for freedom. In Tuscany the suspicion of the Liberal party had been roused by some concessions which the government had made to Pope Gregory at the end of his reign. They now raised their voices for a National Guard, and the Grand Duke was forced to grant it to them. A list of grievances was drawn up by Baron Ricasoli, in which were set forth the number, idleness, and ignorance of the clergy and the monks, the want of popular education, and the general bad administration of the government. Leopold, though he made some concessions, could not begin a large system of reform. In Lucca, under its Bourbon Duke, *Charles Lewis,* the State was managed by one *Ward,* who had been a Yorkshire horse-jockey, and whom the Duke had made a baron and chief minister. In September, 1847, the people rose against the Duke. He managed to appease them at the time, and the next month he sold the duchy to the Grand Duke Leopold. The other changes which had been arranged at Vienna soon followed. On the death of the Duchess Maria Louisa, Charles Lewis took possession of Parma, and the Duke of Modena claimed the Lunigiana. These changes were the cause of some

disturbances. The excitement increased at the end of the year, when it became known that the rulers of Parma and Modena had agreed to allow the Austrians to place troops in their States, to overawe the Italian princes, who were inclined to yield to the people. An insurrection was made at Palermo in the beginning of 1848, and the King was forced to grant his people a constitutional government. His example was quickly followed by the King of Sardinia, the Grand Duke, and the Pope. In February, 1848, Louis Philippe was driven out of France, and a Republic was again set up. This revolution raised the hopes of the Republicans all through Europe. In a short time the disaffection, which had long been felt in Vienna, ended in an open revolt, and the government was further embarrassed by an insurrection in Hungary. The Italians took advantage of the difficulties of their Austrian masters. The Milanese attacked the Austrian troops under Marshal *Radetzky*, and, after a struggle which lasted for five days (March 18-23), drove them out of the city. Vicenza, Padua, Brescia, Bergamo, and other places openly joined the Milanese. The Duke of Modena fled from his dominions. On March 22nd, the Venetians rose against the Austrians, murdered the Commandant of the Arsenal, Colonel *Marinovich*, and raised the cry of *Viva San Marco!* which had not been heard for so many years. The Austrians left the city. A provisional government was set up, and *Daniele Manin*, a Venetian of Jewish blood, who had been foremost in the revolt, was placed at its head. The King of Sardinia seized the opportunity to declare war against Austria. His position was very difficult. He might have set on foot a national league, for his close neighbourhood to the States in revolt would have secured him the headship. Yet had he thus assumed the leadership, the other rulers of Italy would have been jealous. Or he might have taken simply the character of the champion of Italian freedom, and put his kingship in the background. This would have given him the confidence of the cities in revolt, and might have enabled him to give them some power of united action. As it was, he did not enter fully on either course. The Princes were afraid lest his power should become too great for their welfare. The cities had no point of union. He was unhappily mistaken in thinking that the Austrian army was thoroughly disaffected, and that Radetzky was finally beaten. He crossed the Ticino, and defeated the Austrians at *Goito*. He was joined by crowds of volunteers from all parts of Italy. The army of the Pope crossed the Po, and the King of the Two Sicilies was forced to allow General *Pepe* to advance northward. But Charles Albert had no fixed plan, and no military skill. He was successful until Radetzky received reinforcements, and then, July 25th, he was utterly defeated at *Custozza*. The Austrians entered Milan again, and the country was declared under martial law. The people were oppressed by heavy exactions; spies were employed to report any signs of disaffection, and men, and even young girls, were beaten for showing their love for their country and their hatred of the foreigner. Nearly all the north of Italy was subdued. Venice still held out under her *Dictator* Manin, and the Italians of the northern mountains still kept up an irregular warfare. They were led by *Giuseppe Garibaldi*, a native of Nizza. This famous leader had been a sailor; and had been banished from the Sardinian kingdom because it was said that he took part in the plots of Mazzini. He then began a life of adventure, and for a time was in the service of the Republic of *Uruguay*. He offered his services to Charles Albert, but the King was afraid of his republican feelings, and would not accept them. Nevertheless, when the Piedmontese Parliament met in 1848, Giuseppe Garibaldi sat as a deputy from Nizza. He helped the Milanese in their revolt, and for a time defended Brescia, until he was forced to retreat to the Alps. The Austrians occupied Parma and Modena, and put an end to the revolts there. Charles Lewis, Duke of Parma, gave Radetzky leave to enforce martial law in his dominions. France and England kept him from interfering with the government of Tuscany. Meanwhile the Pope and the King of the Two Sicilies betrayed the popular cause. The Pope was afraid when he saw that he would have to fight against Austria, and, on April 29th, 1848, published an *Allocution*, which declared that his troops had crossed the Po without leave. King Ferdinand, on May 15th, slew the people of Naples in the streets, and took away all the liberties which had been forced from him four months before. In September he vainly tried to bring Sicily into obedience by a disgraceful bombardment of Messina.

7. **The End of the Struggle.**—The defeat of Custozza, and the Allocution of April, nearly crushed the moderate party. The Republicans, however, were active in Tuscany and in Rome. The Pope and his ministers were now held to be false to the cause of Italian freedom, and the Roman people became riotous. The wisest of these ministers was Count *Pellegrino Rossi.* He was anxious to avoid an open breach between the frightened Pope and the Republicans, lest Austria should interfere. On the other hand Papalists and Republicans alike longed to push matters to a crisis. On November 15th, the Count was assassinated as he entered the Chamber of Deputies. Then the disorder in Rome became great. The Pope was urged to flee. He yielded to the persuasion of the Austrian representative. In disguise and mounted on the box of a carriage, he fled away to *Gaeta.* In Tuscany the extreme democrats defeated the moderate party, which was led by the Marquess Gino Capponi. *Giuseppe Montanelli,* and the advocate *Guerrazzi,* the two leaders of the democrats, forced the Grand Duke to give his consent to a meeting of a *Constituent Assembly* in Rome.

This demand meant something different in the mouths of different people. The Abbate Gioberti, the minister of Charles Albert, would have had all the States of Italy, whatever might be their form of government, join in a national federation, so that the King of Sardinia and the Republicans of Rome might work together in the common Assembly. In the mouths of the democrats of Rome and Tuscany the demand meant a national but purely democratic Assembly. The Grand Duke Leopold granted the demand, for Leghorn was in revolt, and Florence was in nearly the same state. He then fled away, February 7th, 1849, and the Florentines set up a Provisional government. Early in 1849, the constitutionalists lost ground by the retirement of Gioberti. He was succeeded by *Urbano Rattazzi*, the head of the democratic party in Piedmont. Democracy in the Sardinian kingdom had little in common with democracy in Rome or Tuscany, save that it meant war with Austria. The army of Charles Albert was without generals and without discipline. War was declared against Austria. It did not last quite four days, for, on March 23rd, Radetzky crossed the Ticino, and utterly defeated the Piedmontese at *Novara*. The King gave up his throne to his son *Victor Emmanuel*. He left Italy, broken-hearted, and died four months after his defeat. After the Pope left Rome the city was governed first by the Chamber of Deputies, and then by an Assembly chosen by universal suffrage. There were many people in the city who would gladly have received the Pope back, if he would have yielded some things, but he refused to make any terms with them. The chief place in the Republic was soon taken by Mazzini, who was made the first of the *Triumvirs* (or *three* head magistrates). The cause of the Pope was taken up by the King of the Sicilies, which was natural, and, which sounds more strange, by the French Republic against the Republic of Rome. The French were jealous of the power which Austria had in the peninsula, and seized this opportunity of meddling in the affairs of Italy. The Romans were determined to defend their city. They sent for Garibaldi, who was in the Abruzzi with his volunteers, guarding the frontier, and gave him the chief command. In April, a French army under General *Oudinot* landed at *Civita Vecchia*, expecting to enter Rome without resistance. The French were defeated. They now gave up all hopes of taking the city by storm, and formed the siege. The army of King Ferdinand was sent to help them, and entered the States of the Church at Terracina. It was decisively defeated by Garibaldi at *Palestrina* and *Velletri*. Nevertheless Rome was in great danger, and the government treated with the French envoy, M. de Lesseps, who had come with full powers. A truce was made, and it seemed likely that in the end the French army would be withdrawn. But General Oudinot declared that the envoy had gone beyond his powers. He broke the truce by attacking the *Trastevere* at the gate of *San Pancrazzio*. For nearly four weeks the citizens of Rome and the volunteers of Garibaldi fought for their city. On the night of the 30th a great assault was made, and on July 2nd the gates were opened. The papal government was again declared, and a French garrison was placed in Rome. Garibaldi and Mazzini escaped in safety. The Pope was not brought back until April 1850. He was quite changed. He now rested on the French garrison, he was guided by the Jesuits, and he kept his city under martial law for seven years. After the defeat of Charles Albert, the Austrians besieged Venice. The people under their dictator, Daniele Manin, defended the city bravely. The inhabitants of the *Cannaregio*, which was chiefly exposed to the cannon, left their houses and took shelter round St. Mark's. The Venetians raised new defences, and launched floating batteries against the lines of the enemy. The siege lasted until August 22, 1849, and then the Venetians were forced to surrender, for they were brought to great straits. The Grand Duke of Tuscany, and the Dukes of Modena and Parma, returned to their dominions some months earlier. Thus, by the close of the summer, the Italian insurrection was crushed. The moderate and the democratic parties had both failed. But the struggle was not without its fruits. From this time onwards no Italian statesman believed in the scheme of Federalism. The old Federalists now sought for Italian freedom and union through the House of Savoy. Above all, Mazzini and his party, faulty as their judgment often was, had made their countrymen believe that the freedom and union of Italy were possible. The defenders of Rome and Venice were not kings or nobles, but men of the people, lawyers and poets, clerks and tradesmen. These were the men who kept the armies of France and Austria so long vainly waiting before the gates of their cities. From this time forward the Italians began to hope. The leaders of the democratic party often perplexed the statesmen who worked for Italian freedom. Nevertheless without them the work would never have been begun, and, unless they had continually urged it on, it would have been left half done.

8. **King Victor Emmanuel II.**—From the wars of 1848-9 the King of Sardinia was looked upon by the moderate party as the champion of Italian freedom. Charles Albert had failed: yet his son would not, and indeed could not go back. When Victor Emmanuel began his reign, there were many things against him. As soon as the Genoese heard of the defeat of Novara, they rose against the government. They had only belonged to the kingdom since the Treaty of Vienna, and when they saw the democrats of Rome and Venice fighting for their cities, they hoped that the time was come for them to regain their old republican independence. The revolt was quickly put down by the King's general, *Alfonso della Marmora*. The army of Sardinia was disorganized, the moderate party

was cast down, the Austrians were triumphant, and the democrats were as yet the only successful party in Italy. Nevertheless King Victor Emmanuel did not despair. He was forced first of all to make terms with Radetzky, and England and France persuaded the Austrian Emperor to withdraw his troops from Piedmont. At first people distrusted the new King, for he had been harsh and stern, and both his mother and his wife were Austrians. Great efforts were made to win him over to the Austrian party, but the King was neither cast down by defeat and distrust, nor won over by soft words. He soon showed that, though he had been forced to make a treaty with Austria, yet he would not cast in his lot with the oppressors of Italy. He made *Massimo d'Azeglio* his chief Minister, and *Camillo Benso di Cavour* his Minister of Commerce. With the help of these two men he honestly carried out the reforms which had been granted by his father, and set new ones on foot. No country, save the Papal States, was so weighed down by priests as Piedmont. The Jesuits were driven out in 1848, but there still remained 23,000 ecclesiastics in the Sardinian kingdom, who used their wealth and influence to hinder reform. The Pope was now thoroughly in the hands of the Austrians, and so there was no hope of winning over the clergy to the national cause. It became necessary therefore to weaken their power. The first step towards this was made in 1850 by the *Siccardi Law*, so called from a statesman of that name. This law did away with the Ecclesiastical Courts and privileges. It was soon followed by a law which forbade corporations to buy or receive landed property. In 1854, Urbano Rattazzi brought in a bill, which was at last carried, which gave the government power to abolish monastic bodies. Meanwhile the Piedmontese enjoyed a constitutional government, a free press, and a large share of religious liberty. The King steadily kept his word to all parties, and won for himself the honourable nickname of *Il Re Galantuomo* (the honest King). The quick progress of reform frightened Count Massimo d'Azeglio. He retired from office in 1853. His place was taken by Count Cavour, who made a coalition with the democratic party in Piedmont headed by Urbano Rattazzi. The new chief Minister began to work not only for the good of Piedmont but for Italy at large. The Milanese still listened to the hopes which Mazzini held out, and could not quietly bear their subjection. Count Cavour indignantly remonstrated with Radetzky for his harsh government. He also protested in vain against the oppressive rule of King Ferdinand the Second in Naples. The division and slavery of Italy had shut her out from European politics. Cavour held that, if she was once looked upon as an useful ally, then her deliverance might be hastened by foreign interference. The Sardinian army had been brought into good order by Alfonso della Marmora, and was ready for action. In 1855, Sardinia made alliance with England and France, who were at war with Russia; for Cavour looked on Russia as the chief support of the system of despotism on the Continent, and held that it was necessary for Italian freedom that Russia should be humbled. The Sardinian army was therefore sent to *Crimea*, under La Marmora. This force did good service in the battle of *Tchernaya*, Aug. 16th. In the same month, the Allied Powers remonstrated in vain with King Ferdinand. The next year the *Congress of Paris* was held to arrange terms of peace between the Allies and Russia. At Paris Cavour took the opportunity of laying before the representatives of the European powers the unhappy state of his countrymen under King Ferdinand and the Pope. The Governments of England and France in vain tried to persuade the King to rule better, and at length the dispute became so serious that their ambassadors were withdrawn from Naples. Diplomatic relations were not resumed until after the death of Ferdinand.

9. Freedom of Lombardy and Central Italy, 1859-60. —In December, 1851, Louis-Napoleon Buonaparte, the President of the French Republic, seized the government, and the next year took the title of *Emperor of the French*. He was anxious to weaken the power of Austria, and at the beginning of 1859 it became evident that war would soon break out. As a sign of the friendly feeling of the French Emperor towards the Italian cause, his cousin, *Napoleon Joseph*, married Clotilda, the daughter of Victor Emmanuel. Count Cavour now declared that Sardinia would make war on Austria, unless a separate and national government was granted to Lombardy and Venetia, and unless Austria promised to meddle no more with the rest of Italy. On the other hand, Austria demanded the disarmament of Sardinia. The King would not listen to this demand, and France and Sardinia declared war against Austria. The Emperor Napoleon declared that he would free Italy from the Alps to the Adriatic. Romagna threw off the yoke of the Pope. A revolt was made in Tuscany against the Grand Duke, and he was forced to flee. A few days afterwards the Duchess regent of Parma had to leave her capital. The Piedmontese cavalry helped to defeat the Austrians at Montebello. The Sardinian army under the King and General Cialdini gained a decisive victory at Palestro. The battle of *Magenta*, June 4th, forced the Austrians to retreat from Lombardy. The Duke of Modena thus lost his support, and was forced to flee. On June 24th the Austrians, who had crossed the Mincio, were defeated at *Solferino* by the allied armies of France and Sardinia. It seemed as though the French Emperor would keep his word. But he found that if he went further, Prussia would take up the cause of Austria, and that he would have to fight on the Rhine as well as on the Adige. When, therefore, the French army came before Verona, a meeting was arranged between the two Emperors. This took place at

Villafranca, and there Buonaparte, without consulting his ally, agreed with Francis Joseph to establish an *Italian Confederation.* The Austrian Emperor, as sovereign of Venetia, would have been a member of this Confederation, and therefore this scheme of Buonaparte, which he had learned years before from Gioberti and his party, would not have been likely to help forward Italian independence. Austria gave up Lombardy to the west of the Mincio to the King of Sardinia. The rulers of Tuscany, Modena, and Parma were to return to their Duchies. The proposed Confederation was never made, for the people of Tuscany, Modena, Parma, and Romagna sent to the King to pray that they might be made part of his Kingdom, and Victor Emmanuel refused to enter on the scheme of the French Emperor. In return for allowing the Italians of Central Italy to shake off the yoke, Buonaparte asked for Savoy and Nizza. The annexation of these two provinces would, he said, give France "a guaranty indicated by Nature herself." The possession of Savoy was a check on Italian progress, and in a military point of view was highly dangerous. The Piedmontese monarchs, moreover, had now become thoroughly Italian; and they no longer had need of territory on the other side of the Alps. The King therefore consented to give up the "glorious cradle of his Monarchy" in exchange for Central Italy. In March, 1860, Tuscany, Modena, Parma, and Romagna, by a general vote of the people, became subject to the King of Sardinia. On the loss of Romagna the Pope pronounced the greater form of excommunication against the invaders and usurpers of the Papal States, but without mentioning anyone by name. The next month the people of Savoy and Nizza were joined on to France by the form of a popular vote. Thus the last remains of the Burgundian territories of the Counts of Savoy were severed from their House. It had been agreed at the Treaty of Vienna that these provinces should always be kept neutral, and it had long been understood that, if at any time they were parted from Piedmont, they were to be added to Switzerland. Their annexation by France therefore roused indignation amongst the European powers, but none of them cared to make it a cause of war.

10. **Freedom of Sicily and Naples.**—Ferdinand the Second reigned over Naples and Sicily with stern tyranny. He kept his people quiet by the sheer terror which his cruelty excited. He had bombarded Messina and Palermo, he had caused his people to be shot down in the streets of Naples, and had won for himself the nickname of *King Bomba*. He filled his prisons with political offenders, and these prisons were loathsome dungeons. Amongst the most illustrious of his victims was *Baron Carlo Poerio*. England and other foreign powers remonstrated in vain with the King. Each year many of his subjects fled from his tyranny, and for the most part found a refuge in Piedmont. Baron Poerio, as he was being transported to America, managed to land in Ireland, and thence went to join the refugees in Turin. From their place of shelter the Neapolitan exiles taught their fellow-countrymen to look to Piedmont for deliverance. The union of Lombardy and Central Italy made them feel that the freedom and union of Italy was perhaps not far off. In 1859 King Ferdinand died, and was succeeded by his son, Francis the Second. The new King had been brought up by the Jesuits, and by his Austrian stepmother, and began his reign in a way which did credit to his training. In March 1860, the foreign ambassadors at his Court presented an address to the King, urging him to make some political reforms. It was already too late. In a few days a revolution began in Palermo, Messina, and Catania. Every Italian patriot looked with hope upon the movement. Count Cavour, however, judged that it would be unsafe to interfere, for France could not be trusted, and Austria and the Pope were hostile.

Nevertheless an expedition was made without the King's consent. General Garibaldi raised a body of 1000 volunteers, and, on May 5th, set sail from Genoa. The Government declared its displeasure at this expedition, and it seemed as though it was sure to end in failure. But Garibaldi was not disheartened. He landed at Marsala, and took the title of Dictator of Sicily "in the name of Victor Emmanuel of Italy." With his little band of volunteers he took Palermo, and defeated the troops of the King on the promontory of *Melazzo*. This victory completed the conquest of the island, save that the soldiers of King Francis still defended Messina. The Neapolitans made no movement, for they were kept down by terror. The guns of the fortress of *St. Elmo* seemed daily to threaten Naples with destruction, and the soldiers of the King insulted and ill-used the citizens. All people of every class were in great fear; the more wealthy left the city; trade ceased, and every one who had anything to lose set about seeking for some means of saving it. The King, who was the cause of all this terror, was himself greatly alarmed at the success of Garibaldi. Francis made many promises of reform, and begged the King of Sardinia to interfere on his behalf. Victor Emmanuel and Count Cavour could probably have stopped the expedition at the onset. Instead of doing this, they were contented with declaring that they disapproved it. They would not be responsible for the attack on the King of Naples. Having made this declaration, they did no more, for they considered that they might gain and could not lose. But now, though the King and his minister were willing enough that the Neapolitans and the Sicilians should have an opportunity of rising against their Bourbon King and voluntarily joining themselves to the Sardinian Kingdom, yet they began to be somewhat afraid as to what might be the intentions of the victorious General. The republican ideas of Garibaldi were well known, and there seemed to be a danger lest he should not only embroil Sardinia in war with other powers, but also lest his success should encourage the revolutionary party throughout Italy. The King therefore forbade Garibaldi to take any steps against Naples until the Sicilians had had an opportunity of voting as to whether they would become his subjects. Garibaldi, in answer, expressed his devotion to his sovereign, but refused to obey his command, for he said that, if he hesitated now, he would endanger the cause of Italy, and be faithless to his duty as an Italian. Accordingly, on August 20th, Garibaldi landed at *Spartivento*, and drove back the Neapolitan troops at *Reggio* and *San Giovanni*. King Francis was abandoned by his family, and by a great number of his soldiers, and was afraid to stay in Naples. On September 7th he sailed away in a Spanish ship to *Gaeta*, and the next day Garibaldi entered the capital. The perplexity of King Francis had enabled many political refugees to return to Naples, and thus when the Dictator entered the city, he found a provisional government ready to his hand. Giuseppe Mazzini and a number of extreme democrats quickly joined him in Naples. Great efforts were made to induce Garibaldi to delay giving up his conquests to the King as long as possible, and the hopes and plans of the democrats caused considerable uneasiness at Turin. By this time it became evident that unless the Sardinians invaded the Papal States, the Republicans would invade them. For the mercenary force of the Pope under General *Lamoricière* endangered the success of the Southern expedition. Cavour saw that the union of Southern Italy with Sardinia depended on the King taking the lead in the Italian movement. The French Emperor did not wish for further Republican success, and so did not prevent the invasion of the Papal States by Sardinia. An army under General Cialdini entered the States, and took Urbino, Perugia, and some other places. The Papal General *Lamoricière* was defeated at *Castelfidardo*. This expedition prevented the Pope's army from seriously hindering the union of Southern Italy, but the Pope was still able to disturb its peace, and to thwart the action of the Sardinian government. Meanwhile, Garibaldi was perplexed by different parties, by Mazzinians, by the party for annexation, by those who upheld the scheme of confederation, by his friends and his enemies. At the same time, the people of Naples hailed him as their Deliverer, and crowds of volunteers joined him from all quarters. The Neapolitan Generals attacked the Garibaldian army. They had no experience of war, and their men had no confidence in them. They were defeated in a battle on the *Volturno*. In October, King Victor Emmanuel entered the Abruzzi to receive the fruits of the expedition which he had forbidden. He was met by the Dictator at the head of his red-shirted volunteers, and was hailed as King of Italy. The people of Naples and Sicily joined themselves by vote to the Sardinian Kingdom. Some of the States of Europe expressed their displeasure at the invasion of the Papal States and at the annexation of the Southern provinces. The English government, under *Viscount Palmerston*, boldly announced its warm sympathy with the Italian people. The French were gratified by being allowed to add the tiny principality of *Monaco* to the new department which they made out of Nizza (*Nice*), and the Emperor in return acknowledged Victor Emmanuel as King of Italy. Thus the daring of one man gave freedom to Naples and Sicily.

11. **Difficulties of the Government.**—In February 1861, the first *Italian Parliament* was held at Turin in a wooden building made for the purpose, and there Victor Emmanuel was declared *King of Italy*. Though Garibaldi had thus wonderfully brought about the union of Northern and Southern Italy, the Government had many difficulties to meet. The excitable people of the South had received Garibaldi with enthusiasm, not merely because he gave them freedom,

but chiefly because his dashing bravery and romantic career enlisted their sympathies. They were disappointed at the quiet demeanour of the King. The red shirt which marked the Garibaldian volunteer was in their eyes an emblem of recklessness and romance. The grey coats of the Piedmontese soldiers seemed to foreshadow quietness and order, and these never engage the sympathy of the *Lazzaroni*, as the people of the lowest class of Neapolitans are called. These feelings placed Garibaldi in a very difficult position. This difficulty was increased by the strong dislike and distrust which both he and Count Cavour felt for one another. For these reasons Garibaldi left Naples and retired to his island-home of *Caprera*, and soon afterwards his volunteer army was disbanded. This added to the discontent of the lower orders, for they thought that the object of their admiration had been hardly dealt with. The new government was also distrusted because it offended the religious prejudices of the people. Considerable indignation was felt when Count Cavour began to carry out the same policy against convents which had met with general approval in Piedmont. Francis the Second prepared to defend Gaeta against the Sardinian army, and the siege was begun in November 1860. In Sicily Messina still held out. Brigandage again began to spread in the Abruzzi and Basilicata. It was encouraged by the priests, for the brigands avowed that they fought for King Francis. When they were pursued by the Sardinian army they found a convenient shelter in the Papal States, and, it is said, were supplied with arms by the Papal Treasury. King Francis still had an army in the field, and the brigands tried to make themselves out to be the King's soldiers. During the summer of 1861, they became so powerful that even Naples itself did not seem safe. They fired at railway trains; they attacked and slew men in their own dwellings; they carried off prisoners, who had to buy their release with a large ransom; they sacked villages and slaughtered cattle. In no other country has there been in modern times so little difference between the soldier and the brigand, between the brigand and the labourer, as in Southern Italy. Some of these men, such as *Carmine Crocco* and *Ninco Nanco*, called themselves Generals and Colonels of the King. The peasant as he worked in his garden had at the same time a gun at hand, and would use it as naturally as he did the spade. The real officers of the Bourbon King were not ashamed to act with the brigands. *Don Jose Borjès*, the Catalan, and some others were taken and shot; for, though they were soldiers, they were not only rebels, but the companions and abettors of brigands. The new government had also other difficulties. The men who had to carry out the law, the police and several different officials, were to a large extent disaffected. The government of Victor Emmanuel was forced to employ the old servants of the Bourbon King, because there was no other official staff ready at hand. These officers were not as yet thoroughly loyal to their new King. There was at first also some discontent amongst the upper class. Naples ceased to be a capital city. The Southern Kingdom seemed to some to have become almost subject to Turin. It was moreover impossible to work all the social reforms which the Neapolitans wanted until some time had passed, and there were many who thought that they had gained nothing by being joined to Piedmont. These difficulties gradually disappeared before the vigour and wisdom of the new King of Italy and his ministers. King Francis for a time hoped to receive help from Austria. The French fleet off Gaeta gave him some moral support, and prevented the Italian ships from attacking the town. When, in February 1861, the French fleet was withdrawn, the town was surrendered, and the ex-King took shelter in Rome; General Cialdini, and afterwards Alfonso della Marmora, checked the brigands of Southern Italy, although they were not able to put them down altogether. Before long all classes saw that they could trust their new King, and the progress of social and political reform reconciled the Neapolitans to the lessened importance of their city. In the summer of 1861, the new Italian King and Kingdom suffered a heavy loss by the death of Count Cavour. His name will live for ever, for to his wisdom and energy the Italians owe the regeneration of their land.

12. **The September Convention.** — Venetia under the Austrians, and Rome and the Roman Campagna under Pope Pius, were now the only parts of the peninsula which lay outside the Italian Kingdom. As regards Venetia, all the laity, and indeed nearly all the clergy, were of one mind, for the old Austrian or Retrogressionist party had come to an end. But the powers of Europe would not allow the peace of the Continent to be disturbed by a breach of the Treaty of Villafranca. The Pope was upheld in Rome by the French garrison. The Italian laity were now anxious for the completion of the work of union, while a large number of priests rejoiced at the presence of the French because it acted as a guaranty of the temporal power of the Pope. The French Emperor was pleased to be looked on as the Protector of the Holy See, for this made him sure of the good will of a considerable number of his own subjects. Each party in Italy, save the *Ultramontanes*, or extreme Papalists, now looked forward with hope to gaining Venetia and Rome. The more thorough Republicans, with Mazzini at their head, hoped to accomplish this by some conspiracy. The more moderate Republicans, or Garibaldians, hoped to do so by some sudden attack, such as their leader had made upon the Southern Kingdom. The constitutional party was for waiting until it could make sure of success. After the death of Cavour, Baron Bettino Ricasoli became the head of the Constitutionalists, and the chief minister of the King.

Besides these was the democratic party of Piedmont, which was led by Urbano Rattazzi, the minister of Charles Albert. This party, though it did not agree with the republican theories of Garibaldi, yet felt that there was no great need of waiting. Garibaldi was eager to be again at the head of a volunteer army, and to complete the work of deliverance. In Venetia the hopes of the party of '48 were again revived, and crowds of young men were ready to follow the republican general. Urbano Rattazzi for a while allied himself with the Garibaldians, and encouraged a hope that he would uphold a grant of money for a Garibaldian expedition against Venetia. When however the King appointed him to succeed Baron Ricasoli, he found that such a scheme was impossible. Meanwhile Garibaldi was in Sicily and was set on gaining Rome. He hoped to gather together a volunteer army in the South, and with it to attack the French garrison, and drive the Pope and his protectors out of Rome. Rattazzi hoped that, if he played the same part as Count Cavour had done in 1860, he might reap the benefit of the scheme if it succeeded, without getting into trouble if it came to nought. But, unlike Count Cavour, he had not secured the secret good will of Buonaparte. The French Emperor showed that he would not allow the Italian government to remain a willing spectator of an attack on Rome. Urbano Rattazzi was forced to take active steps to defeat the scheme. As General Garibaldi still followed up his plan, Sicily was declared in a state of siege. The General landed in Italy, but was met at *Reggio* by an Italian army under General Cialdini. The republican volunteers attacked and defeated the royal army, August 28, 1862. The next day Garibaldi was attacked by General *Pallavicino*, at *Aspromonte*. The republican army was defeated, and Garibaldi and one of his sons were wounded. The wounded General was taken to *Spezzia*, and there he put forward his defence. He declared that he had fought with the King's soldiers against his own will, that he had been made the victim of Rattazzi, to whom alone it was owing that the French garrison was still at Rome. Rattazzi was forced to retire from office. This unhappy affair was ended by a general amnesty, and Garibaldi went back to Caprera. Though his expedition thus ended in utter failure, it was not without results. It made the Italians look forward more earnestly than ever to the time when Rome and Venetia should become theirs. It taught them that that time would surely come, and clearly pointed out to them and to Europe what those things were which hindered its coming. It made the ministers of King Victor Emmanuel more eager to complete the union and freedom of Italy, for they saw that the will of the people and the sympathy of foreign powers would uphold them in so doing. It made it impossible for the Emperor Napoleon to hope to keep a French garrison in Rome for many years longer. The Liberals throughout Europe, and especially in England, were moved by the gallant attempt of Garibaldi, and were indignant at the way in which Buonaparte had made the Italian government crush the hopes of the Italian people. In September 1864, an agreement was made between the King of Italy and the French Emperor called the *September Convention*. Buonaparte could no longer act in direct opposition to the Liberal party, by continuing to interfere in Italian affairs. Nevertheless he joined burthensome conditions to his concessions. He agreed to withdraw the French garrison from Rome little by little, so as to give the Pope time to form an army. The evacuation was to be complete by the end of two years. On the other hand, the King had to agree that he would allow no attack to be made on the Pope's territory. This Convention was a great step towards gaining Rome. As the temporal power of the Pope was certain to fall to pieces when it was no longer upheld by the French, Italy would one day be able to act as it chose. Meanwhile the Italian government was bound not to hasten the end. It was moreover highly gratifying to the Italians to be able to look forward to the time when the French would leave the peninsula. By the last article of the Convention it was agreed that Florence should be made the capital of Italy instead of Turin. This change seemed, at first sight, to imply that the Italians would give up all hope of gaining Rome. It did not do so in reality. General Cialdini, in a speech before the Italian Senate, openly declared that he still desired Rome for the capital. He voted for the Convention, because it promised relief from the presence of a foreign power. He approved the change of capital, because so long as the seat of government was kept at Turin, Austria might at any time send out her troops from the fortresses which she occupied in the valley of the Po to overwhelm the capital. At Florence the seat of government would be also more secure from French interference. It would be sheltered by the Apennines and the sea. In Florence a system of general defence might be adopted and preparations made in safety for future action. The people of Turin deeply felt the loss which their city was likely to sustain. For the most part, however, they submitted willingly to the change for the sake of Italy. The rapid increase of Italian prosperity has already made up their losses. Turin, though no longer the abode of royalty, has gained a more solid distinction by commerce and manufactures, while it still remains the seat of a great University.

13. **Freedom of Venetia.**—In 1866 a war broke out between Prussia and Austria. The policy of Cavour in bringing Italy into European politics now bore its fruit. In March an alliance was made between Prussia and Italy. The King of Prussia agreed to carry on the war until Austria gave up to the Italians the whole of the mainland of Venetia, save the city of Venice and the *Quadrilateral* of fortresses formed by Verona, Legnago, Peschiera, and Mantua. Garibaldi came

over from Caprera to Genoa, and the King ordered the formation of twenty battalions of volunteers, which were to be under his command. Unhappily the popularity, zeal, and indiscretion of Garibaldi made the government dislike his presence. On June 20th war was declared between Italy and Austria. Garibaldi and his volunteers were sent to struggle hopelessly in the district of Trent against troops which were far stronger than they were, both in number and skill. The royal army crossed the Mincio, but was defeated at *Custozza*, and Garibaldi was defeated and wounded at *Monte Suello*. The event of the war, however, was decided by the Prussian victory of *Königgrätz*. Austria was no longer able to hold Venetia, and gave it up to the French Emperor, that he might settle the quarrel with Italy. The Italian fleet was defeated a few days afterwards by the Austrians in an engagement off *Lissa*. Nevertheless, the end was gained in spite of all these disasters. Venetia, with the city of Venice, Peschiera, and the other Austrian fortresses, were united to free Italy. Austria retained *Istria* and *Aquileia*, and the old possessions of Venice on the *Dalmatian* coast.

14. **Rome and Garibaldi.**—In accordance with the September Convention, the French troops were withdrawn from Rome at the end of 1866. The King declared that he would try to reconcile the interests of two parties who were contending with each other for Rome, the papal and the national party. On the other hand, the Republicans urged an immediate attack upon the city, and Mazzini prayed the Italians to set their hearts on Rome, which represented, he said, the *eternal gospel of oneness to the peoples*. The King did not consider that it would be consistent with his honour to yield to these wishes. Rattazzi was now again at the head of affairs. He had been placed in office by the democratic party, and had entered into some rash engagements with it. He tried to follow the same policy which had failed in 1862.

He hoped to be able to see an attack made on Rome without bringing any responsibility upon himself, to stand a chance of winning the city without running any risk. Garibaldi began to gather together a band of volunteers. In September 1867, he presided over an *International Peace Congress* at Geneva, and there declared his intention of at once making war upon the Pope. Volunteers joined him in great numbers, and his movements were so open and undisguised that the Italian government considered it necessary for its own safety to make a protest. On September 24th, as the General was making his preparations for invasion, he was arrested at *Sinalunga*. This arrest caused some slight disturbances in some of the cities of the kingdom, but they were quieted without bloodshed. The General was taken first to Alessandria, and then to his own home, the island of Caprera. This arrest, however, was only a pretence. The Garibaldian volunteers on the frontier skirmished with the Papal troops without being checked by the Government, and, on October 14th, Garibaldi was allowed to escape from Caprera. The Italian government was now understood to encourage the movement, and Garibaldi hoped that he would be upheld by the Royal troops. Buonaparte now interfered, and gave Rattazzi notice that he should look upon any further action against the Papal power as a declaration of war against France. This forced the Italian government to give up its present line of policy. Meanwhile Garibaldi went to Florence and harangued the people, calling on them to join his army. Thence he went southward and took the command of his volunteers on the frontier. The republican party in Rome made some serious disturbances. Barricades were raised, and some street-fighting took place between the insurgents and the Papal troops. During this outbreak some conspirators blew up the *Serristori Barracks*, and caused the death of some of the soldiers of the Pope. Garibaldi gained a victory at *Monte Rotondo*, which raised the hopes of his party. But the movement had already failed. The King put out a proclamation in which he declared that he would oppose the further advance of the volunteers, and he called upon his people to trust to his personal honour. The French Emperor considered that the September Convention had been broken, and again sent a garrison into Rome. Garibaldi left his position on Monte Rotondo, and prepared to disband his volunteers, for he said that he would now leave the Roman question to be decided by the Italian and French troops. His garrison at *Mentana*, after some hard fighting, surrendered on November 4th to the French and Papal army, and on the same day Garibaldi was again arrested by order of the Italian government, at *Figline*, as he was on his way to Caprera. Much indignation was expressed by the republican party at his arrest, and a violent riot broke out at Milan, which was happily soon put down. In about three weeks Garibaldi was released and allowed again to retire to his island-farm. The rash attempt of the General and the Minister thus failed utterly. The volunteers met with much loss and suffering. Rattazzi had to leave office. A French garrison again occupied Rome. On the other hand, the people and the government of Italy were stirred up to greater earnestness in their hopes of gaining Rome. The sympathies of the Liberal party in Europe, and above all in England, were enlisted in the cause. In obedience to this feeling, the French Emperor declared that the occupation of Rome was only to last until some satisfactory arrangement was made with the King of Italy.

15. **Rome the Capital.**—In July 1870, war was declared between Prussia and France. The Italians saw that there was hope that now at last Buonaparte would cease to keep them out of Rome. The Republicans were much excited. Bands of young men, wearing the red colour which was the

badge of their party, began to gather together and march about in the Tuscan Maremma and in Calabria. The war with Prussia called for all the forces which France could muster, and, on August 8th, the army of occupation left Rome, and sailed from Civita Vecchia. The Republicans in Rome now became more violent every day. Still the Pope refused to leave the city. This placed the Italian government in some difficulty, for there was reason to fear that the democrats of Rome would attack the Pope on their own account. Mazzini, who was in Italy, strongly urged them to take some decisive step. If Rome had been taken in this way the authority of the King, and the cause of order and union, would have been much shaken throughout the peninsula. If Rome was to be the capital of the Kingdom, it was needful that it should be made so by the King. If it had been gained without him, it might have been the capital of a republican Italy, but it is more than doubtful whether the Italians would in that case have long remained one nation. It was needful that Victor Emmanuel, and no one else, should add Rome to the Italian Kingdom. The King, however, would not stir so long as he was bound by the September Convention. For this reason Mazzini was arrested, August 14th, and sent to Gaeta. He was working for Italy, but he was working in a way which would have overset the established government, and which would probably have really injured his country. Before long Victor Emmanuel felt himself able to act. On September 2nd, the French army, with Buonaparte at its head, surrendered to the King of Prussia at *Sedan*. The government of Buonaparte was ended, and a Republic was proclaimed. *M. Jules Favre*, the Foreign Minister of the new government, declared the September Convention at an end. Within a week the King of Italy announced to the Pope that he took upon himself the duty of keeping order within the peninsula. In other words, he meant for the future to be King of Rome and its territory, as he was of the rest of Italy. The Pope made an appeal to the victorious King *William of Prussia*, and begged him to take the place of Buonaparte, and keep the Italian King out of Rome. King William answered plainly that any such interference was against his policy. In a few days the King's troops entered the Papal territory, and the people of the province of *Viterbo* immediately declared themselves under the King's government. The army advanced to Rome. The Pope allowed just so much resistance to be made as might show that force was used. A small breach was made in the wall at *Porta Pia*, and through it General *Cadorna* and the Royal troops entered the city, September 20th. Rome and its territory were declared part of the Kingdom of Italy, and on the last day of the year King Victor Emmanuel entered the city which was now his capital. The loss of Rome and of all temporal dominions in no way changed the spiritual title and power of the Pope. His personal comfort and dignity were carefully considered by the King. He was even allowed to keep his guards, and an ample income was secured to him. The *Vatican*, the Church of *Sta. Maria Maggiore*, and the *Castel Gandolfo*, with their precincts, were exempted from the law of the State, that the Pope might not be offended by seeing the signs of the King's power. Thus the Pope ceased to be a temporal Prince, and lost all power save that which he exercises over the minds of a large part of the people of the world.

16. **Italy since 1870.**—The entrance of King Victor Emmanuel into Rome was the end of the work of deliverance and union. Italy is now free and united, and has Rome for her capital. The work needed skill, patience, and moderation as well as courage. The work which is going on in the peninsula now needs these qualities in no less degree, for it is the work of regenerating a country which has suffered more

than any other from a long bondage, both mental and physical. It has to be carried on in the face of great difficulties. Pope Pius, by uttering curses and complaints against the policy of the King and his government, made it difficult for the King's ministers to deal with him on those terms of cordial respect which they would wish to observe. On the other hand, the hatred of the Romans against the priests who ruled them so long, forces the government to protect against its own people men who look upon it with abhorrence. Victor Emmanuel steadily kept his word to the Pope, and no condemnation from the Vatican provoked him to curtail the privileges which were granted to Pius in 1870. At the same time the Italian ministers followed the same policy in Rome as they did in Turin, and have curtailed the over-large power and possessions of some of the religious corporations. The country is rapidly growing more prosperous. Sicily and Southern Italy are still the most backward parts of the Kingdom. It may be that the people of the South are less naturally anxious for reform, and less capable of enjoying it, than those of the North. But even there, as in the rest of Italy, education is doing its work. Throughout the Kingdom the education of the people is provided for by the State. In the South the opposition of the priests has long hindered the full working of the system. Brigandage has almost disappeared before an efficient police, and all suspicion of any understanding between the thief and him who should be the thief-catcher is long ago at an end. Schools, railways, an organized body of police, and other suchlike things, which were rare in Italy a few years ago, all cost money, and the Italians are heavily taxed. There are but few imports, for the country brings forth nearly all things which her people want. The burthen therefore falls heavily on landed property. The people, however, feel that the things for which they pay are worth paying for. The increase in the prosperity of the country has also made property rise in value, and lands and houses, even in the de̶c̶a̶y̶e̶d̶ capitals of Turin and Florence, are worth more than they were before the seat of government was moved to Rome. The change of the capital has been accompanied by some drawbacks. One of the greatest of these is the unhealthiness of the *Agro Romano*, the Roman Campagna. The malaria which rises from the marshes and infects all the neighbourhood seems to be the effect of the stagnant water which lies on and just below the surface of the soil. It has been proposed to drain the marshes of *Ostia* and *Maccarese*, which extend over fifteen thousand acres. The water is to be drawn off the higher land to the *Tiber* and the *Arone*, while the land, which lies below the level of the sea, is to be drained by steam-pumps. A large tract of country in *Polesina* and the *Veronese* has been already reclaimed in this way. Plans are also made for the drainage, cultivation, and planting of other large marshes in the neighbourhood of Rome, and there seems reason to hope that these works will in time make these dreary wastes fruitful, and the air which comes from them at least far less hurtful to life than it is at present. The lack of all government offices in the new capital has also been inconvenient, but this is now (1874) being remedied. In one sense it may seem that Rome has lost in dignity. Her position as a national capital in some degree lessens her position as the capital of the world, the City which, as the home either of the Emperor or the Pope, belonged equally to all nations and to none. Nevertheless, in the truest sense she has gained in dignity, for she has become the seat of a liberal and enlightened government, the head of free and united Italy.

INDEX.

A.

Abati, degli, Bocca, 55.
Adalbert, Count of Tuscany, 17.
Adelheid, Queen of Italy, 20.
Æneas Sylvius, 101. *See* Pius II.
Agilulf, King of the Lombards, 8.
Agnadello, battle of, 137.
Agnello, Doge of Pisa, 81.
Alberic, Consul or Senator, 19.
Alberigo, Count of Barbiano, 89, 92.
Albert, King of the Romans, 63.
Albizzi, degli, family, 81; Rinaldo, 98; Antonfrancesco, 141.
Alboin, King of the Lombards, 5, 6.
Aldo Manuzio, 202.
Alexander, Popes, III., 39; IV., 54; V., 94; VI., 114, 123-133.
Alexandria or Alessandria, 41.
Alexios Komnênos, Emperor (East), 28, 32.
Alfieri, Count, 215.
Alfonso of Castile, claimant for Empire, 55.
Alfonso of Aragon and Sicily, 96; gains Naples, 100.
Alfonso II. of Naples, 117.
Alliance, the Grand, 207.
Alliance, the Quadruple, 209.
Amadeus VIII. Duke of Savoy, 101, 193.
Andrea of Pisa, 68.
Angevins, in S. Italy, line founded, 57; becomes extinct, 100; new line founded by adoption of Lewis, 85; its rights centre in Charles VIII., 114.
Architecture, 65-68, 146.
Arcola, battle of, 216.
Arcos, Duke of, 205.
Arduin, King, 25.
Ariosto Lodovico, 148.
Arnulf, King and Emperor, 17.
Arts in Florence, 60.
Arvedo, battle of, 96.
Aspromonte, battle of, 251.
Austria, power in Italy begins, 208; War of Succession, 211; overthrown by Buonaparte, 216; restored by Congress of Vienna, 222; its strength, 225; war with France and Sardinia, 242; loses Lombardy, 243; war with Prussia: the Quadrilateral: loses Venetia, 254.
Autharis, King of the Lombards, 6.
d'Azeglio, Massimo, Count, 231, 240.

B.

Baccio Valori, 174.
Balbo, Counts, Prospero, 226; Cesare, 230.
Bandiera, attempt of the brothers, 230.
Barbarians, use of term, 138, 145.
Barbarossa the Algerine, 180, 189.
Barbavara, Francesco, 91.
Bari, taking of, 14.
Basel. *See* Councils.
Basil, Emperors (East), I., 14; II., 22.
Basilica, nature of a, 66.
Bayard, the Chevalier, 151, 156.
Beccaria, family in Pavia, 80.
Beccaria, Marquess, 215.
Bellarmino, Cardinal, 202.
Bembo, Piero, 148.
Benedict, Pope, XIII., 93.
Benvenuto Cellini, 148.
Berengar, King and Emperor, 17.
Berengar II., King, 20.
Bianchi, faction of the, 63.
Boccaccio, Gio., 77, 90.
Bologna, taken by Visconti, 79; tyranny of Bentivogli, 107, 133; they are expelled and brought back, 138; regained by Julius II., 140; part of

Northern Legations, 222; University of, 49; the Palazzo della Mercanzia, 68.
Bona of Savoy, Duchess of Milan, 107.
Boniface, Popes, VIII., 63; IX., 92.
Bonnivard, "the Prisoner of Chillon," 195.
Bonnivet, Admiral, 155.
Borgia, Roderigo, chosen Pope Alexander VI., 114; Lucrezia, *ib.*; Cesare, 114, 130, 132.
Botta Adorno, Marquess, 212.
Boucicault, Jean, 92, 94.
Bourbon, Charles of, Constable, 155, 164.
Bourbons, the, 211, 213, 216, 218, 219.
Bouvines, battle of, 48.
Braccio, 94.
Bramante, architect, 146.
Brancaleone, Senator, 54.
Brenta, battle on the, 19.
Brigandage, 219, 248, 249, 259.
Brunelleschi, Filippo, architect, 105.
Buonaparte, Napoleon, 216-221; Joseph, 218; Eliza, 220; Napoleon Joseph, 242; L. Napoleon, 242, 247, 250-253, 256, 257.
Buondelmonte, murder of, 45.
Bussolari, Jacopo, of Pavia, 80.
Byng, Admiral, 209.

C.

Cadorna, General, 258.
Cadoro, battle of, 136.
Capponi, Neri, 105; Piero, 122; Marquess Gino, 236.
Caraffa, Gian-Piero. *See* Paul IV.
Caravaggio, battle of, 100.
Carbonari, 225.
Carlo Borromeo, Abp., 187.
Carlo Zeno, 86.
Carloman, King, 16.
Carmagnola, Francesco, 95, 97.
Caroline, Queen of Naples and Sicily, 219.
Carrara, da, Francesco, 85, 87; Francesco Novello, 87.
Carroccio, first used, 25.
Castelfidardo, battle of, 246.
Castruccio Castrucani, 71-73.
Catapan, title of, 15.
Catherine, Duchess of Milan, 91.
Cavour, di, Camillo Benso, Count, 240-251, 253.
Charles the Great, King and Emperor, 11-15.

Charles II. (the Bald), King and Emperor, 14.
Charles III. (the Fat), King and Emperor, 16
Charles IV., King and Emperor, 79.
Charles V., King and Emperor, I. of Spain, 152-170, 183.
Charles VI., King and Emperor, King of the Two Sicilies, 208, 209.
Charles II. of Spain, 206, 207.
Charles III. of Spain (Don Carlos), King of the Two Sicilies, 210.
Charles VI. of France, 86, 88.
Charles VIII. of France, 112; his claim on Naples, 114; enters Italy, 120; his failure, 125, 130, 142.
Charles Martel, Duke of the Franks, 10.
Charles of Anjou, King of Naples and Sicily, 56-59.
Charles II. (son), King of Naples, 59.
Charles of Calabria, Duke, son of Robert, King of Naples, 72.
Charles of Durazzo, nephew of King Robert, 75.
Charles III., Duke of Savoy, 194.
Charles Emmanuel, Duke of Savoy, 197.
Charles Emmanuel III., King of Sardinia, 210, 211, 215.
Charles Emmanuel IV., King of Sardinia, 218.
Charles Felix, King of Sardinia, 226.
Charles Albert of Carignano, 226; King, 227, 233, 235, 237.
Charles Lewis, King of Etruria, 220.
Charles Lewis, Duke of Lucca, 233; of Parma, 236, 239.
Chioggia, war of, 85.
Christina, daughter of Henry IV. of France, Regent of Savoy, 205.
Cimabue, 69.
Ciompi, insurrection of the, 82.
Ciro Menotti, 227.
Civitella, battle of, 28.
Clement, Popes, III., Antipope, 32; IV., 56; V., 63; VI., 75-78; VII., Antipope, 84; VII., 148, 156-165, 171, 175; XIII., 215; XIV., *ib.*
Clotilda, Princess, marriage of, 242.
Colonna, family of, 78, 124; Prospero, 150; Pompeo, Card., 161; Stefano, 172; Marc' Antonio, 183.
Companies, the Free, 76; the Great, *ib.*; the White, 77; St. George, 89.
Concordat of Worms, 34.
Confederation, Italian, idea of, 231, 237, 243.

INDEX.

Conrad II., King and Emperor, 25, 26.
Conrad III., King of the Romans, 36.
Conrad, King, son of Henry IV., 33.
Conrad, King of Sicily, claimant for Empire, 53.
Conradin, King of Sicily, 53, 57.
Constance, Queen of Sicily, 42; daughter of King Manfred, 58.
Constantine, donation of, 11.
Constantine, Emperors (East), II., 8; X., 27.
Constituent Assembly, idea of, 237.
Corte Nuova, battle of, 51.
Councils, of Church, Piacenza, 33; Lyons, 51; Pisa, 93; Constanz, 95; Basel, 98; Pisa (schismatical), 138.
Councils, of Republics, 24, 60, 62, 82.
Counts, official, become territorial lords, 15; their power checked, 26.
Counts, of Tuscany 15, 17, 29; of Tusculum, 23.
Crescentius, Consul, 22.
Crotona, battle of, 22.
Custozza battles of, 235, 254.

D.

Dandolo, Enrico, Doge of Venice, 46.
Dante, Alighieri, his exile, 63; his hopes, 64; the Divine Comedy, 69; De Monarchia, *ib.*
Dominic, St., 50, 186.
Doria, family, 71; Luciano, 86; Andrea, 165, 166; Giannettino, 178.
Drainage and cultivation, 113, 182, 201, 214, 260.

E.

Education directed by Jesuits, 186, 188; in Kingdom of Sardinia, 215; of Italy, 260.
Eiréné, Empress (East), 11.
Emmanuel Filibert, Duke of Savoy, 195-197, 209.
Emperor Elect, title of, 153.
Empire, the, becomes one, 5; Western restored, 11; abolished, 23; Eastern conquered by Latins, 46; reconquered by Greeks, 47; conquered by Ottoman Turks, 103; designs of Charles VIII. upon, 115.
Enzio, son of Emperor Frederic II., 52.
Este, family of, 62.
Estradiots, 119.

Eugène Beauharnais, Viceroy of Italy, 218.
Eugene, Prince, 207.
Eugenius, Pope, IV., 98.
Exarchate, the, 4, 9.

F.

Facino Cane, 95.
Farinata degli Uberti, 55.
Farnese, Alessandro, Pope Paul III., 176; Ottaviano, 177-179; Orazio, Pier-Luigi, 177; Alessandro, Prince of Parma; the Farnesi Dukes, 179; Elizabeth, heiress of, her marriage, 208.
Favre, M. Jules, 257.
Ferdinand, Emperor of Austria, 232.
Ferdinand I. of Naples, 104, 112, 117.
Ferdinand II. of Naples, 123.
Ferdinand of Aragon and Sicily, 124; III. of Naples, 132, 152.
Ferdinand IV. of Naples, III. of Sicily, 219; I. of the Two Sicilies, 223, 226.
Ferdinand II. of the Two Sicilies, 236, 244.
Ferdinand III. Grand Duke of Tuscany, 216.
Feruccio, Francesco, 172-174.
Fieschi, conspiracy of the, 178.
Florence, her position, 30; gains independence, 35; factions of nobles, 45; falls under Ghibelins, 52; return of Guelfs; Year of Victories, 54; taken by Ghibelins, danger of city, 55; return of Guelfs, 57; the Government, the Parte Guelfa, 60, 61; defeat at Montecatini, 70; danger, 74; tyranny of the Duke of Athens, 75; the Eight of War, 81; rise of the Medici, *see* Medici; the Ciompi, 82; withstands Gian-Galeazzo, 87, and King Ladislas, 93; over-great power of Medici, 105, 106; conspiracies against them, 108-110; Florence delivered from them, 121; deceived by Charles VIII., 126; preaching of Fra Girolamo, 127; long war with Pisa, 135; faithful to France, 140; return of the Medici, *ib.*; rising against them, 163; flight of the Medici, 167; the siege, 171; the fall, 174; flight of the Grand Duke, 237; his return, 239; Florence and Tuscany join the kingdom of Sardinia, 243; becomes the capital of Italy, 253; the capital removed, 260; the Duomo; the Baptistery and the Church of Stᵃ Croce, 69, 106;

INDEX.

Palazzo Vecchio, 82, 129, 174, 175; Palazzo Pitti, 106; Carmine Church, 106, 146; Palazzo Riccardi, 175.
Formosus, Pope, 17.
Fornovo, battle of, 128.
Fossombroni, Vittorio, 231.
Francis of Lorraine, 211; Emperor Elect, *ib.*
Francis I. of France, 150-180.
Francis II. of the Two Sicilies. 246, 248, 249.
Francis, Duke of Modena, 227, 233, 239, 243.
Franks burn Milan, 6; withstand the Lombards, 6, 7; defend Rome, 10; their Empire, 11; finally divided, 16.
Frederic I. King and Emperor, 38-42.
Frederic II., birth of, 43; King of Sicily, 47; King and Emperor, 48; quarrel with the Pope, 49-52.
Frederic, his son, 52.
Frederic III. King and Emperor, 100, 103.
Frederic of Aragon, King of Sicily, 63, 71.
Frederic, Don, his defeat, 190; King of Naples, 126.
Frundsberg, George, 158, 162.

G.

Gaimar, Prince of Salerno, 27.
Galileo, 188.
Garibaldi, Giuseppe, early adventures, 235; defends Brescia, *ib.*; defends Rome, 238; delivers Sicily, 246; and Naples, 247; retires to Caprera, 248; attempt on Venetia; Aspromonte, 251, 252; his volunteers defeated, 254; arrested at Sinalunga, 255; Mentana, 256.
Gaston de Foix, 139.
Gavinana, battle of, 174.
Geneva, connexion with Savoy, 194; head-quarters of Mazzini, 229; Garibaldi at Peace Congress, 255.
Gennaro Annesi, 206.
Genoa, her trade, 29; rivalry with Venice; settlement of Galata, 47; joins Guelfic party; defeat of Meloria, 51; victory of Meloria, 61; besieged by Ghibelins, 71; submits to the Visconti, 79; War of Chioggia, 85; Charles VI. of France, Signor, 88; revolts, joined to Duchy of Milan, 104; revolts from Duchess Bona, 111; taken by Lewis XII., 134; frequent changes, 155; submits to Charles V.; power of Andrea Doria, 166; conspiracy of the Fieschi, 178; bombarded by Lewis XIV., 207; frees herself from the Austrians, 212; under the protection of France; cession of Corsica, 213; joined to the kingdom of Sardinia, 222; revolt quelled, 240.
Germans, or East-Franks, uphold Arnulf, 17. *See* Prussians and Austrians.
Ghibelins and Guelfs, name, 36; changes in meaning, 75, 145.
Ghibelins, greatness of, 47, 50, 55, 63, 64, 71.
Giannone, Piero, 214.
Gian-Galeazzo. *See* Visconti.
Giano della Bella, 61.
Gioberti, Vincenzo, 231, 237, 243.
Giordano, Patrician, 37.
Giotto, 68.
Giovanni, Fra, of Vicenza, 50.
Giovanni di Procida, 59.
Girolamo, Fra, Savonarola, his preaching, 113; his followers, 127; ordeal and death, 128; his followers the Frateschi, 167.
Girolamo Morone, 159.
Giusti, Giuseppe, 231
Goito, battle of, 235.
Gonsalvo de Cordova, 125, 131, 132
Grandella, battle of, 56.
Gravelines, battle of, 183.
Greeks in S. Italy, 3, 4; separation of Italy from the East, 9; revival of Greek power; the province of Bari, 14, 15.
Greek literature in Italy, 90, 103.
Gregory, Popes, I., the Great, 8; II., 9; III., 10; VII., Hildebrand, 30-33; IX., 49; X., 57; XI., 78-81; XII., 93; XVI., 232.
Grisons, the Three Leagues, 140, 199.
Guelfs, name, *see* Ghibelins; greatness of, 41. 54, 57, 60.
Guerrazzi, F. D., 236.
Guibert of Ravenna, Antipope Clement III., 32.
Guicciardini, Francesco, 148, 164, 175; Luigi, 163.
Guido, King and Emperor, 17.
Guise, Duke of, 197, 206.

H.

Hadrian, Popes, III., 11; IV., 38; VI., 154.
Hawkwood, Sir John, 81, 87.

INDEX.

Henry, King of the Germans, victory at Merseberg, 21.
Henry II., King and Emperor, 25.
Henry III., King and Emperor, 26.
Henry IV., King and Emperor, 31-33.
Henry V., King and Emperor, 33-35.
Henry VI., King and Emperor, King of Sicily, 42.
Henry VII., King and Emperor, 64, 65, 70.
Henry, King of the Romans, son of Frederic II., 50.
Henry III. of England interferes in affairs of Sicily, 53.
Henry VIII. of England, 139, 159, 161.
Henry II. of France, 180.
Henry IV. of France, 198, 203.
Heribert, Abp. of Milan, 25.
Honorius, Pope, III., 48, 49.
Hugh of Provence, King, 19.
Humbert, Count of Burgundy, 191.
Hungarians, 18, 20.

I.

Iconoclasts, 11.
Ignatius Loyola, 185.
Innocent, Popes, II., 37; III., 43, 48; IV., 52; VI., 78; VII., 93; VIII., 111.
Inquisition, the, 186-188.
Investitures, war of, 30-35.
Isabella of Castile, her marriage, 152.
Isabella, daughter of John King of France, married to Gian-Galeazzo Visconti, 80.
Italian language, 3; begins to be written in S. Italy, 49; in N. Italy, 69.
Italy, physical geography of, 1-3.
Italy, Young, 228.

J.

James I. of England, 203.
Jesuits, their Society founded, 185; they leave Venice, 203; in Piedmont, 209; Order suppressed, 215, 216; re-established, 223; driven out of Piedmont, 240; influence at Court of Naples, 244.
Joachim (Murat), King of Naples, 219, 223.
Joanna I., Queen of Naples, 75, 84.
Joanna II., Queen of Naples, 96, 97.
John Tzimiskês, Emperor (East), 22.

John Cantacuzene, Emperor (East), 85.
John, Popes, VIII., 14; X., defeats the Saracens, 18; XII., the Consul Octavian, 19; deposed, 22; XV., 22; XXII., 71; XXIII., deposed, 94.
John of Bohemia leads the Ghibelins, 73.
John, Duke of Calabria, son of King René, 104.
John, Don, of Austria, natural son of Charles V., at Lepanto, 190.
John, Don, of Austria, natural son of King Philip IV., at Naples, 206.
John Sobieski, King of Poland, 203.
Joseph Buonaparte, King of Naples and of Spain, 218.
Julius, Popes, II., Giuliano della Rovere, 109, 134, 137, 138, 140, 144, 200; III., 179.

K.

Kingdom of Italy, right of the Emperor to, 17, 21.
Königgrätz, battle of, 254.

L.

Ladislas, King of Naples, 85, 93-95.
Lambert, King and Emperor, 17.
Lamoricière, Papal General, 246.
Lando, Michele di, Gonfaloniere, 83.
Lanzo, Milanese popular leader, 26.
Laocoon, group of the, 146.
Lautrec, Marshal de, Odet de Foix, in the Duchy of Milan, 154; in Naples, 165, 166.
Laybach, Congress of, 226.
Leagues, Lombard, 40, 42, 44, 49; of Veronese cities, 40; of Cambray, 136; the Holy, 138; second Holy League, 161, 165.
Lechfeld, battle of, 21.
Legnano, battle of, 41.
Leo, Emperor (East), the Isaurian, 9.
Leo, Popes, VIII., 22; IX., 26; taken prisoner, 28; X., Giovanni de' Medici, 113, 141, 144, 146, 150, 152, 154; XII., 201.
Leonardo da Vinci, 147.
Leopold, Emperor Elect, his alliance with Venice, 203.
Leopold, Peter, Grand Duke of Tuscany, 213; succeeds to the Empire, 214.

Leopold II., Grand Duke of Tuscany, 231, 234, 237, 239, 243.
Lepanto, battle of, 190.
Lesseps, M., at Rome, 238.
Lewis the Pious, King and Emperor, 13.
Lewis II., King and Emperor, 13.
Lewis III. of Provence, King and Emperor, 17.
Lewis IV., of Bavaria, King and Emperor, 72-74.
Lewis the Great, King of Hungary, invades Naples, 75, 84.
Lewis IX., King of France, 56.
Lewis XI., of France, 104.
Lewis XII., of France, 129-150.
Lewis XIII., of France, 199.
Lewis XIV., of France, 206.
Lewis of Anjou, son of John of France, adopted by Queen Joanna I., of Naples, 84.
Lewis II., of Anjou, *ib*.
Lewis III., of Anjou, adopted by Queen Joanna II. of Naples, 96.
Lewis, Duke of Savoy, marries Anne Lusignan, 193.
Lewis, their son, marries Charlotte of Cyprus; claims the kingdom, 194.
Leyva de, Antonio, 157, 166.
Lionel, Duke of Clarence, marries Violante Visconti, 80.
Lissa, sea-fight off, 254.
Liutprand, King of the Lombards, 10.
Lodovico. *See* Sforza.
Lombards, the, 5; conquer Italy, 5-7; their kingdom and duchies, 7-11.
Lothar, King and Emperor, 13.
Lothar II., King, 20.
Lothar II., Emperor, the Saxon, 36.
Lottery, the, in Italy, 225.
Louis Philippe, King of the French, 228.
Lucca, war with Pisa, 35; ruled over by Castruccio, 71; sold and quarrelled over, 73, 74; in power of Pisa, 80; under Gian-Galeazzo, 89; falls under power of Florence; revolts in vain, 97; helps Pisa against Florence, 135; forced to desist, 136; remains a Republic, but without importance, 190; Eliza Buonaparte made Duchess of, 220; given to the Bourbons of Parma, 222; Charles Lewis, Duke, 233; sold to Grand Duke of Tuscany, 222, 233; gains freedom with the rest of the Grand Duchy, 243.
Luna, burnt by the Northmen, 18.
Luther, Martin, 153.

M.

Machiavelli, Niccolo, 148, 172.
Magenta, battle of, 242.
Maida, battle of. 219.
Malaspini, the, 90.
Malatesta Baglioni, 172.
Manfred, King of Sicily, 53-57.
Maniakês, George, Catapan, 27.
Manin, Daniele, Dictator of Venice, 234, 238.
Manini, Luigi, last Doge of Venice, 217.
Manuel, Emperor (East), alliance with Emperor Conrad, 37; attempts to regain Italy, 41.
Manuel Chrysoloras, 90.
Manzoni, Alessandro, 231.
Maramaldo, Fabrizio, 173.
Maria Theresa, Queen of Hungary, 210; marries Francis, afterwards elected Emperor, 211.
Maria Louisa, wife of Napoleon Buonaparte, made Duchess of Parma, 222, 227, 235, 236.
Maria of Sicily, marriage with Martin of Aragon, 93.
Marignano, battle of, 151.
Marinovich, murder of, 234.
Markwald, Regent of Sicily, 43.
Marmora, della, Alfonso, 239, 241, 249.
Marozia, 19.
Martin, Popes, IV., 58; V., 95.
Martin of Aragon and Sicily, 93.
Masaccio, 106, 146.
'Mas Aniello, 205.
Matilda, Countess, 32; her territory left to Popes, 34; disputes concerning, 39, 40, 43, 47, 52.
Maurice, Emperor (East), 8.
Maximilian, Emperor Elect, King of the Romans, 124, 135, 137, 153.
Mazzini, Giuseppe, 228, 237-239, 246, 254, 257.
Medici, Salvestro, Gonfaloniere, 81-83; Cosimo, Father of his Country, 98, 99; his power in Florence, 106. Piero, son, 106. Giuliano, son, 107; assassinated, 110. Lorenzo, son of Piero, "Il Magnifico," 106, 108, 109, 111; his foreign policy, 112. Piero, his son, 114; flight, 121; death, 132. Giovanni, son of Lorenzo, 113, *see* Leo X. Giuliano, son of Lorenzo, *ib*.; returns to Florence, 141, 142. Lorenzo, son of Piero, 142, 150, 152. Catherine, his daughter, Queen of France, 152, 197. Giulio, natural son of Giuliano, 152, 156, *see* Clement

INDEX.

VII. Giovanni delle Bande Nere, 158, 162. Ippolito, natural son of Giuliano, 163. Alessandro, his cousin, 163, 169; returns to Florence, 175. Clarice, 167. Lorenzo, descendant of brother of Cosimo the elder, 175. Cosimo, son of Giovanni, Lord of Florence, 176. Duke of Florence and Siena, 182; the Medicean Grand Dukes of Tuscany, 177. Cosimo II., 177, 188. Ferdinand, 177, 197. Cosimo III., 207. Gian-Gastone, last of the Medici, 177, 208, 210.
Medici, Gian-Jacopo de', Marquess of Marignano, 181.
Melazzo, battle of, 245.
Meloria, sea-fights off, 51, 61.
Mentana, battle at, 256.
Michael Palaiologos, Emperor (East), 47, 59.
Michel-Angelo Buonarroti, 147, 172, 175.
Milan, burnt by Franks, 6; place of coronation, 21; rivalry of Pavia, 25; its rise under Abp. Heribert, 25; disturbances in, 26; centre of history of N. Republics, 29; withstands Francis, 38; destroyed, 40; rebuilt, 41; defeat at Corte Nuova, 51; influence of Guelfic della Torre, 51; of Ghibelin Visconti, 58; the Guelfs driven out; the city under the Visconti, 65—*see* Visconti—struggle for freedom; falls under F. Sforza, 101; *see* Sforza; claim of Lewis, Duke of Orleans, 117; conquered by Lewis XII., 129; held by Swiss Mercenaries in the name of Duke Massimiliano, 140; Duchy invaded by Lewis XII., 149; taken by Francis I., 151; by Charles V., 153; unsuccessful invasion of French, 155-158; conspiracy of the Great Chancellor, 159; sufferings of the people, 161; under Spain, 170, 180; passes to the Austrians, 207; invasion of Charles Emmanuel, 210; Novara and Tortona, taken from the Duchy, added to Sardinia, 211; sufferings during the war of the Austrian succession, 211; N. Buonaparte enters, 216; part of Cisalpine Republic, 217; N. Buonaparte crowned king, 218; given back to the Austrians, 222; plot of the Carbonari, 225; the Five Days of Milan, 234; the Austrians re-enter, 235; regains freedom, 243; short riot, 256; the Church of St. Ambrose, 33, 65, 66, 218; the Duomo, 68.

Milan, Abp. of, 6, 15, 24, 25, *see* Heribert, and Carlo Borromeo.
Mola, battle of, 132.
Monaco, sold to France, 247.
Monteaperto, battle of, 55.
Montecatini, battle of, 70.
Montefeltri, lords of Urbino, 71; Federigo, Duke of, 111; Guidobaldo, 133; Guido, 152; end of family, 200.
Monte Rotondo, battle of, 256.
Monte Suello, battle of, 254.
Montferrat, Marquesses of, 120, 192, 198, 199.
Montpensier, Count of, 125.
Monza, 33; the iron crown kept there, 65.
Morosini, Francesco, Doge of Venice, conquers Peloponnesos, 203.

N.

Naples—Greek maritime city, 4; resists Saracens, 13; in alliance with them, 14; continues faithful to Eastern Cæsar, 14; crushed by Normans, 28; University founded, 49; becomes the capital of kingdom of the Angevins, 59, 65, 75; wars of succession, 85, 95, 97; joined to Aragon and Sicily, 100; separated under Aragonese kings, 104; claim of Charles VIII., 114; conquered by French, 124; reconquered, 126; conquered by Spaniards, 132; insurrection, 204; under Austrian Charles VI., 207; under Spanish Bourbons, Charles III., 211; surrenders to French; capital of Parthenopean Republic, 218; French Kings, Joseph and Joachim; the brigands, 219; the Bourbons restored, 222; the Carbonari, 225; joins National cause, 236; the massacre of May 15, 236; tyranny of Ferdinand and Francis, 244; deliverance, 248. Naples ceases to be a capital; discontent and brigandage, 248-9, 250; present state, 259, 260.
Narses, 5.
National Guard, 232, 233.
Neri, faction of the, 62.
Niccolo Piccinino, 97.
Nicolas, Popes, II., 28; III., the Ghibelin. 58; V., 103.
Nicolas of Pisa, architect and sculptor, 68.
Nikêphoros Phokas, Emperor (East), 22.

INDEX

Nizza (Nice), 193, 196, 243, 247.
Normans, the, conquer Apulia, 27; Calabria and Sicily, 28; in alliance with the Popes, 28, 32, 37, 39; end of their kingdom, 42.
Northmen, the, 18.
Novara, battles of, 149, 237.

O.

Octavian, Consul and Pope, 19.
Odoacer, the Herulian King, 4.
Orange, Prince of. Philibert, 165, 174.
Orleans, Dukes of, Lewis marries Violante Visconti, 88; Lewis, grandson, claim on Milan, 117. *See* Lewis XII.
Orsini, family, 78, 124, 133; Gianpagolo, 174; Giulio, 183.
Ostrogoths, 4.
Otto the Great, German King, 20; crowned King and Emperor, 21, 22.
Otto II., King and Emperor, 22.
Otto III., King and Emperor, 22, 23.
Oudinot, General, 238.

P.

Padua, destroyed, 7; heretics in, 50; falls under Eccelino da Romano, *ib.*; under Can' Grande della Scala, 71; under Francesco da Carrara, 85; under Venice, 93; claimed as an Imperial fief, 136.
Painting, 68, 106, 147, 148, 188.
Palestrina, battle of, 238.
Pallavicini, General, 253.
Palmerston, Viscount, 247.
Paoli, General, 213.
Paolo Veronese, 148.
Papacy, the, absence of the Emperor, 8; period of degradation, 19; reformed by Emperor Otto, 21; period of degradation, 23; reformed by Henry III., 26; simony and celibacy, 26, 30; its relations with Empire, 31; Investitures, 31-35; quarrel with Frederic, 38; its causes, 38-42; greatness under Innocent III., 48; injury done by Boniface VIII., 63, 64, 77; Babylonish captivity, 78; the Great Schism, 84, 93; restored strength, 101; change in policy, 108; worldliness, 145; effect on religion, 184; the Jesuit reformation, 186; the Jesuit difficulty, 215, 216; depressed by Buonaparte, 218, 220; restored, 222, 223; its position towards free Italy, 243, 250-259.
Parma, 140, 152, 154, 179, 210, 211, 217, 222, 227, 236, 243; Baptistery, 67.
Paterines persecuted, 50.
Patrician, title of, 10, 15.
Paul, Popes, II., 107; III., 177; IV., 183; V., 201.
Pavia, capital of Lombard Kingdom, 6; taken by Charles the Great, 11; rivalry in Milan, 25; Ghibelin, 39; hostile to the Lombard League, 41; upholds Frederic, 48; falls under Matteo Visconti, 71; power of the Beccarias; taken by Visconti, 80; under Duke of Milan, but separate from Duchy, 88; attempt for freedom, 101; siege of, 157; battle of, 158; sack of, 165; St. Michael's Church, 67.
Pazzi, conspiracy of the, 108.
Pepe, General, 235.
Pergola della, Agnolo, 96.
Pescara, Marquess of, Ferdinando, 154, 159.
Peter, Leopold. *See* Leopold.
Peter, King of Aragon and Sicily, 59.
Petrarca, Francesco, 90.
Philip of Swabia, King, 43, 44.
Philip II. of Spain, 182, 200.
Philip III. of Spain, 199.
Philip IV. of Spain, 199.
Philip V. of Spain, 207, 208, 210.
Philip of Valois, 71.
Philip of Commines, 120, 124.
Piacenza, battle of, 211.
Piedmont, position in the Duchy of Savoy, 196; insurrection in, 226; the Moderate party, 230; the Democratic party, 237; the power of the priests, 240.
Pippin, King of the Franks, Patrician, 10.
Pisa, her power and splendour, 28, 29; alliance with Florence, 35; victory off Meloria, 51; defeated by Florence, 54; Ghibelin policy, 55; defeat off Meloria, and decline, 61; receives Henry VII., his burial-place, 65; falls before Castruccio, 73; under Agnello, 81; under Gian-Galeazzo, 90; under Gabriello, 92; sold to Florence, 93; liberty restored by Charles VIII., 122, 126; enslaved by Florence, 136; Baptistery and Campanile, 67; Church of St. Michael, 138; University, 188.
Pitti, Luca, 105.

INDEX. 269

Pius, Popes, II., 103; III., 133; V., 190; VI., 201, 218; VII., 201, 218, 222; IX., 232, 236, 237, 239, 243, 259, 260.
Plague, the, 77, 88.
Podesta, 44, 60, 136.
Poggio Bracciolini, 106.
Polish Succession, war of the, 210.
Ponza, battle off, 99.
Popes, temporal power, rise of, 8; first temporal dominion, 10, 11; the house of Tusculum, 19, 23; territory of Countess Matilda, which *see*, 34; become a great Italian power, 102; begin to found houses of Italian Princes, 109, 111; States of the Church increased by Julius II., 137, 143; treated as private property, 143, 144, 200; *see* Bologna, Parma, and Urbino; position by Treaty of Vienna, 222; government of Gregory XVI., 232; loses Romagna, 243; the Pope's troops, 246; end of the temporal power, 258.
Prato, massacre at, 141.
Prussia, war with Austria, 253; with France, 256; King William and the Pope, 258.

Q.

Quadrilateral, the Austrian, 253.

R.

Radetzki, Marshal, 234.
Raffaello Sanzio d'Urbino, 147.
Rapallo, battle of, 119.
Ravenna, 10; architecture, 67; Church of St. Vital, *ib*., battle of, 139.
Raymond of Cardona, Viceroy of Naples, 139, 149.
Raymond Beranger, Count of Provence, his daughters, 56, 191, 193.
Religious movements of 16th century, 184-188.
Renaissance, the, 145.
René I. of Anjou, adoption of, 97.
René II., Duke of Lorraine, 114.
Richard of Cornwall, King of the Romans, 53.
Richelieu, Cardinal, 204.
Rienzi, Cola di, 78.
Rivoli, battle of, 216.
Robert Wiscard, Count, 28, 32, 33

Robert, King of Naples, 65, 72, 73-75.
Rocca Secca, battle of, 94.
Roger I., Count, 28.
Roger II., the Great Count, King of Sicily and Apulia, 28.
Roger of Loria, Catalan Admiral, 59.
Romagna, old exarchate, 4; given to the Popes, 10; independent position of its lords, 132; Cæsar Borgia, Duke of, 133, *see* Popes; part of Cisalpine Republic, 217; the Legations, 222; revolts from Pope, 227; joins the Kingdom of Sardinia, 243.
Romano, da, Eccelino, 50-54; Alberigo, 54.
Rōmanos II., Emperor (East), 22.
Rome, without Emperor, 3; defended by Pope, 8; again seat of Empire, 12; Consuls, 12, 22, 23; taken by Henry IV., 32; by Robert Wiscard, 33; Neapolitan garrison, 65; without Pope, 78; Stefano Porcaro, 103; Vatican and St. Peter's plundered, 161; City sacked, 164; Buonaparte in Rome, 217; National Guard, 232; the Republic, the siege, 237; the French garrison, 238, 251, 254, 256; finally leave, 258; the capital of Italy, 259, 260; the Basilican Churches, 65; the Vatican, 102, 147; St. Peter's, 146; the Sistine Chapel, 147.
Romulus Augustulus, Emperor, 3.
Rossi, Pellegrino, Count, 236.
Rovere, della, family, 200; Giuliano, 108. *See* Julius II.
Rudolf of Habsburg, King of the Romans, 58.
Rudolf of Swabia, 32.
Rudolf of Burgundy, King, 190.
Rupert, King of the Romans, 88.

S.

San Marino, 190.
Saracens, 13, 18; garrison of Frederic II., 49, 57; influence on Sicilian architecture, 68.
Sardinia island, 28, 93, 207, 214, 221; kingdom of, 209; extended, 211; despotism in, 214; overrun by French, 218; King restored; addition of Genoa, 222; becomes truly Italian, 224, 231; constitution granted, 234; government, 240; Crimean war, 241; Lombardy and

Central Italy added, 242; merged in kingdom of Italy, 247, 248.
Sarpi, Paolo, Fra, 202.
Savona, Conference at, 135.
Savonarola. *See* Girolamo, Fra.
Savoy, County of, 192; Duchy of, became Italian State, 193; claim on Cyprus, 194; headship of Italian part, 196; finally shut out from Provence, 198; *see* Kingdom of Sicily, 208, and of Sardinia, *ib.*; cession of, 243, 244.
Scala, della, lords of Verona, 63; Can' Grande, 71; Mastino, 74; Antonio, 87.
Sedan, battle of, 257.
Serristori Barracks blown up, 255.
Sesia, battle near the, 156.
Sforza, Attendolo, 94; Francesco, son, 97, 99; Duke of Milan, 101; Galleazzo, son, 107; Bona of Savoy, widow, 107; Gian-Galeazzo Maria, son, 107, 120; Lodovico, uncle, 108, 111, 112, 114, 117, 131; Massimiliano, son, 140, 149; Francesco, brother, 153, 159, 160, 165, 170, 180.
Sicily, colonised by Greeks, 3; conquered by Normans, 28; Norman Kingdom, 28, 37, 40, 42; claim of the Pope, 47; under Frederic II., 48, 49, 52; claimants for the Crown, 53, 56; conquered by Charles of Anjou, 57; the Sicilian Vespers, 59; the Aragonese Kingdom, 60; rejoined to Aragon, 93; and to Naples, 97, 104; revolt in Palermo, 205; Lewis XIV. proclaimed King, 207; Kingdom given to Victor Amadeus, 209; the Kingdom of the Two Sicilies under Austrian Charles VI., 209; under Spanish Bourbons, 211, 213; King Ferdinand retreats to, 219; restored as King of the Two Sicilies, 223; tyranny of Ferdinand II. and Francis II., 224; deliverance of, by Garibaldi, 245, 247.
Siena, 35, 54, 55, 65, 89, 93, 170, 180-182; the Palazzo Publico, 68.
Sigismund, King and Emperor, 97.
Sixtus, Pope IV., 108, 110.
Soderini, Tommaso, 106; Piero 140; Tommaso, 168.
Soncino, battle of, 97.
Spalato, Palace of Diocletian, 66.
Spaniards, Aragon kings of Sicily, 93; union of Castile and Aragon, 124; gain Naples, 132; advance into Central Italy, 140, 144; become masters of Milan, 153, 154; in Rome, 165; master of Italy, 170, 171; decline of power, 204; end of Austrian line, 207; and of power, 208; the Bourbon line in Sicily and Naples, 211-247.
St. Quentin, battle of, 184.
Stanislas receives Lorraine, 210.
Stefano Porcaro, 103.
Stephania, wife of Crescentius, 23.
Stephen, Pope, 10.
Stewart, John, Duke of Albany, 157.
Strozzi, Filippo, 167, 176; Alfonso, 168; Piero, 176, 180, 181; Leone, 181.
Stuart, Sir John, 219.
Swiss or Confederates, 96, 118, 131, 140, 149, 150, 194.

T.

Tagliacozzo, battle of, 57.
Tancred, King of Sicily, 42
Taxation in Italy, 260.
Tchernaya, battle of, 241.
Thaddeus of Sessa, 52.
Theodora, 19.
Theodoric, the Ostrogoth, Lieutenant of the Emperor, 4.
Theophanó, Empress, wife of Otto III., 22.
Tiepolo, Podesta of Milan, 51.
Tintoretto, Jacopo Robusti, 148.
Tiziano Vecellio, 148.
Torcello, Church of St. Fosca, 68.
Torre, della, Pagano, 51; greatness of house, 58; Guido, 64.
Treaties, Aix-la-Chapelle, 213; Barcelona, 169; Cambray, 170; Campo Formio, 217; Câteau Cambresis, 184; Constanz, 42; Lodi, 102; Lyons, 198; Madrid, 160; Nimwegen, 206; Passarowitz, 203; Pyrenees, the, 205; Paris, Congress, 241; San Germano, 49; September Convention, 252, 258; Turin, 86; Utrecht, 207; Vercelli, 125; Verdun, 13; Verviers, 198; Villafranca, 150; Vienna, 210; Vienna Congress, 221; Westphalia, 205; Worms, Concordat of, 34.
Trivulzio Gian Jacopo, 123, 130, 150.
Turin, made a capital by Emmanuel Filibert, 196; ceases to be a capital, 253.
Turks in Italy, 103, 185.

INDEX.

U.

Ugolino della Gherardesca, 61.
Urban, Popes, IV., 55; V., 81; VI., 84.
Urbino, the Montefeltri, lords and dukes of, 71, 111; twice seized by Cæsar Borgia, 133; the Duchy seized by Leo X. for Lorenzo de' Medici, 154; the family of Rovere; Urbino lapses to Holy See, 200.
Uri, men of, 96, 111, 131.
Uscocchi, 203.

V.

Vachero, Giulio Cesare, conspiracy of, 199.
Val d'Ossola, 96, 192.
Val Levantina, 96, 131.
Vallais, men of, 192.
Valtellina, 140, 199.
Vaud, the Catholic nobles of, 195.
Venice, 2; faithful to Emperor, 6, 7; reigning in East, 28; trade in Levant, 29; independent position, 46; share in Fourth Crusade, 47; joins Lombard League, 51; its government, 62; war with the Visconti, 79, 80; war of Chioggia, 85, 87; war with Francesco da Carrara, 92; power on the mainland, 93; Italian policy, 101, 112, 121. 125; wars with Turks, 103, 188, 189, 203; the League of Cambray, 136; the Holy League, 138; the Second Holy League, 161; quarrel with Paul V., 201; decline, 203; taken by Buonaparte, 217; given to Austria, 217, 222; insurrection, 235; defence, *ib.*; fall, 239; hopes of Venetians, 250; deliverance, 254; Church of St. Mark, 67.
Venice, truce of, 41.
Veniero, Sebastiano, Venetian commander at Lepanto, 190.
Verona, 6, 40, 50, 71, 92, 136, 217.

Victor Amadeus II., Duke of Savoy, 207, 208; King of Sicily, 209; King of Sardinia, 209.
Victor Amadeus III., King of Sardinia, 215, 216.
Victor Emmanuel I., King of Sardinia, 221, 224, 226.
Victor Emmanuel II., King of Sardinia, 237, 239, 240, 243, 245; King of Italy, 247, 256-258.
Victor IV., Antipope, 39.
Villani, Giovanni, Matteo, Filippo, 91.
Visconti, Otho, Archbishop Elect and Lord of Milan, 58; Matteo, nephew, 63, 65, 71; Galeazzo, son, 72; family depressed by Emperor Lewis, 73; Azzo, son, 73; Luchino, son of Matteo, 74; Gian, Abp. brother, 79; Matteo, Bernabo, Galeazzo, nephews of Gian, 80; foreign alliances: Violante, 81; Gian-Galeazzo, son of Galeazzo, 80, 86; made Duke, 88; Gian-Maria, Filippo Maria, sons, 92; Gabriello, natural son of Gian-Galeazzo, 92; Bianca, Valentina 100.
Vittorio Pisani, 85.
Volta, Alessandro, 215.

W.

Waldenses, 187.
Walter of Brienne, 43.
Walter of Brienne, Duke of Athens, 74.
Warfare, Italian, 89, 118.
Waterloo, battle of, 221.
Welfs of Bavaria. *See* Guelfs.
Wenceslas, 88.
William, King of Prussia, 258.

Z.

Zachary, Pope, 10.
Zeno, sole Emperor, 3.
Zizim, 123.

LONDON:
R. CLAY, SONS, AND TAYLOR, PRINTERS,
BREAD STREET HILL.

MACMILLAN & CO.'S PUBLICATIONS.

HISTORICAL COURSE FOR SCHOOLS.

Edited by EDWARD A. FREEMAN, D.C.L., late Fellow of Trinity College, Oxford.

I. *GENERAL SKETCH OF EUROPEAN HISTORY.* By EDWARD A. FREEMAN, D.C.L. New Edition, revised and enlarged, with Chronological Table, Maps, and Index. 18mo. 3s. 6d.

> "It supplies the great want of a good foundation for historical teaching. The scheme is an excellent one, and this instalment has been executed in a way that promises much for the volumes that are yet to appear."—EDUCATIONAL TIMES.

II. *HISTORY OF ENGLAND.* By EDITH THOMPSON. New Edition, revised and enlarged, with Coloured Maps. 18mo. 2s. 6d.

III. *HISTORY OF SCOTLAND.* By MARGARET MACARTHUR. New Edition. 18mo. 2s.

> "An excellent summary, unimpeachable as to facts, and putting them in the clearest and most impartial light attainable."—GUARDIAN.

IV. *HISTORY OF ITALY.* By the Rev. W. HUNT, M.A. New Edition, with Coloured Maps. 18mo.

> "It possesses the same solid merit as its predecessors . . . . the same scrupulous care about fidelity in details. . . . It is distinguished, too, by information on art, architecture, and social politics, in which the writer's grasp is seen by the firmness and clearness of his touch."—EDUCATIONAL TIMES.

V. *HISTORY OF GERMANY.* By J. SIME, M.A. 18mo. 3s.

> "A remarkably clear and impressive history of Germany. Its great events are wisely kept as central figures, and the smaller events are carefully kept, not only subordinate and subservient, but most skilfully woven into the texture of the historical tapestry presented to the eye."—STANDARD.

VI. *HISTORY OF AMERICA.* By JOHN A. DOYLE. With Maps. 18mo. 4s. 6d.

> "Mr. Doyle has performed his task with admirable care, fulness, and clearness, and for the first time we have for schools an accurate and interesting history of America, from the earliest to the present time."—STANDARD.

MACMILLAN AND CO., LONDON.

Messrs. Macmillan & Co.'s Publications.

Historical Course for Schools—*continued.*

EUROPEAN COLONIES. By E. J. PAYNE, M.A. With Maps. 18mo. 4s. 6d.

"We have seldom met with an Historian capable of forming a more comprehensive, far-seeing, and unprejudiced estimate of events and peoples, and we can commend this little work as one certain to prove of the highest interest to all thoughtful readers."—TIMES.

FRANCE. By CHARLOTTE M. YONGE. With Coloured Maps. 18mo. 3s. 6d.

"An admirable text-book for the lecture-room."—ACADEMY.

GREECE. By EDWARD A. FREEMAN, D.C.L. [*In preparation.*

ROME. By EDWARD A. FREEMAN, D.C.L. [*In the press.*

By **John Richard Green**, M.A., LL.D., &c.

A SHORT HISTORY OF THE ENGLISH PEOPLE. With Coloured Maps, Genealogical Tables and Chronological Annals. Crown 8vo. 8s. 6d. Eighty-eighth Thousand.

"Stands alone as the one general history of the country, for the sake of which all others, if young and old are wise, will be speedily and surely set aside."—ACADEMY.

READINGS FROM ENGLISH HISTORY. Selected and Edited by JOHN RICHARD GREEN, M.A., LL.D., Honorary Fellow of Jesus College, Oxford. Three Parts. Globe 8vo. 1s. 6d. each. I. Hengist to Cressy. II. Cressy to Cromwell. III. Cromwell to Balaklava.

ANALYSIS OF ENGLISH HISTORY, based on Green's 'Short History of the English People.' By C. W. A. TAIT, M.A., Assistant-Master, Clifton College. Crown 8vo. 3s. 6d.

By **E. A. Freeman**, D.C.L., LL.D.

OLD-ENGLISH HISTORY. With Five Coloured Maps. New Edition. Extra fcap. 8vo. half-bound. 6s.

LECTURES ON THE HISTORY OF ENGLAND. By M. J. GUEST. With Maps. Crown 8vo. 6s.

"It is not too much to assert that this is one of the very best class books of English History for young students ever published."—SCOTSMAN.

MACMILLAN AND CO., LONDON.

Messrs. Macmillan & Co.'s Publications.

PICTURES OF OLD ENGLAND. By Dr. R. PAULI. Translated with the sanction of the Author by E. C. OTTÉ. Cheaper Edition. Crown 8vo. 6s.

By **Charlotte M. Yonge.**

A PARALLEL HISTORY OF FRANCE AND ENGLAND: consisting of Outlines and Dates. Oblong 4to. 3s. 6d.

CAMEOS FROM ENGLISH HISTORY. By the Author of 'The Heir of Redclyffe.' Extra fcap. 8vo. Price Five Shillings each volume. FIRST SERIES—FROM ROLLO TO EDWARD II. —SECOND SERIES—THE WARS IN FRANCE.—THIRD SERIES—THE WARS OF THE ROSES. — FOURTH SERIES—REFORMATION TIMES.

EUROPEAN HISTORY. Narrated in a Series of Historical Selections from the Best Authorities. Edited and arranged by E. M. SEWELL and C. M YONGE. First Series, 1003—1154. Third Edition. Crown 8vo. 6s. Second Series, 1088—1228. New Edition. Crown 8vo. 6s.

FRENCH HISTORY FOR ENGLISH CHILDREN. By SARAH BROOK. With Coloured Maps. Crown 8vo. 6s.

A SUMMARY OF MODERN HISTORY. Translated from the French of M. MICHELET, and continued to the Present Time, by M. C. M. SIMPSON. Globe 8vo. 4s. 6d.

SCANDINAVIAN HISTORY. By E. C. OTTÉ. With Maps. Globe 8vo. 6s.

A SHORT HISTORY OF INDIA AND OF THE FRONTIER STATES OF AFGHANISTAN, NEPAUL, AND BURMA. By J. TALBOYS WHEELER. With Maps. Crown 8vo. 12s.

"It is the best book of the kind we have ever seen, and we recommend it to a place in every school library."—EDUCATIONAL TIMES.

A SHORT MANUAL OF THE HISTORY OF INDIA. With an Account of INDIA AS IT IS. The Soil, Climate, and Productions; the People, their Races, Religions, Public Works, and Industries; the Civil Services, and System of Administration. By ROPER LETHBRIDGE, M.A., C.I.E., late Scholar of Exeter College, Oxford, formerly Principal of Kishnaghur College, Bengal, Fellow and sometime Examiner of the Calcutta University. With Maps. Crown 8vo. 5s.

MACMILLAN & CO., LONDON.

Messrs. Macmillan & Co.'s Publications.

THE ROMAN SYSTEM OF PROVINCIAL ADMINISTRATION TO THE ACCESSION OF CONSTANTINE THE GREAT. By W. T. ARNOLD, B.A. Crown 8vo. 6s.

"Ought to prove a valuable handbook to the student of Roman history."—GUARDIAN.

STORIES FROM THE HISTORY OF ROME. By Mrs. BEESLY. Fcap. 8vo. 2s. 6d.

"The attempt appears to us in every way successful. The stories are interesting in themselves, and are told with perfect simplicity and good feeling."—DAILY NEWS.

AN EPITOME OF THE HISTORY OF THE CHRISTIAN CHURCH. By WILLIAM SIMPSON, M.A. New Edition. Fcap. 8vo. 3s. 6d.

HISTORY AND LITERATURE PRIMERS.

Edited by John JOHN RICHARD GREEN. 18mo. 1s. each.

Homer. By the Right Hon. W. E. GLADSTONE, M.P.
English Grammar. By R. MORRIS, LL.D.
Exercises on Morris's Primer of English Grammar. By JOHN WETHERELL, M.A.
Rome. By M. CREIGHTON, M.A. Maps.
Greece. By C. A. FYFFE, M.A. Maps.
English Literature. By STOPFORD BROOKE, M.A.
Europe. By E. A. FREEMAN, D.C.L.
Greek Antiquities. By J. P. MAHAFFY, M.A.
Roman Antiquities. By Professor A. S. WILKINS.
Classical Geography. By H. F. TOZER, M.A.
Geography. By GEORGE GROVE, F.R.G.S. Maps.
Children's Treasury of Lyrical Poetry. By F. T. PALGRAVE. In two Parts, each 1s.
Shakspere. By Professor DOWDEN.
Philology. By J. PEILE, M.A.
Greek Literature. By Professor JEBB.
English Grammar Exercises. By R. MORRIS, LL.D., and H. C. BOWEN, M.A.
France. By C. M. YONGE. Maps.
English Composition. By Professor NICHOL.

** Others to follow.

MACMILLAN & CO., LONDON.

Primary French and German Reading Books.

De Maistre—La Jeune Sibérienne et Le Lépreux de la Cité d'Aoste. Edited by STEPHANE BARLET, B.Sc. 1s. 6d.
Florian. Fables selected and edited by Rev. C. YELD. With Exercises. 1s. 6d.
Grimm—Kinder und Hausmärchen. Edited by G. E. FASNACHT With Exercises. 2s. 6d.
Hauff—Die Karavane. Edited by HERMAN HAGER, Ph.D. With Exercises by G. E. FASNACHT. 3s.
La Fontaine—A Selection of Fables. Edited by L. M. MORIARTY. 2s.
Perrault—Contes de Fees. Edited by G. E FASNACHT. With Exercises. 1s. 6d.
G. Schwab—Odysseus By the same Editor. [*In preparation.*

Foreign School Classics

Edited by G. EUGENE FASNACHT 18mo.
Corneille—Le Cid. By G. E. FASNACHT. 1s.
Dumas—Les Demoiselles de St. Cyr. Edited by VICTOR OGER. 1s. 6d.
Molière—Les Femmes Savantes. By G E FASNACHT 1s.
LE MISANTHROPE. By G. E. FASNACHT. 1s.
L'AVARE. By L. M. MORIARTY. 1s.
LE MÉDECIN MALGRÉ LUI. By G. E. FASNACHT. 1s.
LE BOURGEOIS GENTILHOMME. By L. M. MORIARTY. 1s. 6d.
Goethe—Götz von Berlichingen. By H A. BULL, M.A. 2s.
FAUST Part I. Edited by JANE LEE. 4s. 6d.
Heine—Selections from ProseWorks. By C. COLBECK. 2s. 6d.
Racine- Brittanicus Edited by E. PELLISIER. 2s.
George Sand La Mare au Diable. By W. E. RUSSELL. 1s.
Sandeau, Jules—Mlle. de la Seiglière. H. C. STEEL. 1s. 6d.
Schiller—Die Jungfrau von Orleans. By JOSEPH GOSTWICK.
MARIA STUART By C SHELDON, M.A. 2s. 6d. [2s. 6d.
SELECTIONS FROM SCHILLER'S LYRICAL POEMS. Ed by E. J. TURNER, and E. D. A. MORSHEAD, 2s. 6d
WALLENSTEIN. Part 1. Das Lager. By H. B. COTTERILL. 2s.
WILHELM TELL. By G. E. FASNACHT 2s. 6d.
French Readings from Roman History. Selected from Various Authors and Edited by C. COLBECK, M.A. 4s. 6d.
Uhland's Ballads and Romances. Selections. By G. E. FASNACHT. 1s.
Voltaire—Charles XII. By G. E. FASNACHT. 3s. 6d.
*** *A prospectus of this series will be sent on application.*
Progressive French Course. By G. E. FASNACHT. 1st Year, 1s. ; 2nd Year, 2s. ; 3rd Year, 2s. 6d.
Teacher's Companion to Above. Each Year, 4s. 6d.
Progressive French Reader By the same Author. First Year, 2s. 6d. ; Second Year, 2s. 6d.
A French Grammar for Schools. By the Same. 3s. 6d.
Progressive German Course. By the Same. First Year, 1s. 6d. ; Second Year, 3s. 6d.
Teacher's Companion to Above. 1st Year, 4s. 6d. ; 2nd Year, 4s. 6d. [18mo. 1s.
First Lessons in French. By H. COURTHOPE BOWEN, M.A.
French Dictionary. By G. MASSON. 6s.
German Dictionary. By Prof. WHITNEY and A. H. EDGREN. 7s. 6d. German-English Part. 5s.

Macmillan's Science Primers.

Professors HUXLEY, ROSCOE, and BALFOUR STEWART.

18mo. Cloth.

INTRODUCTORY. By T. H. HUXLEY, F.R.S.
CHEMISTRY. By Sir H. E. ROSCOE, F.R.S. Questions.
PHYSICS. By BALFOUR STEWART, F.R.S. Questions.
PHYSICAL GEOGRAPHY. By A. GEIKIE, F.R.S. With Questions.
GEOLOGY. By ARCHIBALD GEIKIE, F.R.S.
PHYSIOLOGY. By Prof. M. FOSTER, M.D., F.R.S.
ASTRONOMY. By J. N. LOCKYER, F.R.S.
BOTANY. By Sir J. D. HOOKER, K.C.S.I., F.R.S.
LOGIC. By W. STANLEY JEVONS, F.R.S.
POLITICAL ECONOMY. By W. STANLEY JEVONS, F.R.S.

*** Others to follow.

AGRICULTURE, THE ALPHABET OF
PRINCIPLES OF; being a First Lesson Book on Agriculture Schools. By Prof. HENRY TANNER. First Book. Second Book, 1s. Third Book 1s.

FIRST PRINCIPLES OF AGRICULTURE
HENRY TANNER, F.C.S. 18mo. 1s.

FIRST LESSONS IN PRACTICAL BOTANY
By G. T. BETTANY. 18mo. 1s.

HOUSEHOLD MANAGEMENT and COOKERY
With an Appendix of Receipts used by the Teachers of the N. School of Cookery. Compiled by W. B. TEGETMEIER. 18mo.

THE SCHOOL COOKERY BOOK. Compiled Arranged by C. E. GUTHRIE WRIGHT. 18mo. 1s.

MACMILLAN AND CO., LONDON.

www.ingramcontent.com/pod-product-compliance
Lightning Source LLC
Chambersburg PA
CBHW032100220426
43664CB00008B/1079